W.B. YEATS
SELECTED PLAYS

W.B. YEATS
SELECTED PLAYS

*Edited with an introduction
and notes by*

A. NORMAN JEFFARES

PAPERMAC

This selection first published 1964 by
Macmillan London Limited

Later edition published 1974 by
Pan Books Limited

This revised and expanded edition first published 1991 by
PAPERMAC
a division of Macmillan Publishers Limited
Cavaye Place London SW10 9PG
and Basingstoke

Associated companies in Auckland, Delhi, Dublin, Gaborone, Hamburg,
Harare, Hong Kong, Johannesburg, Kuala Lumpur, Lagos, Manzini,
Melbourne, Mexico City, Nairobi, New York, Singapore and Tokyo

ISBN 0-333-05375-3

A CIP catalogue record for this book is available from the British Library

Typeset by Macmillan Production Limited

Printed in Hong Kong

CONTENTS

CONTENTS

INTRODUCTION

We think of Yeats primarily as a poet, yet throughout his life he devoted much of his energy to writing plays and for many years his time was taken up as Manager of the Abbey Theatre with 'theatre business, management of men'. The second (posthumous) edition of his *Collected Plays* (1952),[1] though it does not include all his published dramatic work,[1] contains over seven hundred pages of text, and this gives some indication of the scope of his dramatic work.

Yeats began to write play after play in imitation of Spenser and Shelley in his teens. His father, who exercised a strong influence over him at this period of his life, used to read aloud the most dramatic passages of whatever play or poem was at the time engaging his capacity for acute, original, speculative appreciation. His son read his own lines aloud as he wrote them; as he did not understand prosody, he discovered that, in order to create some common music for his lines, he needed a listener, an audience. He developed a habit of acting what he wrote and spoke. Indeed, when he left the High School and joined the School of Art in Dublin he sometimes adopted an artificial stride, seeing himself as a kind of Hamlet seeking for heroic self-possession as he was torn by inner struggles.

His concern in drama was largely with the heroic. His early plays were romantic and mournful, preoccupied with loneliness and beauty. *The Island of Statues*[2] of 1885, for instance, though cast in dramatic form, was a romantic poem with little dramatic content. About 1886, under the influence of John O'Leary and his own developing nationalism, he had

decided to write out of his emotions; he had come to believe
a new kind of Irish literature was needed. As he began to
explore through translations a new world of Gaelic literature,
and also to build up a deep knowledge of nineteenth-century
Irish writing in English, he left behind conventional themes
and derivative romance.

  The Countess Kathleen (1892)[3] bears witness to this change in
his style and aims. His falling in love with Maud Gonne in 1889
and his realization that he would need 'a very public talent'
to commend himself to this beautiful, dashing, and ruthless
revolutionary were reasons for his writing this verse play for
her. But he was also deeply impressed by Florence Farr's
verse speaking in John Todhunter's *A Sicilian Idyll* (1890),
performed at Bedford Park in 1890. He based *The Countess
Cathleen* on a story he had found and thought suitable for a
poetic drama when he was preparing his *Fairy and Folk Tales
of the Irish Peasantry* (1888). He drafted it in prose, beginning
work in February or March 1889, and finishing the first version
in verse in October 1891.

  The play has a simple episodic plot. The Countess leaves
her dreams for the reality of life; she opposes the efforts
of two demon-merchants to buy the souls of her starving
peasants. Finally she sells her own soul to prevent this.
Yeats wrote *The Countess Cathleen* out of a general ambition
to create a 'great distinctive poetic literature' out of Ireland's
pagan and Christian traditions: in contrast to his long poem
The Wanderings of Oisin (1889), which was concerned with
pagan legends, this play was to mingle his personal thought
and feeling with the beliefs and customs of Christian Ireland.
He regarded the pagan and Christian elements in Irish tradition
as a kind of double fountain head of inspiration. His personal
feelings are contained in the play, when the poet Kevin vainly
attempts to sell his own soul to prevent the Countess from
selling hers. He believes that she should leave the ultimate
salvation of the peasants to the builder of the heavens, that her
concern should be with marriage and children. This was an
indirect message for Maud Gonne, which becomes stronger

in later versions of the play, when Kevin, altered to Aleel, puts the claims of subjective life (the beautiful life of artists which Yeats dreamed of for Maud Gonne) as opposed to the grey realities of 'the evil of the times'.

Yeats revised the text extensively, in 1895, 1901, 1912, and 1919, making minor alterations at other times. The first of these major revisions[4] was stimulated by the performance in 1894 of *The Land of Heart's Desire* (1894) at the Avenue Theatre. Yeats wrote this slight play at Florence Farr's suggestion, so that her niece Dorothy Paget could play the role of a fairy child who tempts a young woman away from a respectable cottage marriage to the timelessness of life with the faery host.

The Shadowy Waters (1900),[5] also a much revised play, on which Yeats worked from 1885 to 1905 or later,[6] explores a different kind of situation: it is a study of the heroic gesture, the union of hearts. More a ritual than a play, according to Yeats, it is a symbolic drama of escape, in which the hero and heroine, lily and rose, seek death and life respectively. The symbols are meant – like those in his poems of the 1890s – to carry a weight of cryptic meaning. Through their shadows they suggest the lovers' contrasting dreams of love and also they symbolize a love beyond this, of superhuman kind.

Yeats's twilight *fin de siècle* weariness changed into a new harsh realism after the turn of the century, and he devoted most of his energy and a great deal of courage to launching, administering, and championing the Irish dramatic movement. He visited Lady Gregory in 1896 and spent subsequent summers in Coole, gathering folklore with her in the west of Ireland, and finding in her the ally he sought in creating an Irish theatre. Together they established the Irish Literary Theatre, with Edward Martyn and George Moore as co-directors, and in 1899 Martyn's *The Heather Field* and Yeats's *The Countess Cathleen* were performed in Dublin. There was a baptism of fire for *The Countess Cathleen*, which incurred moral, political, and religious opposition on the grounds that the people of Ireland would never sell their souls, and the play was performed with police protection.

The Irish Literary Theatre continued to function until the end of 1902: by then Martyn and Moore dropped out of the movement, but not before Yeats and Moore had quarrelled violently over their joint play *Diarmuid and Grania*[7] and then over a story intended to provide the basis for further collaboration. Yeats hastily wrote *Where There is Nothing* (1902)[8] to stop Moore using the subject. This was an account of an anarchistic country gentleman who, after joining a group of tinkers, marries one of them, dissociates himself from his respectable neighbours, enters a monastery where he becomes heretical, is banished and finally killed by a mob. Nietzsche, whom Yeats began reading in 1902, may well have influenced the superman element in this hero.

The Irish National Dramatic Society, with Yeats as its president, replaced the Irish Literary Theatre; this new group contained the Fay brothers, and it provided Yeats with the Irish actors and actresses he had wanted. He gave it his *Cathleen ni Hoolihan* (1902), and Maud Gonne acted in the title role. The play was almost terrifyingly successful in its revolutionary message, in its portrayal of Ireland as the traditional wronged old woman, calling on her children for help. On the news of the landing of a French force at Killala,[9] she is suddenly seen as a young girl with 'the walk of a queen'. The play is simple and dramatically very effective indeed. In old age Yeats, remembering its startling effect on the audience, wondered

> Did that play of mine send out
> Certain men the English shot?[10]

The Pot of Broth (1904)[11] was an adaptation of a folk tale for which Lady Gregory wrote some dialogue. *The Hour-Glass* (1903), originally a prose morality play, in which a Wise Man humbles himself to a Fool and receives salvation,[12] was rewritten in verse. These plays are due to the aim Yeats and Lady Gregory had formed of bringing the poetical tradition contained in the speech of the countryside to the city. They, along with Synge, thought

> All that we did, all that we said or sang
> Must come from contact with the soil, from that
> Contact everything Antaeus-like grew strong.[13]

Synge's first plays to be performed in Dublin were *In the Shadow of the Glen* (1903) and *Riders to the Sea* (1904). The melancholia and vitality of Synge's genius (which Yeats felt he had discovered and guided into its right channels) made for a different use of peasant speech and idiom, and Yeats fully realized and wrote enthusiastically of its merits.[14] He and Lady Gregory fought unselfishly for Synge's work, especially *The Playboy of the Western World* (1907), the exuberant yet profound sense of comedy of which aroused vociferous hostility from a section of Irish and later Irish-American public opinion. The poetical quality of Synge's prose drama was, however, *sui generis*, and when, after the success of Yeats's *The Countess Cathleen*, *The Pot of Broth*, and *The Hour-Glass*, and Lady Gregory's *Twenty Five* in London in 1903, the Abbey Theatre was opened in Dublin in 1904 Yeats was writing a very different kind of play.

The King's Threshold (1904) was first performed in 1903. This play was founded on a middle-Irish story of the demands of the poets at the court of King Guaire at Gort, Co. Galway; it also owed something to Edwin Ellis's play *Sancan the Bard* (1905). It marks, according to S.B. Bushrui,[15] the point at which Yeats abandoned passivity – the idealism of Kevin in *The Countess Cathleen*, the isolation of Forgael in *The Shadowy Waters* – and descended into the world of reality. In this play Seanchan the bard is prepared to become part of the real world and struggle with its trivialities in order to assert his view of the place of poetry in the life of the nation. This is an aristocratic view of poetry. It has moved away from any desire to become an instrument of nationalistic politics. As J.I.M. Stewart remarked, 'Yeats was at least as shrewd as he was mystical,' and must have realized that the forces Maud Gonne wished to unleash would be as hostile in the end to Coole Park as to Dublin Castle.[16]

Yeats's romantic dreams were over once Maud Gonne had married John MacBride in 1903. His new love poetry, now devoid of decorative trappings, recorded movingly the losses caused by his barren passion. Maud Gonne had not understood his aims for Ireland and Ireland itself seemed not to want the new culture he and his friends were creating. Like Seanchan, Yeats was ready to enter the real world; he became Manager of the Abbey and soon his heartfelt curse lay on plays

> That have to be set up in fifty ways,
> On the day's war with every knave and dolt . . .[17]

But despite Yeats's preoccupation with the fascination of what was difficult his own verse plays were not popular with the Abbey audience:

> When we are high and airy hundreds say
> That if we hold that flight they'll leave the place.[18]

The audience preferred realism, and Yeats was unselfish enough to work for the kind of play the younger dramatists were writing. But his own preoccupation was still with the heroic.

In 1892 he had written 'The Death of Cuchulain', a poem based largely on folk-tale sources and on the work of Sir Samuel Ferguson and Standish O'Grady. Cuchulain continued to occupy his mind as a subject throughout his life, especially at critical periods in it.[19] In 1901 he was working on the play *On Baile's Strand* (1903),[20] which also deals with Cuchulain's unwitting killing of his own son. Birgit Bjersby has shown how Cuchulain grows older in Yeats's work along with Yeats himself; in the revised version of *On Baile's Strand* of 1905 (when Yeats was forty) we are told he is about forty, though, traditionally, he was twenty-seven when he died.[21]

This, then, is a play with reflections of Yeats's frustrated love and frustrated desire for a son: in it he is beginning to stylize the form of the play, and to make the characters reflect the abstract ideas that were persecuting him,[22] for the Fool and the Blind Man are shadows of Cuchulain and Conchubar, and are later to become important symbols in *A Vision* (1926, 1937). They affect the play's events and yet are detached from it: they reveal Yeats's increasing interest in extremes and oppositions. The play has a sense of impending doom; its irony and inexorability inevitably remind us of Greek tragedy.

In *Deirdre* (1907) Yeats attempted a more difficult subject, concentrating into one act the treachery and terror that kill Naoise, the pity provoked by Deirdre's suicide. The suspense is skilfully built up, the poetry sensuous and sinister. This is the story of a quarrel that knows no mending, the legend of 'one woman and two men', and the circumstances of Yeats's life gave it imaginative intensity. Naoise plays a self-conscious role, but Deirdre triumphs finally over Conchubar; theirs are 'contrasted sorrows'. The attention of the audience, indeed, is meant to centre on her and her situation. Though the play departs from the simplicity of its sources it has a strange, lofty dignity about it.

Though Yeats returned to the Cuchulain theme in his next play his treatment of the heroic Gaelic material was very different. *The Golden Helmet* (1908), rewritten in verse as *The Green Helmet* (1910), founded on an old Irish tale, 'The Feast of Bricriu', was an ironical farce, a farce being for Yeats 'a moment of intense life'. Though the play reflects quarrels and controversies it praises Cuchulain's joyful fighting and powers of reconciliation:

> And I choose the laughing lip
> That shall not turn from laughing, whatever rise or fall;
> The heart that grows no bitterer although betrayed by all;
> The hand that loves to scatter; the life like a gambler's throw . . . [23]

The Unicorn from the Stars (1908) was a rewriting of *Where There is Nothing*: it replaces the unsatisfactory episodic activities of the hero of the earlier play with a new concentrated action and a more convincing hero, Martin Hearne. This young coachbuilder has a vision of the unicorns which will destroy the existing order of things; he collects beggars, initiates a drunken revel, and finally realizes, before he is shot, that he has been mistaken in giving way to the attraction of destructive violence.

Yeats's concern with the end of one era and the beginning of a new, symbolized by the iron-clawed beast of *Where There is Nothing* and the unicorns of *The Unicorn from the Stars*, was taken up yet again in the unicorn of *The Player Queen* (1922), the genesis of which is described in a note:

> I began in, I think, 1907, a verse tragedy, but at that time the thought I have set forth in *Per Amica Silentia Lunae* was coming into my head, and I found examples of it everywhere. I wasted the best working months of several years in an attempt to write a poetical play where every character became an example of the finding or not finding of what I have called the Antithetical Self; and because passion and not thought makes tragedy, what I made had neither simplicity nor life. I knew precisely what was wrong and yet could neither escape from thought nor give up my play. At last it came into my head all of a sudden that I could get rid of the play if I turned it into a farce; and never did I do anything so easily, for I think I wrote the present play in about a month . . . [24]

This 'wild comedy' (first performed in 1919) is extremely effective on the stage. It can be enjoyed as a prose farce as well as an extension of the theory of the mask which finds expression in *Per Amica Silentia Lunae* (1918).[25] There are other, obscurer elements of Yeats's 'system' in the play. Decima, according to Professor Ure, is both harlot and artist seeking her anti-self, and she can be explained in terms of Yeats's story 'The Adoration of the Magi' (1897, 1925). F.A.C. Wilson sees the unicorn as the form in which divinity is to descend to Decima[26] (as the swan descends to Leda), but Professor Ure argues against this (since Decima does not marry a unicorn but the Prime Minister) and suggests that beneath the farce lies the tragedy, that Decima finds, instead of death, her anti-self and happiness, but, as a condition of this, has to unite with a buffoon.[27]

There had been difficulty earlier in getting the right actress for the initial production of *Deirdre*. Miss Darragh (Letitia Marion Dallas) was chosen; this appointment displeased the Abbey actors; and the part was subsequently played by Mrs Patrick Campbell. For the part of Decima, Yeats had Mrs Campbell in mind when he began to write the play that became *The Player Queen*. A possible reason for this move from tragedy to the farce of *The Golden Helmet* and *The Player Queen* may have been a desire to provide plays that would suit the Abbey actors. But what Yeats wanted was an audience and actors to suit himself, and this situation was achieved in Lady Cunard's drawing room on 2 April 1916. Here was performed *At the Hawk's Well* (1917),[28] the first of the four *Plays for Dancers* (1921). These were plays written out of his interest in the Japanese Noh drama, to which Ezra Pound had introduced him. This offered him a new, simple technique. He could do without an orthodox theatre – an unpopular one was better since he wanted a mysterious art, a ritual helped into being by music and dancing. This would allow him to make credible strange events and elaborate words.

At the Hawk's Well sums up some personal disillusion and uncertainty. It symbolizes man's search for the unobtainable, the hawk suggesting the persecution of the abstract, and Cuchulain the contradictory nature of carnage. *The Only Jealousy of Emer* (1919)[29] is more complicated in structure, and its account of Emer's renunciation of Cuchulain, a solitary act of sacrifice which is unknown to her husband, is encumbered by the ambiguous temptation offered by Fand, the woman of the Sidhe. *The Dreaming of the Bones* (1919)[30] is more successful in its mixture of the supernatural and the political. A revolutionary soldier meets the ghosts of Dermot and Dervorgilla who were responsible for bringing Strongbow and the Normans into Ireland in the twelfth century. They reveal their identity; their anguished separation can be ended if someone of their own race forgives them. But the soldier cannot bring himself to do this, and their remorseful dance of longing ends the play.

Calvary (1921)[31] possesses the musicians' songs, the dance and masked actors, the grouped images of the other Noh-style plays. Its subject, however, marks it off as different, and it requires some knowledge of *A Vision* for its understanding. Christ, himself a victim of intellectual despair, can help neither the Roman soldiers, who are a form of objectivity, nor Lazarus, nor Judas, nor the heron, eagle, and swan, who are content with solitude. The play consists, in Professor Ure's words, of 'four variations on the theme of Christ's powerlessness to save those who can live without salvation'.

Yeats wrote *The Cat and the Moon* (1926),[32] a brief, curiously Synge-like exercise,[33] and followed it with his two translations, *Sophocles' 'King Oedipus'* (1928) and *Sophocles' 'Oedipus at Colonus'* (1934). *The Resurrection* (1931)[34] occupied him from 1925 to 1930; it develops the static attitudes of *Calvary* into a far livelier, more effective play which has structure and development. The plot rests on Yeats's view of history as antithetical; he thought Christianity brought radical thought into the world and with it a new historical period. He makes his abstract system live, first through explanatory dialogue, then through the explosive tension generated out of the situation, an undercurrent of Dionysiac irrational force, beating through the play, contrasting ironically with the talk of the two main characters, the Greek and the Hebrew. This is a masterpiece of dramatic intensity and economy. The stagecraft has a confidence, the dialogue an assurance that reflects the effect that writing *A Vision*, 'getting it all in order', had on Yeats's poetry.

The same superb dramatic skill is at work in *The Words upon the Window-pane* (1934). Yeats's sense of dialogue and of construction allow him to vary the tension of the play, to make realistic use of a seance to communicate the terror in his sense of Swift's agony of spirit:

> . . . beating on his breast in sibylline frenzy blind
> Because the heart in his blood-sodden breast had dragged
>   him down into mankind.[35]

The King of the Great Clock Tower (1934) was 'the most popular of my dance plays', and *A Full Moon in March* (1935) was a second version of the idea based on Oscar Wilde's *Salomé*. The characters are not convincing as people; they are in fact parts of a ritual. *The Herne's Egg* (1938) – 'the strangest wildest thing I have ever written' – seemed to Yeats to have more tragedy and philosophic depth than *The Player Queen*. The hero, Congal, is at war with the bird-god, the Great Herne: but he does not fully understand what he fights. He is obtuse, he falls into a state of mind where he decides the rape of Attracta will restore the state of disorder which existed before he stole the herne's egg and so began the quarrel that led to his killing of Aedh. The 'first bout' with the god led to disorder, the second to the violation of Attracta, which Congal fails to understand in its fullest meaning. The third bout leads to his death in terms of the curse at the hands of a fool, and his reincarnation as a donkey. Congal is a tragic hero of the Othello or Coriolanus kind, limited because his virtues are also his flaws; he makes mistakes, and misunderstands the situation into which his mistakes lead him. The Great Herne has an impersonality and mystery which perhaps reinforce the unimportance of Congal's heroic activity, his inability to realize the difference between fighting against men and against the god.

Purgatory[36] (1939) dramatizes some elements of a ghost story Yeats told earlier about Castle Dargan, near Sligo; in the play the protagonist is an old pedlar, who tells his bastard son the history of the ruined house and its inhabitants. The ghosts of the house appear to the old man – and then, finally, to the boy, as he and his father grapple together, fighting for the pedlar's money. The murder of the son, however, fails to arrest the haunting of the place, centred on the pedlar's mother's dream. This is a play, its theme Oresteia-like, on the problem of the possible purification of a family and of the sexual act that began it. The irony of the repeated pattern of the murders adds to the horror of the play; the circle cannot be broken by mankind, and the old man prays, finally, to God to appease the misery of the living as well as the remains of the dead.

Yeats wrote *The Death of Cuchulain* (1939)[37] shortly before his death. Here he again returned to the material of Lady Gregory's *Cuchulain of Muirthemne*; he also weighted the play with the intimations of the system of *A Vision*. Cuchulain is given a false message by his mistress Eithne, who is under the spell of the goddess of war, which will lead him into hopeless battle; he faces the prospect of death with his usual bravery, forgiving Eithne with a magnanimity that is ironic. He is mortally wounded, and, though Aoife is about to revenge upon him the death of their son Conlaech, the actual death is, ironically, administered by a blind man for a paltry reward. This is the Cuchulain, blinded by heroism, butchered by a clown, who is envisaged in the final song of the play as resuming his place in the folk memory of Irish tradition with the occurrence of the Easter Rising of 1916:

> What stood in the Post Office
> With Pearse and Connolly?
> What comes out of the mountain
> Where men first shed their blood?
> Who thought Cuchulain till it seemed
> He stood where they had stood?
>
> No body like his body
> Has modern woman borne,
> But an old man looking back on life

Imagines it in scorn.
A statue's there to mark the place,
By Oliver Sheppard done.

Yeats had aimed to 'make the old stories as familiar to
Irishmen at any rate as are the stories of King Arthur and his
Knights to all readers of books'. In doing so he had helped
to bring a regenerated nation into being, and it was fitting
that his hero met death with the proud disdain he sought to
achieve himself.

1 For details of some unpublished manuscripts see G.B. Saul,
 Prolegomena to the Study of Yeats's Plays (1958), pp. 99–100.
2 Included in the *Dublin University Review*, April, May,
 June, and July 1885.
3 The original spelling, 'Kathleen', was altered to 'Cathleen'
 in 1895; the latter spelling is subsequently used in this
 edition.
4 They are described in Peter Ure, *Yeats the Playwright*
 (1963), pp. 13–15.
5 First published in the *North American Review*, May 1900.
6 It was first produced at the Molesworth Hall, Dublin, on
 14 January 1904. The acting version was first published in
 1907.
7 The text has been published by W. Becker, *Dublin Magazine*,
 April–June 1951.
8 First published as supplement to the *United Irishman*,
 1 November 1902.
9 The play is based on the *Shan Van Vocht*, a well-known
 street ballad which celebrated French aid for Irish rebellions.
 General Humbert landed his men at Killala in 1798. The idea
 of the play was Yeats's, but Lady Gregory wrote a great deal
 of it.
10 W.B. Yeats, 'The Man and the Echo', *Yeats's Poems* (2nd
 ed., 1991), p. 469.
11 First published in the *Gael*, September 1903; then in
 The Hour-Glass and Other Plays (1904).
12 It was founded on a story, 'The Priest's Soul', recorded

in Lady Wilde, *Ancient Legends of Ireland* (1887), I, pp. 60–67.

13 W.B. Yeats, 'The Municipal Gallery Revisited', *Yeats's Poems*, p. 438.

14 Cf. W.B. Yeats, *Plays in Prose and Verse* (1922), p. 421: 'The first use of Irish dialect, rich, abundant and correct, for the purposes of creative art, was in J.M. Synge's *Riders to the Sea* and Lady Gregory's *Spreading the News*.'

15 '"The King's Threshold": A Defence of Poetry', *A Review of English Literature*, IV, 3 July 1963, p. 83.

16 *Eight Modern Writers, Oxford History of English Literature* (1963), p. 326.

17 W.B. Yeats, 'The Fascination of What's Difficult', *Yeats's Poems*, p. 188.

18 W.B. Yeats, 'At the Abbey Theatre', *Yeats's Poems*, p. 190.

19 There were seven main treatments: 'The Death of Cuchulain' (poem, 1892); *On Baile's Strand* (1903); *The Golden Helmet* (1908) and *The Green Helmet* (1910); *At the Hawk's Well* (1917), *The Only Jealousy of Emer* (1919), and *Fighting the Waves* (1934); *The Death of Cuchulain* (1939) and 'Cuchulain Comforted' (poem, 1939).

20 First published in *The Seven Woods* (1903).

21 *The Interpretation of the Cuchulain Legend in the Works of W.B. Yeats* (1950), p. 79.

22 Cf. W.B. Yeats, *Wheels and Butterflies* (1934), p. 102.

23 W.B. Yeats, *The Green Helmet, Collected Plays* (1952), p. 243. *The Golden Helmet* was first performed on 19 March 1908; *The Green Helmet* on 10 February 1910, both at the Abbey Theatre, Dublin.

24 W.B. Yeats, *Plays in Prose and Verse* (1922), p. 428.

25 See W.B. Yeats, 'Ego Dominus Tuus', *Yeats's Poems*, p. 264; 'The Phases of the Moon', ibid., p. 183, is a similar exposition of Yeats's 'system'.

26 F.A.C. Wilson, *Yeats and Tradition* (1958), p. 182.

27 P. Ure, *Yeats the Playwright* (1963), p. 144.

28 First published in *Harper's Bazaar*, March 1917.

29 First published in *Poetry* (Chicago), January 1919.

30 First published in *The Little Review*, January 1919 and subsequently in *Two Plays for Dancers* (1919).

31 *Four Plays for Dancers* (1921).

32 First published in the *Criterion*, July 1924, and in the *Dial*, July 1924.
33 The play describes the friendship of George Moore and Edward Martyn. Cf. W.B. Yeats, *Autobiographies* (1956), p. 482.
34 First published in *Adelphi*, June 1927; then in *Stories of Michael Robartes and His Friends* (1931).
35 W.B. Yeats, 'Blood and the Moon', *Yeats's Poems*, p. 391.
36 *Last Poems and Two Plays* (1939).
37 Ibid.

NOTE ON THE TEXT

The copy-text used is that of *Collected Plays* (1952). The text of *Cathleen Ni Hoolihan*, however, is taken from *Samhain*, 1902, in which it first appeared, in view of the play's immediate effect on its audience. As the dates given in that edition (in the list of contents and under the title of each play) for the first published versions are not always correct they have been omitted from the body of this text. The notes of this edition attempt to establish where possible the dates of the first publication and production of each play included in the selection. The order of the plays in *Collected Plays* (1952) is followed. I am greatly indebted to the late Mrs W.B. Yeats for her aid in correcting the text of *Collected Plays* (1952) and for other assistance in annotation. Professor Brendan Kennelly and the late Professor David Greene also helped me greatly with the identification of Gaelic material.

CATHLEEN NI HOOLIHAN

PERSONS IN THE PLAY

PETER GILLANE

MICHAEL GILLANE, *His son, going to be married*

PATRICK GILLANE, *A lad of twelve, Michael's brother*

BRIDGET GILLANE, *Peter's wife*

DELIA CAHEL, *Engaged to Michael*

THE POOR OLD WOMAN

NEIGHBOURS

Interior of a cottage close to Killala, in 1798. BRIDGET *is standing at a table undoing a parcel.* PETER *is sitting at one side of the fire,* PATRICK *at the other.*

PETER: What is that sound I hear?

PATRICK: I don't hear anything. (*He listens.*) I hear it now. It's like cheering. (*He goes to the window and looks out.*) I wonder what they are cheering about. I don't see anybody.

PETER: It might be a hurling match.

PATRICK: There's no hurling today. It must be down in the town the cheering is.

BRIDGET: I suppose the boys must be having some sport of their own.

PATRICK: There is an old woman coming down the road. I don't know is it here she's coming.

BRIDGET: It will be a neighbour coming to hear about Michael's wedding. Can you see who it is?

PATRICK: I think it is a stranger, and she's not coming to the house. She has not turned up the path. She's turned into the gap that goes down where Maurteen and his sons are shearing sheep. (*He turns towards them.*) Do you remember what Winnie of the Cross Roads was saying the other night about the strange woman that goes through the country the time there's war or trouble coming?

BRIDGET: Don't be bothering us about Winnie's talk, but go and open the door for your brother. I hear him coming up the path. Come over here, Peter, and look at Michael's wedding clothes.

(PETER *shifts his chair to table.*)

3

Those are grand clothes, indeed. You hadn't clothes like
that when you married me, and no coat to put on of a
Sunday more than any other day.

PETER: That is true, indeed. We never thought a son
of our own would be wearing a suit of that sort at his
wedding, or have so good a place to bring a wife to.

PATRICK: (*Who is still at the window*) Here is Michael coming
back, Father.

PETER: I hope he has brought Delia's fortune with him
safe, for fear her people might go back of the bargain,
and I after making it. Trouble enough I had making it.

(PATRICK *opens the door, and* MICHAEL *comes in.*)

BRIDGET: What kept you, Michael? We were looking
out for you this long time.

MICHAEL: I went round by the priest's house to bid him be
ready to marry us tomorrow.

BRIDGET: Did he say anything?

MICHAEL: He said it was a very nice match, and that he
was never better pleased to marry two in his parish than
myself and Delia Cahel.

PETER: Have you got the fortune, Michael?

MICHAEL: Here it is.

(*He puts bag on the table and goes over and leans against
chimney jamb.* BRIDGET, *who has been all this time
examining the clothes, pulling the seams and trying the lining
of the pockets, etc., puts the clothes on the dresser.*)

PETER (*Getting up and taking the bag in his hand and
turning out the money.*) Yes, I made the bargain well for
you, Michael. Old John Cahel would sooner have kept a
share of this a while longer. 'Let me keep the half of it
till the first boy is born,' says he. 'You will not,' says
I. 'Whether there is or is not a boy, the whole hundred
pounds must be in Michael's hands before he brings your
daughter to the house.' The wife spoke to him then, and
he gave in at the end.

BRIDGET: You seem well pleased to be handling the money,
Peter.

PETER: Indeed, I wish I'd had the luck to get a hundred pounds, or twenty pounds itself, with the wife I married.

BRIDGET: Well, if I didn't bring much I didn't get much. What had you the day I married you but a flock of hens and you feeding them, and a few lambs and you driving them to the market at Ballina. (*She is vexed, and bangs a jug on the dresser.*) If I brought no fortune I worked it out in my bones, laying down the baby – Michael, that is standing there now, on a stook of straw, while I dug the potatoes, and never asking big dresses or anything, but to be working.

PETER: That is true, indeed.

(*He pats her arm.*)

BRIDGET: Leave me alone now till I ready the house for the woman that is to come into it.

PETER: You are the best woman in Ireland, but money is good, too. (*He begins handling the money again and sits down.*) I never thought to see so much money within my four walls. We can do great things now we have it. We can take the ten acres of land we have a chance of since Jamsie Dempsey died, and stock it. We will go the fair of Ballina to buy the stock. Did Delia ask any of the money for her own use, Michael?

MICHAEL: She did not, indeed. She did not seem to take much notice of it, or to look at it at all.

BRIDGET: That's no wonder. Why would she look at it when she had yourself to look at – a fine strong young man; it is proud she must be to get you; a good, steady boy, that will make use of the money, and will not be running through it, or spending it on drink, like another.

PETER: It's likely Michael himself was not thinking much of the fortune either, but of what sort the girl was to look at.

MICHAEL: (*Coming over towards the table*) Well, you would like a nice comely girl to be beside you, and to go walking with you. The fortune only lasts for a while, but the woman will be there always.

PATRICK: (*Turning round from the window*) They are cheering again down in the town. Maybe they are landing horses from Enniscrone. They do be cheering when the horses take the water well.

MICHAEL: There are no horses in it. Where would they be going and no fair at hand! Go down to the town, Patrick, and see what is going on.

(PATRICK *opens the door to go out, but stops for a moment on the threshold.*)

PATRICK: Will Delia remember, do you think, to bring the greyhound pup she promised me when she would be coming to the house?

MICHAEL: She will surely.

(PATRICK *goes out, leaving the door open.*)

PETER: It will be Patrick's turn next to be looking for a fortune, but he won't find it so easy to get it, and he with no place of his own.

BRIDGET: I do be thinking sometimes, now things are going so well with us, and the Cahels such a good back to us in the district, and Delia's own uncle a priest, we might be put in the way of making Patrick himself a priest some day, and he so good at his books.

PETER: Time enough, time enough; you have always your head full of plans.

BRIDGET: We will be well able to give him learning, and not to send him tramping the country like a poor scholar that lives on charity.

MICHAEL: They're not done cheering yet.

(*He goes over to the door and stands there for a moment, putting up his hand to shade his eyes.*)

BRIDGET: Do you see anything?

MICHAEL: I see an old woman coming up the path.

BRIDGET: Who is it, I wonder?

MICHAEL: I don't think it's one of the neighbours, but she has her cloak over her face.

BRIDGET: Maybe it's the same woman Patrick saw a while ago. It might be some poor woman heard we were making ready for the wedding, and came to look for her share.

PETER: I may as well put the money out of sight. There's no use leaving it out for every stranger to look at.

(*He goes over to a large box by the wall, opens it and puts the bag in, and fumbles with the lock.*)

MICHAEL: There she is, Father!

(*An* OLD WOMAN *passes the window slowly. She looks at* MICHAEL *as she passes.*)

I'd sooner a stranger not to come to the house the night before the wedding.

BRIDGET: Open the door, Michael, don't keep the poor woman waiting.

(*The* OLD WOMAN *comes in,* MICHAEL *stands aside to make way for her.*)

OLD WOMAN: God save all here!

PETER: God save you kindly.

OLD WOMAN: You have good shelter here.

PETER: You are welcome to whatever shelter we have.

BRIDGET: Sit down there by the fire and welcome.

OLD WOMAN: (*Warming her hands*) There's a hard wind outside.

(MICHAEL *watches her curiously from the door.* PETER *comes over to the table.*)

PETER: Have you travelled far today?

OLD WOMAN: I have travelled far, very far; there are few have travelled so far as myself.

PETER: It is a pity, indeed, for any person to have no place of their own.

OLD WOMAN: That is true for you, indeed, and it is long I am on the road since I first went wandering. It is seldom I have any rest.

BRIDGET: It is a wonder you are not worn out with so much wandering.

OLD WOMAN: Sometimes my feet are tired and my hands are quiet, but there is no quiet in my heart. When the people see me quiet they think old age has come on me, and that all the stir has gone out of me.

BRIDGET: What was it put you astray?

OLD WOMAN: Too many strangers in the house.

BRIDGET: Indeed you look as if you had had your share of trouble.

OLD WOMAN: I have had trouble indeed.

BRIDGET: What was it put the trouble on you?

OLD WOMAN: My land that was taken from me.

PETER: Was it much land they took from you?

OLD WOMAN: My four beautiful green fields.

PETER: (*Aside to* BRIDGET) Do you think could she be the Widow Casey that was put out of her holding at Kilglas a while ago?

BRIDGET: She is not. I saw the Widow Casey one time at the market in Ballina, a stout, fresh woman.

PETER: (*To* OLD WOMAN) Did you hear a noise of cheering, and you coming up the hill?

OLD WOMAN: I thought I heard the noise I used to hear when my friends came to visit me.

(*She begins singing half to herself:*)

I will go cry with the woman,
For yellow-haired Donough is dead;
With a hempen rope for a neckcloth
And a white cloth on his head.

MICHAEL: (*Coming from the door*) What is that you are singing, ma'am?

(*She goes on singing, much louder.*)

OLD WOMAN: Singing I am about a man I knew one time, yellow-haired Donough, that was hanged in Galway.

I am come to cry with you, woman,
My hair is unwound and unbound;
I remember him ploughing his field,
Turning up the red side of the ground.

And building his barn on the hill
With the good mortared stone;
O! we'd have pulled down the gallows
Had it happened in Enniscrone!

MICHAEL: What was it brought him to his death?

OLD WOMAN: He died for love of me; many a man has died for love of me.

PETER: (*Aside to* BRIDGET) Her trouble has put her wits astray.

MICHAEL: Is it long since that song was made? Is it long since he got his death?

OLD WOMAN: Not long, not long. But there were others that died for love of me a long time ago.

MICHAEL: Were they neighbours of your own, ma'am?

OLD WOMAN: Come here beside me and I'll tell you about them. (MICHAEL *sits down beside her at the hearth.*)
There was a red man of the O'Donells from the North, and a man of the O'Sullivans from the South, and there was one Brian that lost his life at Clontarf, by the sea, and there were a great many in the West, some that died hundreds of years ago, and there are some that will die tomorrow.

MICHAEL: Is it in the West that men will die tomorrow?

OLD WOMAN: Come nearer, nearer to me.

BRIDGET: Is she right, do you think? or is she a woman from the North?

PETER: She doesn't know well what she's talking about, with the want and the trouble she has gone through.

BRIDGET: The poor thing, we should treat her well.

PETER: Give her a drink of milk, and a bit of the oaten cake.

BRIDGET: Maybe we should give her something along with that to bring her on her way; a few pence, or a shilling itself, and we with so much money in the house.

PETER: Indeed, I'd not begrudge it to her if we had it to spare, but if we go running through what we have, we'll soon have to break the hundred pounds, and that would be a pity.

BRIDGET: Shame on you, Peter. Give her the shilling and your blessing with it, or our own luck will go from us.
(PETER *goes to the box and takes out a shilling.*)
(*To the old woman*) Will you have a drink of milk?

OLD WOMAN: It is not food or drink that I want.

PETER: (*Offering the shilling*) Here is something for you.

OLD WOMAN: That is not what I want. It is not silver I want.

PETER: What is it you would be asking for?

OLD WOMAN: If anyone would give me help he must give me himself, he must give me all.

(PETER *goes over to the table staring at the shilling in his hand in a bewildered way and stands whispering to* BRIDGET.)

MICHAEL: Have you no man of your own, ma'am?

OLD WOMAN: I have not. With all the lovers that brought me their love, I never set out the bed for any.

MICHAEL: Are you lonely going the roads, ma'am?

OLD WOMAN: I have my thoughts and I have my hopes.

MICHAEL: What hopes have you to hold to?

OLD WOMAN: The hope of getting my beautiful fields back again; the hope of putting the strangers out of my house.

MICHAEL: What way will you do that, ma'am?

OLD WOMAN: I have good friends that will help me. They are gathering to help me now. I am not afraid. If they are put down today, they will get the upper hand tomorrow. (*She gets up.*) I must be going to meet my friends. They are coming to help me, and I must be there to welcome them. I must call the neighbours together to welcome them.

MICHAEL: I will go with you.

BRIDGET: It is not her friends you have to go and welcome, Michael; it is the girl coming into the house you have to welcome. You have plenty to do; it is food and drink you have to bring to the house. The woman that is coming is not coming with empty hands; you would not have an empty house before her. (*To the* OLD WOMAN) Maybe you don't know, ma'am, that my son is going to be married tomorrow.

OLD WOMAN: It is not a man going to his marriage that I look to for help.

PETER: (*To* BRIDGET) Who is she, do you think, at all?

BRIDGET: You did not tell us your name yet, ma'am.

OLD WOMAN: Some call me the Poor Old Woman, and there are some that call me Cathleen ny Hoolihan.

PETER: I think I knew some one of that name once. Who

was it, I wonder? It must have been someone I knew when I was a boy. No, no, I remember I heard it in a song.

OLD WOMAN: (*Who is standing in the doorway*) They are wondering that there were songs made for me; there have been many songs made for me. I heard one on the wind this morning. (*She sings:*)

Do not make a great keening
When the graves have been dug tomorrow,
Do not call the white-scarfed riders
To the burying that shall be tomorrow.

Do not spread food to call strangers
To the wakes that shall be tomorrow;
Do not give money for prayers
For the dead that shall die tomorrow . . .

They will have no need of prayers, they will have no need of prayers.

MICHAEL: I do not know what that song means; but tell me something I can do for you.

PETER: Come over to me, Michael.

MICHAEL: Hush, Father; listen to her.

OLD WOMAN: It is a hard service they take that help me. Many that are red-cheeked now will be pale-cheeked; many that have been free to walk the hills and the bogs and the rushes will be sent to walk hard streets in far countries; many a good plan will be broken; many that have gathered money will not stay to spend it; many a child will be born and there will be no father at its christening to give it a name. They that had red cheeks will have pale cheeks for my sake; and for all that they will think they are well paid.

(*She goes out. Her voice is heard outside singing:*)

They shall be remembered for ever;
They shall be alive for ever;
They shall be speaking for ever;
The people shall hear them for ever.

BRIDGET: (*To* PETER) Look at him, Peter; he has the look of a man that has got the touch. (*Raising her voice*)

Look here, Michael, at the wedding clothes. (*Taking clothes from dresser*) You have a right to fit them on now; it would be a pity tomorrow if they did not fit; the boys would be laughing at you. Take them, Michael, and go into the room and fit them on.

(*She puts them on his arm.*)

MICHAEL: What wedding are you talking of? What clothes will I be wearing tomorrow?

BRIDGET: These are the clothes you are going to wear when you marry Delia Cahel tomorrow.

MICHAEL: I had forgotten that.

(*He looks at the clothes and turns towards the inner room, but stops at the sound of cheering outside.*)

PETER: There is the shouting come to our own door. What is it has happened?

(NEIGHBOURS *come crowding in,* PATRICK *and* DELIA *with them.*)

PATRICK: There are ships in the bay; the French are landing at Killala.

(PETER *takes his pipe from his mouth and his hat off and stands up. The clothes slip from* MICHAEL'S *arm.*)

DELIA: Michael!

(*He takes no notice.*)

Michael!

(*He turns towards her.*)

Why do you look at me like a stranger?

(*She drops his arm.* BRIDGET *goes over towards her.*)

PATRICK: The boys are all hurrying down the hillsides to meet the French.

DELIA: Michael won't be going to join the French.

BRIDGET: (*To* PETER) Tell him not to go, Peter.

PETER: It's no use. He doesn't hear a word we're saying.

BRIDGET: Try, Delia, and coax him over to the fire.

DELIA: Michael, Michael, you won't leave me! You won't join the French and we going to be married tomorrow!

(*She puts her arms about him. He turns to her as if about to yield.*)

OLD WOMAN'S VOICE: (*Outside*)
    They shall be remembered for ever;
    The people shall hear them for ever.
    (MICHAEL *breaks away from* DELIA *and goes towards*
    NEIGHBOURS *at the door.*)
MICHAEL: Come, we have no time to lose; we must
    follow her.
    (MICHAEL *and the* NEIGHBOURS *go out.*)
PETER: (*Laying his hand on* PATRICK's *arm*) Did you
    see an old woman going down the path?
PATRICK: I did not; but I saw a young girl, and she
    had the walk of a queen.

ON BAILE'S STRAND

TO

WILLIAM FAY

because of the beautiful fantasy of his
playing in the character of the Fool

PERSONS IN THE PLAY

A FOOL
A BLIND MAN
CUCHULAIN, *King of Muirthemne*
CONCHUBAR *(pronounced 'Conohar'), High King of Uladh*
A YOUNG MAN, *son of Cuchulain*
KINGS *and* SINGING WOMEN

*A great hall at Dundealgan, not 'Cuchulain's great ancient
house' but an assembly house nearer to the sea. A big door
at the back, and through the door misty light as of sea mist.
There are many chairs and one long bench. One of these chairs,
which is towards the front of the stage, is bigger than the others.
Somewhere at the back there is a table with flagons of ale upon it
and drinking-horns. There is a small door at one side of the hall. A*
FOOL *and* BLIND MAN, *both ragged, and their features made
grotesque and extravagant by masks, come in through the door at
the back. The* BLIND MAN *leans upon a staff.*

FOOL: What a clever man you are though you are blind!
There's nobody with two eyes in his head that is as clever as
you are. Who but you could have thought that the hen-wife
sleeps every day a little at noon? I would never be able to
steal anything if you didn't tell me where to look for it.
And what a good cook you are! You take the fowl out of
my hands after I have stolen it and plucked it, and you
put it into the big pot at the fire there, and I can go out
and run races with the witches at the edge of the waves
and get an appetite, and when I've got it, there's the hen
waiting inside for me, done to the turn.

BLIND MAN: (*Who is feeling about with his stick*) Done to
the turn.

FOOL: (*Putting his arm round* BLIND MAN's *neck*) Come
now, I'll have a leg and you'll have a leg, and we'll draw
lots for the wish-bone. I'll be praising you, I'll be praising
you while we're eating it, for your good plans and for your
good cooking. There's nobody in the world like you, Blind
Man. Come, come. Wait a minute. I shouldn't have closed

17

the door. There are some that look for me, and I wouldn't like them not to find me. Don't tell it to anybody, Blind Man. There are some that follow me. Boann herself out of the river and Fand out of the deep sea. Witches they are, and they come by in the wind, and they cry, 'Give a kiss, Fool, give a kiss', that's what they cry. That's wide enough. All the witches can come in now. I wouldn't have them beat at the door and say, 'Where is the Fool? Why has he put a lock on the door?' Maybe they'll hear the bubbling of the pot and come in and sit on the ground. But we won't give them any of the fowl. Let them go back to the sea, let them go back to the sea.

BLIND MAN: (*Feeling legs of big chair with his hands*) Ah! (*Then, in a louder voice as he feels the back of it*) Ah – ah –

FOOL: Why do you say 'Ah–ah'?

BLIND MAN: I know the big chair. It is today the High King Conchubar is coming. They have brought out his chair. He is going to be Cuchulain's master in earnest from this day out. It is that he's coming for.

FOOL: He must be a great man to be Cuchulain's master.

BLIND MAN: So he is. He is a great man. He is over all the rest of the kings of Ireland.

FOOL: Cuchulain's master! I thought Cuchulain could do anything he liked.

BLIND MAN: So he did, so he did. But he ran too wild, and Conchubar is coming today to put an oath upon him that will stop his rambling and make him as biddable as a house-dog and keep him always at his hand. He will sit in this chair and put the oath upon him.

FOOL: How will he do that?

BLIND MAN: You have no wits to understand such things. (*He has got into the chair.*) He will sit up in this chair and he'll say, 'Take the oath, Cuchulain. I bid you take the oath. Do as I tell you. What are your wits compared with mine, and what are your riches compared with mine? And what sons have you to pay your debts and to put a stone over you when you die? Take the oath, I tell you. Take a strong oath.'

FOOL: (*Crumpling himself up and whining*) I will not. I'll take no oath. I want my dinner.

BLIND MAN: Hush, hush! It is not done yet.

FOOL: You said it was done to a turn.

BLIND MAN: Did I, now? Well, it might be done, and not done. The wings might be white, but the legs might be red. The flesh might stick hard to the bones and not come away in the teeth. But, believe me, Fool, it will be well done before you put your teeth in it.

FOOL: My teeth are growing long with the hunger.

BLIND MAN: I'll tell you a story – the kings have story-tellers while they are waiting for their dinner – I will tell you a story with a fight in it, a story with a champion in it, and a ship and a queen's son that has his mind set on killing somebody that you and I know.

FOOL: Who is that? Who is he coming to kill?

BLIND MAN: Wait, now, till you hear. When you were stealing the fowl, I was lying in a hole in the sand, and I heard three men coming with a shuffling sort of noise. They were wounded and groaning.

FOOL: Go on. Tell me about the fight.

BLIND MAN: There had been a fight, a great fight, a tremendous great fight. A young man had landed on the shore, the guardians of the shore had asked his name, and he had refused to tell it, and he had killed one, and others had run away.

FOOL: That's enough. Come on now to the fowl. I wish it was bigger. I wish it was as big as a goose.

BLIND MAN: Hush! I haven't told you all. I know who that young man is. I heard the men who were running away say he had red hair, that he had come from Aoife's country, that he was coming to kill Cuchulain.

FOOL: Nobody can do that.

(*To a tune:*)

   Cuchulain has killed kings,
   Kings and sons of kings,
   Dragons out of the water,

And witches out of the air,
Banachas and Bonachas and people of the woods.

BLIND MAN: Hush! hush!

FOOL: (*Still singing:*)

Witches that steal the milk,
Fomor that steal the children,
Hags that have heads like hares,
Hares that have claws like witches,
All riding a-cock-horse

(*Spoken:*) Out of the very bottom of the bitter black North.

BLIND MAN: Hush, I say!

FOOL: Does Cuchulain know that he is coming to kill him?

BLIND MAN: How would he know that with his head in the clouds? He doesn't care for common fighting. Why would he put himself out, and nobody in it but that young man? Now if it were a white fawn that might turn into a queen before morning –

FOOL: Come to the fowl. I wish it was as big as a pig; a fowl with goose grease and pig's crackling.

BLIND MAN: No hurry, no hurry. I know whose son it is. I wouldn't tell anybody else, but I will tell you, – a secret is better to you than your dinner. You like being told secrets.

FOOL: Tell me the secret.

BLIND MAN: That young man is Aoife's son. I am sure it is Aoife's son, it flows in upon me that it is Aoife's son. You have often heard me talking of Aoife, the great woman-fighter Cuchulain got the mastery over in the North?

FOOL: I know, I know. She is one of those cross queens that live in hungry Scotland.

BLIND MAN: I am sure it is her son. I was in Aoife's country for a long time.

FOOL: That was before you were blinded for putting a curse upon the wind.

BLIND MAN: There was a boy in her house that had her own red colour on him, and everybody said he was to be brought up to kill Cuchulain, that she hated Cuchulain. She used to put a helmet on a pillar-stone and call it Cuchulain and set

him casting at it. There is a step outside – Cuchulain's step.
(CUCHULAIN *passes by in the mist outside the big door*.)

FOOL: Where is Cuchulain going?

BLIND MAN: He is going to meet Conchubar that has bidden him to take the oath.

FOOL: Ah, an oath, Blind Man. How can I remember so many things at once? Who is going to take an oath?

BLIND MAN: Cuchulain is going to take an oath to Conchubar who is High King.

FOOL: What a mix-up you make of everything, Blind Man! You were telling me one story, and now you are telling me another story . . . How can I get the hang of it at the end if you mix everything at the beginning? Wait till I settle it out. There now, there's Cuchulain (*he points to one foot*), and there is the young man (*he points to the other foot*) that is coming to kill him, and Cuchulain doesn't know. But where's Conchubar? (*Takes bag from side.*) That's Conchubar with all his riches – Cuchulain, young man, Conchubar. – And where's Aoife? (*Throws up cap.*) There is Aoife, high up on the mountains in high hungry Scotland. Maybe it is not true after all. Maybe it was your own making up. It's many a time you cheated me before with your lies. Come to the cooking-pot, my stomach is pinched and rusty. Would you have it to be creaking like a gate?

BLIND MAN: I tell you it's true. And more than that is true. If you listen to what I say, you'll forget your stomach.

FOOL: I won't.

BLIND MAN: Listen. I know who the young man's father is, but I won't say. I would be afraid to say. Ah, Fool, you would forget everything if you could know who the young man's father is.

FOOL: Who is it? Tell me now quick, or I'll shake you. Come, out with it, or I'll shake you.
(*A murmur of voices in the distance.*)

BLIND MAN: Wait, wait. There's somebody coming . . . It is Cuchulain is coming. He's coming back with the High King. Go and ask Cuchulain. He'll tell you. It's little you'll care about the cooking-pot when you have asked Cuchulain, that . . .

(*The* BLIND MAN *goes out by side door*.)

FOOL: I'll ask him. Cuchulain will know. He was in Aoife's country. (*Goes upstage*.) I'll ask him. (*Turns and goes downstage*.) But, no, I won't ask him, I would be afraid. (*Going up again*.) Yes, I will ask him. What harm in asking? The Blind Man said I was to ask him. (*Going down*.) No, no. I'll not ask him. He might kill me. I have but killed hens and geese and pigs. He has killed kings. (*Goes up again almost to big door*.) Who says I'm afraid? I'm not afraid. I'm no coward. I'll ask him. No, no, Cuchulain, I'm not going to ask you.

> He has killed kings,
> Kings and the sons of kings,
> Dragons out of the water,
> And witches out of the air.

Banachas and Bonachas and people of the woods.

(*The* FOOL *goes out by side door, the last words being heard outside*. CUCHULAIN *and* CONCHUBAR *enter through the big door at the back. While they are still outside*, CUCHULAIN'S *voice is heard raised in anger. He is a dark man, something over forty years of age*. CONCHUBAR *is much older and carries a long staff, elaborately carved or with an elaborate gold handle*.)

CUCHULAIN: Because I have killed men without your bidding
> And have rewarded others at my own pleasure,
> Because of half a score of trifling things,
> You'd lay this oath upon me, and now – and now
> You add another pebble to the heap,
> And I must be your man, wellnigh your bondsman,
> Because a youngster out of Aoife's country
> Has found the shore ill-guarded.

CONCHUBAR: He came to land
> While you were somewhere out of sight and hearing,
> Hunting or dancing with your wild companions.

CUCHULAIN: He can be driven out. I'll not be bound.
　　I'll dance or hunt, or quarrel or make love,
　　Wherever and whenever I've a mind to.
　　If time had not put water in your blood,
　　You never would have thought it.
CONCHUBAR:　　　　　　　　　　　I would leave
　　A strong and settled country to my children.
CUCHULAIN: And I must be obedient in all things;
　　Give up my will to yours; go where you please;
　　Come when you call; sit at the council-board
　　Among the unshapely bodies of old men;
　　I whose mere name has kept this country safe,
　　I that in early days have driven out
　　Maeve of Cruachan and the northern pirates,
　　The hundred kings of Sorcha, and the kings
　　Out of the Garden in the East of the World.
　　Must I, that held you on the throne when all
　　Had pulled you from it, swear obedience
　　As if I were some cattle-raising king?
　　Are my shins speckled with the heat of the fire,
　　Or have my hands no skill but to make figures
　　Upon the ashes with a stick? Am I
　　So slack and idle that I need a whip
　　Before I serve you?
CONCHUBAR:　　　　　　No, no whip, Cuchulain,
　　But every day my children come and say:
　　'This man is growing harder to endure.
　　How can we be at safety with this man
　　That nobody can buy or bid or bind?
　　We shall be at his mercy when you are gone;
　　He burns the earth as if he were a fire,
　　And time can never touch him.'
CUCHULAIN:　　　　　　　　　And so the tale
　　Grows finer yet; and I am to obey
　　Whatever child you set upon the throne,
　　As if it were yourself!
CONCHUBAR:　　　　　Most certainly.

I am High King, my son shall be High King;
And you for all the wildness of your blood,
And though your father came out of the sun,
Are but a little king and weigh but light
In anything that touches government,
If put into the balance with my children.

CUCHULAIN: It's well that we should speak our minds
    out plainly,
For when we die we shall be spoken of
In many countries. We in our young days
Have seen the heavens like a burning cloud
Brooding upon the world, and being more
Than men can be now that cloud's lifted up,
We should be the more truthful. Conchubar,
I do not like your children – they have no pith,
No marrow in their bones, and will lie soft
Where you and I lie hard.

CONCHUBAR: You rail at them
Because you have no children of your own.

CUCHULAIN: I think myself most lucky that I leave
No pallid ghost or mockery of a man
To drift and mutter in the corridors
Where I have laughed and sung.

CONCHUBAR: That is not true,
For all your boasting of the truth between us;
For there is no man having house and lands,
That have been in the one family, called
By that one family's name for centuries,
But is made miserable if he know
They are to pass into a stranger's keeping,
As yours will pass.

CUCHULAIN: The most of men feel that,
But you and I leave names upon the harp.

CONCHUBAR: You play with arguments as lawyers do,
And put no heart in them. I know your thoughts,
For we have slept under the one cloak and drunk
From the one wine-cup. I know you to the bone,

I have heard you cry, aye, in your very sleep,
'I have no son', and with such bitterness
That I have gone upon my knees and prayed
That it might be amended.

CUCHULAIN: For you thought
That I should be as biddable as others
Had I their reason for it; but that's not true;
For I would need a weightier argument
Than one that marred me in the copying,
As I have that clean hawk out of the air
That, as men say, begot this body of mine
Upon a mortal woman.

CONCHUBAR: Now as ever
You mock at every reasonable hope,
And would have nothing, or impossible things.
What eye has ever looked upon the child
Would satisfy a mind like that?

CUCHULAIN: I would leave
My house and name to none that would not face
Even myself in battle.

CONCHUBAR: Being swift of foot,
And making light of every common chance,
You should have overtaken on the hills
Some daughter of the air, or on the shore
A daughter of the Country-under-Wave.

CUCHULAIN: I am not blasphemous.

CONCHUBAR: Yet you despise
Our queens, and would not call a child your own,
If one of them had borne him.

CUCHULAIN: I have not said it.

CONCHUBAR: Ah! I remember I have heard you boast,
When the ale was in your blood, that there was one
In Scotland, where you had learnt the trade of war,
That had a stone-pale cheek and red-brown hair;
And that although you had loved other women,
You'd sooner that fierce woman of the camp
Bore you a son than any queen among them.

CUCHULAIN: You call her a 'fierce woman of the camp',
    For, having lived among the spinning-wheels,
    You'd have no woman near that would not say,
    'Ah! how wise!' 'What will you have for supper?'
    'What shall I wear that I may please you, sir?'
    And keep that humming through the day and night
    For ever. A fierce woman of the camp!
    But I am getting angry about nothing.
    You have never seen her. Ah! Conchubar, had you seen her
    With that high, laughing, turbulent head of hers
    Thrown backward, and the bowstring at her ear,
    Or sitting at the fire with those grave eyes
    Full of good counsel as it were with wine,
    Or when love ran through all the lineaments
    Or her wild body – although she had no child,
    None other had all beauty, queen or lover,
    Of was so fitted to give birth to kings.
CONCHUBAR: There's nothing I can say but drifts you
      farther
    From the one weighty matter. That very woman –
    For I know well that you are praising Aoife –
    Now hates you and will leave no subtlety
    Unknotted that might run into a noose
    About your throat, no army in idleness
    That might bring ruin on this land you serve.
CUCHULAIN: No wonder in that, no wonder at all in that.
    I never have known love but as a kiss
    In the mid-battle, and a difficult truce
    Of oil and water, candles and dark night,
    Hillside and hollow, the hot-footed sun
    And the cold, sliding, slippery-footed moon –
    A brief forgiveness between opposites
    That have been hatreds for three times the age
    Of this long-'stablished ground.
CONCHUBAR: Listen to me.
    Aoife makes war on us, and every day
    Our enemies grow greater and beat the walls

More bitterly, and you within the walls
Are every day more turbulent; and yet,
When I would speak about these things, your fancy
Runs as it were a swallow on the wind.

(*Outside the door in the blue light of the sea mist are many old and young* KINGS; *among them are three* WOMEN, *two of whom carry a bowl of fire. The third, in what follows, puts from time to time fragrant herbs into the fire so that it flickers up into brighter flame.*)

Look at the door and what men gather there –
Old counsellors that steer the land with me,
And younger kings, the dancers and harp-players
That follow in your tumults, and all these
Are held there by the one anxiety.
Will you be bound into obedience
And so make this land safe for them and theirs?
You are but half a king and I but half;
I need your might of hand and burning heart,
And you my wisdom.

CUCHULAIN: (*Going near to door*) Nestlings of a high nest,
Hawks that have followed me into the air
And looked upon the sun, we'll out of this
And sail upon the wind once more. This king
Would have me take an oath to do his will,
And having listened to his tune from morning,
I will no more of it. Run to the stable
And set the horses to the chariot-pole,
And send a messenger to the harp-players.
We'll find a level place among the woods,
And dance awhile.

A YOUNG KING: Cuchulain, take the oath.
There is none here that would not have you take it.

CUCHULAIN: You'd have me take it? Are you of one mind?

THE KINGS: All, all, all, all!

A YOUNG KING: Do what the High King bids you.

CONCHUBAR: There is not one but dreads this turbulence
Now that they're settled men.

CUCHULAIN: Are you so changed,
   Or have I grown more dangerous of late?
   But that's not it. I understand it all.
   It's you that have changed. You've wives and children
     now,
   And for that reason cannot follow one
   That lives like a bird's flight from tree to tree. –
   It's time the years put water in my blood
   And drowned the wildness of it, for all's changed,
   But that unchanged. – I'll take what oath you will:
   The moon, the sun, the water, light, or air,
   I do not care how binding.
CONCHUBAR: On this fire
   That has been lighted from your hearth and mine;
   The older men shall be my witnesses,
   The younger, yours. The holders of the fire
   Shall purify the thresholds of the house
   With waving fire, and shut the outer door,
   According to the custom; and sing rhyme
   That has come down from the old law-makers
   To blow the witches out. Considering
   That the wild will of man could be oath-bound,
   But that a woman's could not, they bid us sing
   Against the will of woman at its wildest
   In the Shape-Changers that run upon the wind.
   (CONCHUBAR *has gone on to his throne*.)
THE WOMEN: (*They sing in a very low voice after the first few
   words so that the others all but drown their words*.)
   May this fire have driven out
   The Shape-Changers that can put
   Ruin on a great king's house
   Until all be ruinous.
   Names whereby a man has known
   The threshold and the hearthstone,
   Gather on the wind and drive
   The women none can kiss and thrive,
   For they are but whirling wind,

Out of memory and mind.
They would make a prince decay
With light images of clay
Planted in the running wave;
Or, for many shapes they have,
They would change them into hounds
Until he had died of his wounds,
Though the change were but a whim;
Or they'd hurl a spell at him,
That he follow with desire
Bodies that can never tire
Or grow kind, for they anoint
All their bodies, joint by joint,
With a miracle-working juice
That is made out of the grease
Of the ungoverned unicorn.
But the man is thrice forlorn,
Emptied, ruined, wracked, and lost,
That they follow, for at most
They will give him kiss for kiss
While they murmur, 'After this
Hatred may be sweet to the taste.'
Those wild hands that have embraced
All his body can but shove
At the burning wheel of love
Till the side of hate comes up.
Therefore in this ancient cup
May the sword-blades drink their fill
Of the home-brew there, until
They will have for masters none
But the threshold and hearthstone.

CUCHULAIN: (*Speaking, while they are singing*) I'll take
    and keep this oath, and from this day
    I shall be what you please, my chicks, my nestlings.
    Yet I had thought you were of those that praised
    Whatever life could make the pulse run quickly,
    Even though it were brief, and that you held

That a free gift was better than a forced. –
But that's all over. – I will keep it, too;
I never gave a gift and took it again.
If the wild horse should break the chariot-pole,
It would be punished. Should that be in the oath?

(*Two of the* WOMEN, *still singing, crouch in front of him holding the bowl over their heads. He spreads his hands over the flame.*)

I swear to be obedient in all things
To Conchubar, and to uphold his children.

CONCHUBAR: We are one being, as these flames are one:
I give my wisdom, and I take your strength.
Now thrust the swords into the flame, and pray
That they may serve the threshold and the hearthstone
With faithful service.

(*The* KINGS *kneel in a semicircle before the two* WOMEN *and* CUCHULAIN, *who thrusts his sword into the flame. They all put the points of their swords into the flame. The third* WOMAN *is at the back near the big door.*)

CUCHULAIN: O pure, glittering ones
That should be more than wife or friend or mistress,
Give us the enduring will, the unquenchable hope,
The friendliness of the sword! –

(*The song grows louder, and the last words ring out clearly. There is a loud knocking at the door, and a cry of 'Open! open!'*)

CONCHUBAR: Some king that has been loitering on the
    way.
Open the door, for I would have all know
That the oath's finished and Cuchulain bound,
And that the swords are drinking up the flame.

(*The door is opened by the third* WOMAN, *and a* YOUNG MAN *with a drawn sword enters.*)

YOUNG MAN: I am of Aoife's country.

(*The* KINGS *rush towards him.* CUCHULAIN *throws him-self between.*)

CUCHULAIN: Put up your swords.
He is but one. Aoife is far away.

YOUNG MAN: I have come alone into the midst of you
    To weigh this sword against Cuchulain's sword.

CONCHUBAR: And are you noble? for if of common seed,
    You cannot weigh your sword against his sword
    But in mixed battle.

YOUNG MAN: I am under bonds
    To tell my name to no man; but it's noble.

CONCHUBAR: But I would know your name and not your
       bonds.
    You cannot speak in the Assembly House,
    If you are not noble.

FIRST OLD KING: Answer the High King!

YOUNG MAN: I will give no other proof than the hawk gives
    That it's no sparrow!
    (He is silent for a moment, then speaks to all.)
                  Yet look upon me, kings.
    I, too, am of that ancient seed, and carry
    The signs about this body and in these bones.

CUCHULAIN: To have shown the hawk's grey feather is
       enough,
    And you speak highly, too. Give me that helmet.
    I'd thought they had grown weary sending champions.
    That sword and belt will do. This fighting's welcome.
    The High King there has promised me his wisdom;
    But the hawk's sleepy till its well-beloved
    Cries out amid the acorns, or it has seen
    Its enemy like a speck upon the sun.
    What's wisdom to the hawk, when that clear eye
    Is burning nearer up in the high air?
    (Looks hard at YOUNG MAN; *then comes down steps and grasps* YOUNG MAN *by shoulder.)*
    Hither into the light.
    (To CONCHUBAR*)*   The very tint
    Of her that I was speaking of but now.
    Not a pin's difference.
    (To YOUNG MAN*)*   You are from the North,
    Where there are many that have that tint of hair –

Red-brown, the light red-brown. Come nearer, boy,
For I would have another look at you.
There's more likeness – a pale, a stone-pale cheek.
What brought you, boy? Have you no fear of death?

YOUNG MAN: Whether I live or die is in the gods' hands.

CUCHULAIN: That is all words, all words; a young man's
    talk.
I am their plough, their harrow, their very strength;
For he that's in the sun begot this body
Upon a mortal woman, and I have heard tell
It seemed as if he had outrun the moon
That he must follow always through waste heaven,
He loved so happily. He'll be but slow
To break a tree that was so sweetly planted.
Let's see that arm. I'll see it if I choose.
That arm had a good father and a good mother,
But it is not like this.

YOUNG MAN: You are mocking me;
You think I am not worthy to be fought.
But I'll not wrangle but with this talkative knife.

CUCHULAIN: Put up your sword; I am not mocking you.
I'd have you for my friend, but if it's not
Because you have a hot heart and a cold eye,
I cannot tell the reason.

(*To* CONCHUBAR)   He has got her fierceness,
And nobody is as fierce as those pale women.
But I will keep him with me, Conchubar,
That he may set my memory upon her
When the day's fading. – You will stop with us,
And we will hunt the deer and the wild bulls;
And, when we have grown weary, light our fires
Between the wood and water, or on some mountain
Where the Shape-Changers of the morning come.
The High King there would make a mock of me
Because I did not take a wife among them.
Why do you hang your head? It's a good life:
The head grows prouder in the light of the dawn,

And friendship thickens in the murmuring dark
Where the spare hazels meet the wool-white foam.
But I can see there's no more need for words
And that you'll be my friend from this day out.

CONCHUBAR: He has come hither not in his own name
But in Queen Aoife's, and has challenged us
In challenging the foremost man of us all.

CUCHULAIN: Well, well, what matter?

CONCHUBAR: You think it does not matter,
And that a fancy lighter than the air,
A whim of the moment, has more matter in it.
For, having none that shall reign after you,
You cannot think as I do, who would leave
A throne too high for insult.

CUCHULAIN: Let your children
Re-mortar their inheritance, as we have,
And put more muscle on. – I'll give you gifts,
But I'd have something too – that arm-ring, boy.
We'll have this quarrel out when you are older.

YOUNG MAN: There is no man I'd sooner have my friend
Than you, whose name has gone about the world
As if it had been the wind; but Aoife'd say
I had turned coward.

CUCHULAIN: I will give you gifts
That Aoife'll know, and all her people know,
To have come from me.

(Showing cloak)

                    My father gave me this.
He came to try me, rising up at dawn
Out of the cold dark of the rich sea.
He challenged me to battle, but before
My sword had touched his sword, told me his name,
Gave me this cloak, and vanished. It was woven
By women of the Country-under-Wave
Out of the fleeces of the sea. O! tell her
I was afraid, or tell her what you will.
No; tell her that I heard a raven croak

On the north side of the house, and was afraid.

CONCHUBAR: Some witch of the air has troubled
    Cuchulain's mind.

CUCHULAIN: No witchcraft. His head is like a woman's
    head
    I had a fancy for.

CONCHUBAR: A witch of the air
    Can make a leaf confound us with memories.
    They run upon the wind and hurl the spells
    That make us nothing, out of the invisible wind.
    They have gone to school to learn the trick of it.

CUCHULAIN: No, no – there's nothing out of common
    here;
    The winds are innocent. – That arm-ring, boy.

A KING: If I've your leave I'll take this challenge up.

ANOTHER KING: No, give it me, High King, for this wild Aoife
    Has carried off my slaves.

ANOTHER KING: No, give it me,
    For she has harried me in house and herd.

ANOTHER KING: I claim this fight.

OTHER KINGS: (*Together*)   And I! And I! And I!

CUCHULAIN: Back! back! Put up your swords! Put up your
    swords!
    There's none alive that shall accept a challenge
    I have refused. Laegaire, put up your sword!

YOUNG MAN: No, let them come. If they've a mind for it,
    I'll try it out with any two together.

CUCHULAIN: That's spoken as I'd
    have spoken it at your age.
    But you are in my house. Whatever man
    Would fight with you shall fight it out with me.
    They're dumb, they're dumb. How many of you would
    meet
  (*Draws sword.*)
    This mutterer, this old whistler, this sand-piper,
    This edge that's greyer than the tide, this mouse
    That's gnawing at the timbers of the world,

This, this – Boy, I would meet them all in arms
If I'd a son like you. He would avenge me
When I have withstood for the last time the men
Whose fathers, brothers, sons, and friends I have killed
Upholding Conchubar, when the four provinces
Have gathered with the ravens over them.
But I'd need no avenger. You and I
Would scatter them like water from a dish.

YOUNG MAN: We'll stand by one another from this out.
Here is the ring.

CUCHULAIN: No, turn and turn about.
But my turn's first because I am the older.
(Spreading out cloak)
Nine queens out of the Country-under-Wave
Have woven it with the fleeces of the sea
And they were long embroidering at it. – Boy,
If I had fought my father, he'd have killed me,
As certainly as if I had a son
And fought with him, I should be deadly to him;
For the old fiery fountains are far off
And every day there is less heat o' the blood.

CONCHUBAR: (*In a loud voice*) No more of this. I will not
have this friendship.
Cuchulain is my man, and I forbid it.
He shall not go unfought, for I myself –

CUCHULAIN: I will not have it.

CONCHUBAR: You lay commands on me?

CUCHULAIN: (*Seizing* CONCHUBAR) You shall not stir, High
King.
I'll hold you there.

CONCHUBAR: Witchcraft has maddened you.

THE KINGS: (*Shouting*)   Yes, witchcraft! witchcraft!

FIRST OLD KING: Some witch has worked upon your mind,
Cuchulain.
The head of that young man seemed like a woman's
You'd had a fancy for. Then of a sudden
You laid your hands on the High King himself!

CUCHULAIN: And laid my hands on the High King himself?

CONCHUBAR: Some witch is floating in the air above us.

CUCHULAIN: Yes, witchcraft! witchcraft! Witches of the air!

(*To* YOUNG MAN) Why did you? Who was it set you to this work?

Out, out! I say, for now it's sword on sword!

YOUNG MAN: But . . . but I did not.

CUCHULAIN: Out, I say, out, out!

(YOUNG MAN *goes out followed by* CUCHULAIN. *The* KINGS *follow them out with confused cries, and words one can hardly hear because of the noise. Some cry,* 'Quicker, quicker!' 'Why are you so long at the door?' 'We'll be too late!' 'Have they begun to fight?' 'Can you see if they are fighting?' *and so on. Their voices drown each other. The three* WOMEN *are left alone.*)

FIRST WOMAN: I have seen, I have seen!

SECOND WOMAN: What do you cry aloud?

FIRST WOMAN: The Ever-living have shown me what's to come.

THIRD WOMAN: How? Where?

FIRST WOMAN: In the ashes of the bowl.

SECOND WOMAN: While you were holding it between your hands?

THIRD WOMAN: Speak quickly!

FIRST WOMAN: I have seen Cuchulain's roof-tree Leap into fire, and the walls split and blacken.

SECOND WOMAN: Cuchulain has gone out to die.

THIRD WOMAN: O! O!

SECOND WOMAN: Who could have thought that one so great as he
Should meet his end at this unnoted sword!

FIRST WOMAN: Life drifts between a fool and a blind man
To the end, and nobody can know his end.

SECOND WOMAN: Come, look upon the quenching of this greatness.

(The other two go to the door, but they stop for a moment upon the threshold and wail.)

FIRST WOMAN: No crying out, for there'll be need of cries
  And rending of the hair when it's all finished.

(The WOMEN *go out. There is the sound of clashing swords from time to time during what follows. Enter the* FOOL *dragging the* BLIND MAN.)

FOOL: You have eaten it, you have eaten it! You have left me nothing but the bones.

(He throws the BLIND MAN *down by big chair.)*

BLIND MAN: O, that I should have to endure such a plague! O, I ache all over! O, I am pulled to pieces! This is the way you pay me all the good I have done you.

FOOL: You have eaten it! You have told me lies. I might have known you had eaten it when I saw your slow, sleepy walk. Lie there till the kings come. O, I will tell Conchubar and Cuchulain and all the kings about you!

BLIND MAN: What would have happened to you but for me, and you without your wits? If I did not take care of you, what would you do for food and warmth?

FOOL: You take care of me? You stay safe, and send me into every kind of danger. You sent me down the cliffs for gulls' eggs while you warmed your blind eyes in the sun; and then you ate all that were good for food. You left me the eggs that were neither egg nor bird.

(The BLIND MAN *tries to rise; the* FOOL *makes him lie down again.)*

Keep quiet now, till I shut the door. There is some noise outside – a high vexing noise, so that I can't be listening to myself. *(Shuts the big door.)* Why can't they be quiet? Why can't they be quiet?

(The BLIND MAN *tries to get away.)*

Ah! you would get away, would you? *(Follows the* BLIND MAN *and brings him back.)* Lie there! lie there! No, you won't get away! Lie there till the kings come. I'll tell them all about you. I will tell it all. How you sit warming yourself, when you have made me light a fire of sticks, while I sit blowing it with my mouth. Do you not always make me take the windy side of the bush when it blows, and the rainy side when it rains?

BLIND MAN: O, good Fool! listen to me. Think of the care I have taken of you. I have brought you to many a warm hearth, where there was a good welcome for you, but you would not stay there; you were always wandering about.

FOOL: The last time you brought me in, it was not I who wandered away, but you that got put out because you took the crubeen out of the pot when nobody was looking. Keep quiet, now!

CUCHULAIN: (*Rushing in*) Witchcraft! There is no witch-craft on the earth, or among the witches of the air, that these hands cannot break.

FOOL: Listen to me, Cuchulain. I left him turning the fowl at the fire. He ate it all, though I had stolen it. He left me nothing but the feathers.

CUCHULAIN: Fill me a horn of ale!

BLIND MAN: I gave him what he likes best. You do not know how vain this Fool is. He likes nothing so well as a feather.

FOOL: He left me nothing but the bones and feathers. Nothing but the feathers, though I had stolen it.

CUCHULAIN: Give me that horn. Quarrels here, too! (*Drinks*.) What is there between you two that is worth a quarrel? Out with it!

BLIND MAN: Where would he be but for me? I must be always thinking – thinking to get food for the two of us, and when we've got it, if the moon is at the full or the tide on the turn, he'll leave the rabbit in the snare till it is full of maggots, or let the trout slip back through his hands into the stream.

(*The* FOOL *has begun singing while the* BLIND MAN *is speaking.*)

FOOL: (*Singing:*)

When you were an acorn on the tree-top,
    Then was I an eagle-cock;
Now that you are a withered old block,
    Still am I an eagle-cock.

BLIND MAN: Listen to him, now. That's the sort of talk I have to put up with day out, day in.

(*The* FOOL *is putting the feathers into his hair.* CUCHULAIN *takes a handful of feathers out of a heap the* FOOL *has on the bench beside him, and out of the* FOOL's *hair, and begins to wipe the blood from his sword with them.*)

FOOL: He has taken my feathers to wipe his sword. It is blood that he is wiping from his sword.

CUCHULAIN: (*Goes up to door at back and throws away feathers.*) They are standing about his body. They will not awaken him, for all his witchcraft.

BLIND MAN: It is that young champion that he has killed. He that came out of Aoife's country.

CUCHULAIN: He thought to have saved himself with witchcraft.

FOOL: That Blind Man there said he would kill you. He came from Aoife's country to kill you. That Blind Man said they had taught him every kind of weapon that he might do it. But I always knew that you would kill him.

CUCHULAIN: (*To the* BLIND MAN) You knew him, then?

BLIND MAN: I saw him, when I had my eyes, in Aoife's country.

CUCHULAIN: You were in Aoife's country?

BLIND MAN: I knew him and his mother there.

CUCHULAIN: He was about to speak of her when he died.

BLIND MAN: He was a queen's son.

CUCHULAIN: What queen? what queen? (*Seizes the* BLIND MAN, *who is now sitting upon the bench.*) Was it Scathach? There were many queens. All the rulers there were queens.

BLIND MAN: No, not Scathach.

CUCHULAIN: It was Uathach, then? Speak! speak!

BLIND MAN: I cannot speak; you are clutching me too tightly. (CUCHULAIN *lets him go.*)

I cannot remember who it was. I am not certain. It was some queen.

FOOL: He said a while ago that the young man was Aoife's son.

CUCHULAIN: She? No, no! She had no son when I was there.

FOOL: That Blind Man there said that she owned him for her son.

CUCHULAIN: I had rather he had been some other woman's son. What father had he? A soldier out of Alba? She was an amorous woman – a proud, pale, amorous woman.

BLIND MAN: None knew whose son he was.

CUCHULAIN: None knew! Did you know, old listener at doors?

BLIND MAN: No, no; I knew nothing.

FOOL: He said a while ago that he heard Aoife boast that she'd never but the one lover, and he the only man that had overcome her in battle.

(*Pause.*)

BLIND MAN: Somebody is trembling, Fool! The bench is shaking. Why are you trembling? Is Cuchulain going to hurt us? It was not I who told you, Cuchulain.

FOOL: It is Cuchulain who is trembling? It is Cuchulain who is shaking the bench.

BLIND MAN: It is his own son he has slain.

CUCHULAIN: 'Twas they that did it, the pale windy people.
  Where? where? where? My sword against the thunder!
  But no, for they have always been my friends;
  And though they love to blow a smoking coal
  Till it's all flame, the wars they blow aflame
  Are full of glory, and heart-uplifting pride,
  And not like this. The wars they love awaken
  Old fingers and the sleepy strings of harps.
  Who did it then? Are you afraid? Speak out!
  For I have put you under my protection,
  And will reward you well. Dubthach the Chafer?
  He'd an old grudge. No, for he is with Maeve.
  Laegaire did it! Why do you not speak?
  What is this house? (*Pause.*) Now I remember all.

(*Comes before* CONCHUBAR's *chair, and strikes out with his sword, as if* CONCHUBAR *was sitting upon it.*)

'Twas you who did it – you who sat up there
With your old rod of kingship, like a magpie
Nursing a stolen spoon. No, not a magpie,
A maggot that is eating up the earth!
Yes, but a magpie, for he's flown away.
Where did he fly to?

BLIND MAN: He is outside the door.

CUCHULAIN: Outside the door?

BLIND MAN: Between the door and the sea.

CUCHULAIN: Conchubar, Conchubar! the sword into your
   heart!

(*He rushes out. Pause. The* FOOL *creeps up to the big door and
looks after him.*)

FOOL: He is going up to King Conchubar. They are all
   about the young man. No, no, he is standing still. There
   is a great wave going to break, and he is looking at it. Ah!
   now he is running down to the sea, but he is holding up his
   sword as if he were going into a fight. (*Pause.*) Well struck!
   well struck!

BLIND MAN: What is he doing now?

FOOL: O! he is fighting the waves!

BLIND MAN: He sees King Conchubar's crown on every one
   of them.

FOOL: There, he has struck at a big one! He has struck
   the crown off it; he has made the foam fly. There again,
   another big one!

BLIND MAN: Where are the kings? What are the kings doing?

FOOL: They are shouting and running down to the shore,
   and the people are running out of the houses. They are all
   running.

BLIND MAN: You say they are running out of the houses?
   There will be nobody left in the houses. Listen, Fool!

FOOL: There, he is down! He is up again. He is going out in
   the deep water. There is a big wave. It has gone over him. I
   cannot see him now. He has killed kings and giants, but the
   waves have mastered him, the waves have mastered him!

BLIND MAN: Come here, Fool!

FOOL: The waves have mastered him.

BLIND MAN: Come here!

FOOL: The waves have mastered him.

BLIND MAN: Come here, I say.

FOOL: (*Coming towards him, but looking backwards towards the door*) What is it?

BLIND MAN: There will be nobody in the houses. Come this way; come quickly! The ovens will be full. We will put our hands into the ovens.

(*They go out.*)

DEIRDRE

PERSONS IN THE PLAY

MUSICIANS
FERGUS, *an old man*
NAOISE (*pronounced 'Neesh-e'*), *a young king*
DEIRDRE, *his queen*
A DARK-FACED MESSENGER
CONCHUBAR (*pronounced 'Conohar'*), *the old King of Uladh,
     who is still strong and vigorous*
A DARK-FACED EXECUTIONER

A guest-house in a wood. It is a rough house of timber; through the doors and some of the windows one can see the great spaces of the wood, the sky dimming, night closing in. But a window to the left shows the thick leaves of a coppice; the landscape suggests silence and loneliness. There is a door to right and left, and through the side windows one can see anybody who approaches either door, a moment before he enters. In the centre, a part of the house is curtained off; the curtains are drawn. There are unlighted torches in brackets on the walls. There is, at one side, a small table with a chessboard and chessmen upon it. At the other side of the room there is a brazier with a fire; two WOMEN, with musical instruments beside them, crouch about the brazier: they are comely women of about forty. Another WOMAN, who carries a stringed instrument, enters hurriedly; she speaks, at first standing in the doorway.

FIRST MUSICIAN: I have a story right, my wanderers,
    That has so mixed with fable in our songs
    That all seemed fabulous. We are come, by chance,
    Into King Conchubar's country, and this house
    Is an old guest-house built for travellers
    From the seashore to Conchubar's royal house,
    And there are certain hills among these woods
    And there Queen Deirdre grew.
SECOND MUSICIAN: That famous queen
    Who has been wandering with her lover Naoise
    Somewhere beyond the edges of the world?
FIRST MUSICIAN: (*Going nearer to the brazier*) Some dozen
      years ago, King Conchubar found
    A house upon a hillside in this wood,

45

And there a child with an old witch to nurse her,
And nobody to say if she were human,
Or of the gods, or anything at all
Of who she was or why she was hidden there,
But that she'd too much beauty for good luck.
He went up thither daily, till at last
She put on womanhood, and he lost peace,
And Deirdre's tale began. The King was old.
A month or so before the marriage day,
A young man, in the laughing scorn of his youth,
Naoise, the son of Usna, climbed up there,
And having wooed, or, as some say, been wooed,
Carried her off.

SECOND MUSICIAN: The tale were well enough
Had it a finish.

FIRST MUSICIAN: Hush! I have more to tell;
But gather close about that I may whisper
The secrets of a king.

SECOND MUSICIAN: There's none to hear!

FIRST MUSICIAN: I have been to Conchubar's house and fol-
lowed up
A crowd of servants going out and in
With loads upon their heads: embroideries
To hang upon the walls, or new-mown rushes
To strew upon the floors, and came at length
To a great room.

SECOND MUSICIAN: Be silent; there are steps!

(*Enter* FERGUS, *an old man, who moves about from door to window excitedly through what follows.*)

FERGUS: I thought to find a message from the King.
You are musicians by these instruments,
And if as seems – for you are comely women –
You can praise love, you'll have the best of luck,
For there'll be two, before the night is in,
That bargained for their love, and paid for it
All that men value. You have but the time
To weigh a happy music with a sad,

To find what is most pleasing to a lover,
Before the son of Usna and his queen
Have passed this threshold.

FIRST MUSICIAN: Deirdre and her man!

FERGUS: I was to have found a message in this house,
And ran to meet it. Is there no messenger
From Conchubar to Fergus, son of Rogh?

FIRST MUSICIAN: Are Deirdre and her lover tired of life?

FERGUS: You are not of this country, or you'd know
That they are in my charge and all forgiven.

FIRST MUSICIAN: We have no country but the roads of the
world.

FERGUS: Then you should know that all things change in
the world,
And hatred turns to love and love to hate,
And even kings forgive.

FIRST MUSICIAN: An old man's love
Who casts no second line is hard to cure;
His jealousy is like his love.

FERGUS: And that's but true.
You have learned something in your wanderings.
He was so hard to cure that the whole court,
But I alone, thought it impossible;
Yet after I had urged it at all seasons,
I had my way, and all's forgiven now;
And you shall speak the welcome and the joy
That I lack tongue for.

FIRST MUSICIAN: Yet old men are jealous.

FERGUS: (Going to door) I am Conchubar's near friend,
and that weighed somewhat,
And it was policy to pardon them.
The need of some young, famous, popular man
To lead the troops, the murmur of the crowd,
And his own natural impulse, urged him to it.
They have been wandering half a dozen years.

FIRST MUSICIAN: And yet old men are jealous.

FERGUS: (Coming from door)   Sing the more sweetly

Because, though age is arid as a bone,
This man has flowered. I've need of music, too;
If this grey head would suffer no reproach,
I'd dance and sing –

(*Dark-faced* MEN *with strange, barbaric dress and arms begin to pass by the doors and windows. They pass one by one and in silence.*)

                              and dance till the hour ran out,
Because I have accomplished this good deed.

FIRST MUSICIAN: Look there – there at the window, those
          dark men,
     With murderous and outlandish-looking arms –
     They've been about the house all day.

FERGUS: (*Looking after them*)   What are you?
     Where do you come from, who is it sent you here?

FIRST MUSICIAN: They will not answer you.

FERGUS: They do not hear.

FIRST MUSICIAN: Forgive my open speech, but to these eyes
     That have seen many lands they are such men
     As kings will gather for a murderous task
     That neither bribes, commands, nor promises
     Can bring their people to.

FERGUS: And that is why
     You harped upon an old man's jealousy.
     A trifle sets you quaking. Conchubar's fame
     Brings merchandise on every wind that blows.
     They may have brought him Libyan dragon-skin,
     Or the ivory of the fierce unicorn.

FIRST MUSICIAN: If these be merchants, I have seen the goods
     They have brought to Conchubar, and understood
     His murderous purpose.

FERGUS: Murderous, you say?
     Why, what new gossip of the roads is this?
     But I'll not hear.

FIRST MUSICIAN: It may be life or death.
     There is a room in Conchubar's house, and there –

FERGUS: Be silent, or I'll drive you from the door.

There's many a one that would do more than that,
And make it prison, or death, or banishment
To slander the High King.
(*Suddenly restraining himself and speaking gently*)
                                    He is my friend;
I have his oath, and I am well content.
I have known his mind as if it were my own
These many years, and there is none alive
Shall buzz against him, and I there to stop it.
I know myself, and him, and your wild thought
Fed on extravagant poetry, and lit
By such a dazzle of old fabulous tales
That common things are lost, and all that's strange
Is true because 'twere pity if it were not.
(*Going to the door again*)
Quick! quick! your instruments! they are coming now.
I hear the hoofs a-clatter. Begin that song!
But what is it to be? I'd have them hear
A music foaming up out of the house
Like wine out of a cup. Come now, a verse
Of some old time not worth remembering,
And all the lovelier because a bubble.
Begin, begin, of some old king and queen,
Of Lugaidh Redstripe or another; no, not him,
He and his lady perished wretchedly.

FIRST MUSICIAN: (*Singing:*) 'Why is it', Queen Edain said,
        'If I do but climb the stair . . . '

FERGUS: Ah! that is better . . . They are alighted now.
    Shake all your cockscombs, children; these are lovers.
    (FERGUS *goes out*.)

FIRST MUSICIAN: (*Singing:*) 'Why is it', Queen Edain said,
        'If I do but climb the stair
    To the tower overhead,
        When the winds are calling there,
    Or the gannets calling out
        In waste places of the sky,
    There's so much to think about

That I cry, that I cry?'
SECOND MUSICIAN: (*Singing:*) But her goodman answered her:
    'Love would be a thing of naught
Had not all his limbs a stir
    Born out of immoderate thought;
Were he anything by half,
    Were his measure running dry.
Lovers, if they may not laugh,
    Have to cry, have to cry.'
   (DEIRDRE, NAOISE *and* FERGUS *have been seen for a moment
through the windows, but now they have entered.*)
THE THREE MUSICIANS: (*Together, singing:*) But is Edain worth
    a song
    Now the hunt begins anew?
Praise the beautiful and strong;
    Praise the redness of the yew;
Praise the blossoming apple-stem.
    But our silence had been wise.
What is all our praise to them
    That have one another's eyes?
DEIRDRE: Silence your music, though I thank you for it;
But the wind's blown upon my hair, and I
Must set the jewels on my neck and head
For one that's coming.
NAOISE: Your colour has all gone
As 'twere with fear, and there's no cause for that.
DEIRDRE: These women have the raddle that they use
To make them brave and confident, although
Dread, toil, or cold may chill the blood o' their cheeks.
You'll help me, women. It is my husband's will
I show my trust in one that may be here
Before the mind can call the colour up.
My husband took these rubies from a king
Of Surracha that was so murderous
He seemed all glittering dragon. Now wearing them
Myself wars on myself, for I myself –
That do my husband's will, yet fear to do it –

Grow dragonish to myself.

(*The* WOMEN *have gathered about her.* NAOISE *has stood looking at her, but* FERGUS *brings him to the chess table.*)

NAOISE: No messenger!
It's strange that there is none to welcome us.

FERGUS: King Conchubar has sent no messenger
That he may come himself.

NAOISE: And being himself,
Being High King, he cannot break his faith.
I have his word and I must take that word,
Or prove myself unworthy of my nurture
Under a great man's roof.

FERGUS: We'll play at chess
Till the King comes. It is but natural
That she should doubt him, for her house has been
The hole of the badger and the den of the fox.

NAOISE: If I had not King Conchubar's word I'd think
That chessboard ominous.

FERGUS: How can a board
That has been lying there these many years
Be lucky or unlucky?

NAOISE: It is the board
Where Lugaidh Redstripe and that wife of his,
Who had a seamew's body half the year,
Played at the chess upon the night they died.

FERGUS: I can remember now, a tale of treachery,
A broken promise and a journey's end –
But it were best forgot.

(DEIRDRE *has been standing with the* WOMEN *about her. They have been helping her to put on her jewels and to put the pigment on her cheeks and arrange her hair. She has gradually grown attentive to what* FERGUS *is saying.*)

NAOISE: If the tale's true,
When it was plain that they had been betrayed,
They moved the men and waited for the end
As it were bedtime, and had so quiet minds
They hardly winked their eyes when the sword flashed.

FERGUS: She never could have played so, being a woman,
    If she had not the cold sea's blood in her.

DEIRDRE: The gods turn clouds and casual accidents
    Into omens.

NAOISE: It would but ill become us,
    Now that King Conchubar has pledged his word,
    Should we be startled by a cloud or a shadow.

DEIRDRE: There's none to welcome us.

NAOISE: Being his guest,
    Words that would wrong him can but wrong ourselves.

DEIRDRE: An empty house upon the journey's end!
    Is that the way a king that means no mischief
    Honours a guest?

FERGUS: He is but making ready
    A welcome in his house, arranging where
    The moorhen and the mallard go, and where
    The speckled heathcock on a golden dish.

DEIRDRE: Had he no messenger?

NAOISE: Such words and fears
    Wrong this old man who's pledged his word to us.
    We must not speak or think as women do,
    That when the house is all abed sit up
    Marking among the ashes with a stick
    Till they are terrified. – Being what we are
    We must meet all things with an equal mind.
(To FERGUS) Come, let us look if there's a messenger
    From Conchubar. We cannot see from this
    Because we are blinded by the leaves and twigs,
    But it may be the wood will thin again.
    It is but kind that when the lips we love
    Speak words that are unfitting for kings' ears
    Our ears be deaf.

FERGUS: But now I had to threaten
    These wanderers because they would have weighed
    Some crazy fantasy of their own brain
    Or gossip of the road with Conchubar's word.
    If I had thought so little of mankind

I never could have moved him to this pardon.
I have believed the best of every man,
And find that to believe it is enough
To make a bad man show him at his best,
Or even a good man swing his lantern higher.

(NAOISE *and* FERGUS *go out. The last words are spoken as they go through the door. One can see them through part of what follows, either through door or window. They move about, talking or looking along the road towards Conchubar's house.*)

FIRST MUSICIAN: If anything lies heavy on your heart,
Speak freely of it, knowing it is certain
That you will never see my face again.

DEIRDRE: You've been in love?

FIRST MUSICIAN: If you would speak of love
Speak freely. There is nothing in the world
That has been friendly to us but the kisses
That were upon our lips, and when we are old
Their memory will be all the life we have.

DEIRDRE: There was a man that loved me. He was old;
I could not love him. Now I can but fear.
He has made promises, and brought me home;
But though I turn it over in my thoughts,
I cannot tell if they are sound and wholesome,
Or hackles on the hook.

FIRST MUSICIAN: I have heard he loved you
As some old miser loves the dragon-stone
He hides among the cobwebs near the roof.

DEIRDRE: You mean that when a man who has loved like that
Is after crossed, love drowns in its own flood,
And that love drowned and floating is but hate;
And that a king who hates sleeps ill at night
Till he has killed; and that, though the day laughs,
We shall be dead at cock-crow.

FIRST MUSICIAN: You've not my thought.
When I lost one I loved distractedly,

I blamed my crafty rival and not him,
And fancied, till my passion had run out,
That could I carry him away with me,
And tell him all my love, I'd keep him yet.

DEIRDRE: Ah! now I catch your meaning, that this king
Will murder Naoise, and keep me alive.

FIRST MUSICIAN: 'Tis you that put that meaning upon words
Spoken at random.

DEIRDRE: Wanderers like you,
Who have their wit alone to keep their lives,
Speak nothing that is bitter to the ear
At random; if they hint at it at all
Their eyes and ears have gathered it so lately
That it is crying out in them for speech.

FIRST MUSICIAN: We have little that is certain.

DEIRDRE: Certain or not,
Speak it out quickly, I beseech you to it;
I never have met any of your kind
But that I gave them money, food, and fire.

FIRST MUSICIAN: There are strange, miracle-working, wicked
     stones,
Men tear out of the heart and the hot brain
Of Libyan dragons.

DEIRDRE: The hot Istain stone,
And the cold stone of Fanes, that have power
To stir even those at enmity to love.

FIRST MUSICIAN: They have so great an influence, if but sewn
In the embroideries that curtain in
The bridal bed.

DEIRDRE: O Mover of the stars
That made this delicate house of ivory,
And made my soul its mistress, keep it safe!

FIRST MUSICIAN: I have seen a bridal bed, so curtained in,
So decked for miracle in Conchubar's house,
And learned that a bride's coming.

DEIRDRE: And I the bride?
Here is worse treachery than the seamew suffered,

For she but died and mixed into the dust
Of her dear comrade, but I am to live
And lie in the one bed with him I hate.
Where is Naoise? I was not alone like this
When Conchubar first chose me for his wife;
I cried in sleeping or waking and he came,
But now there is worse need.

NAOISE: (*Entering with Fergus*)   Why have you called?
    I was but standing there, without the door.

DEIRDRE: I have heard terrible mysterious things,
    Magical horrors and the spells of wizards.

FERGUS: Why, that's no wonder. You have been listening
    To singers of the roads that gather up
    The stories of the world.

DEIRDRE: But I have one
    To make the stories of the world but nothing.

NAOISE: Be silent if it is against the King
    Whose guest you are.

FERGUS: No, let her speak it out.
    I know the High King's heart as it were my own,
    And can refute a slander, but already
    I have warned these women that it may be death.

NAOISE: I will not weigh the gossip of the roads
    With the King's word. I ask your pardon for her:
    She has the heart of the wild birds that fear
    The net of the fowler or the wicker cage.

DEIRDRE: Am I to see the fowler and the cage
    And speak no word at all?

NAOISE: You would have known,
    Had they not bred you in that mountainous place,
    That when we give a word and take a word
    Sorrow is put away, past wrong forgotten.

DEIRDRE: Though death may come of it?

NAOISE: Though death may come.

DEIRDRE: When first we came into this empty house
    You had foreknowledge of our death, and even
    When speaking of the paleness of my cheek

Your own cheek blanched.

NAOISE: Listen to this old man.
He can remember all the promises
We trusted to.

DEIRDRE: You speak from the lips out,
And I am pleading for your life and mine.

NAOISE: Listen to this old man, for many think
He has a golden tongue.

DEIRDRE: Then I will say
What it were best to carry to the grave.
Look at my face where the leaf raddled it
And at these rubies on my hair and breast.
It was for him, to stir him to desire,
I put on beauty; yes, for Conchubar.

NAOISE: What frenzy put these words into your mouth?

DEIRDRE: No frenzy, for what need is there for frenzy
To change what shifts with every change of the wind,
Or else there is no truth in men's old sayings?
Was I not born a woman?

NAOISE: You're mocking me.

DEIRDRE: And is there mockery in this face and eyes,
Or in this body, in these limbs that brought
So many mischiefs? Look at me and say
If that that shakes my limbs be mockery.

NAOISE: What woman is there that a man can trust
But at the moment when he kisses her
At the first midnight?

DEIRDRE: Were it not most strange
That women should put evil in men's hearts
And lack it in themselves? And yet I think
That being half good I might change round again
Were we aboard our ship and on the sea.

NAOISE: We'll to the horses and take ship again.

FERGUS: Fool, she but seeks to rouse your jealousy
With crafty words.

DEIRDRE: Were we not born to wander?
These jewels have been reaped by the innocent sword

Upon a mountain, and a mountain bred me;
But who can tell what change can come to love
Among the valleys? I speak no falsehood now.
Away to windy summits, and there mock
The night-jar and the valley-keeping bird!

FERGUS: Men blamed you that you stirred a quarrel up
That has brought death to many. I have made peace,
Poured water on the fire, but if you fly
King Conchubar may think that he is mocked
And the house blaze again: and in what quarter,
If Conchubar were the treacherous man you think,
Would you find safety now that you have come
Into the very middle of his power,
Under his very eyes?

DEIRDRE: Under his eyes
And in the very middle of his power!
Then there is but one way to make all safe:
I'll spoil this beauty that brought misery
And houseless wandering on the man I loved.
These wanderers will show me how to do it;
To clip this hair to baldness, blacken my skin
With walnut juice, and tear my face with briars.
O that the creatures of the woods had torn
My body with their claws!

FERGUS: What, wilder yet!

DEIRDRE: (*To* NAOISE) Whatever were to happen to my face
I'd be myself, and there's not any way
But this to bring all trouble to an end.

NAOISE: Leave the gods' handiwork unblotched, and wait
For their decision, our decision is past.

(*A Dark-faced* MESSENGER *comes to the threshold.*)

FERGUS: Peace, peace; the messenger is at the door;
He stands upon the threshold; he stands there;
He stands, King Conchubar's purpose on his lips.

MESSENGER: Supper is on the table. Conchubar
Is waiting for his guests.

FERGUS: All's well again!

All's well! All's well! You cried your doubts so loud
That I had almost doubted.

NAOISE: We doubted him,
And he the while but busy in his house
For the more welcome.

DEIRDRE: The message is not finished.

FERGUS: Come quickly. Conchubar will laugh, that I –
Although I held out boldly in my speech –
That I, even I –

DEIRDRE: Wait, wait! He is not done.

MESSENGER: Deirdre and Fergus, son of Rogh, are summoned;
But not the traitor that bore off the Queen.
It is enough that the King pardon her,
And call her to his table and his bed.

NAOISE: So, then, it's treachery.

FERGUS: I'll not believe it.

NAOISE: Lead on and I will follow at your heels
That I may challenge him before his court
To match me there, or match me in some place
Where none can come between us but our swords,
For I have found no truth on any tongue
That's not of iron.

MESSENGER: I am Conchubar's man,
I am content to serve an iron tongue:
That Tongue commands that Fergus, son of Rogh,
And Deirdre come this night into his house,
And none but they.

(*He goes, followed by* NAOISE.)

FERGUS: Some rogue, some enemy,
Has bribed him to embroil us with the King;
I know that he has lied because I know
King Conchubar's mind as if it were my own,
But I'll find out the truth.

(*He is about to follow* NAOISE, *but* DEIRDRE *stops him.*)

DEIDRE: No, no, old man.
You thought the best, and the worst came of it;
We listened to the counsel of the wise,

And so turned fools. But ride and bring your friends.
Go, and go quickly. Conchubar has not seen me;
It may be that his passion is asleep,
And that we may escape.
FERGUS: But I'll go first,
And follow up that Libyan heel, and send
Such words to Conchubar that he may know
At how great peril he lays hands upon you.
(NAOISE *enters*.)
NAOISE: The Libyan, knowing that a servant's life
Is safe from hands like mine, but turned and mocked.
FERGUS: I'll call my friends, and call the reaping-hooks,
And carry you in safety to the ships.
My name has still some power. I will protect,
Or, if that is impossible, revenge.
(*He goes out by the other door.*)
NAOISE: (*Who is calm, like a man who has passed beyond life*)
The crib has fallen and the birds are in it;
There is not one of the great oaks about us
But shades a hundred men.
DEIRDRE: Let's out and die,
Or break away, if the chance favour us.
NAOISE: They would but drag you from me, stained with
    blood.
Their barbarous weapons would but mar that beauty,
And I would have you die as a queen should —
In a death-chamber. You are in my charge.
We will wait here, and when they come upon us,
I'll hold them from the doors, and when that's over,
Give you a cleanly death with this grey edge.
DEIRDRE: I will stay here; but you go out and fight.
Our way of life has brought no friends to us,
And if we do not buy them leaving it,
We shall be ever friendless.
NAOISE: What do they say?
That Lugaidh Redstripe and that wife of his
Sat at this chessboard, waiting for their end.

They knew that there was nothing that could save them,
And so played chess as they had any night
For years, and waited for the stroke of sword.
I never heard a death so out of reach
Of common hearts, a high and comely end.
What need have I, that gave up all for love,
To die like an old king out of a fable,
Fighting and passionate? What need is there
For all that ostentation at my setting?
I have loved truly and betrayed no man.
I need no lightning at the end, no beating
In a vain fury at the cage's door.
(*To* MUSICIANS) Had you been here when that man and his
    queen
Played at so high a game, could you have found
An ancient poem for the praise of it?
It should have set out plainly that those two,
Because no man and woman have loved better,
Might sit on there contentedly, and weigh
The joy comes after. I have heard the seamew
Sat there, with all the colour in her cheeks,
As though she'd say: 'There's nothing happening
But that a king and queen are playing chess.'
DEIRDRE: He's in the right, though I have not been born
Of the cold, haughty waves, my veins being hot,
And though I have loved better than that queen,
I'll have as quiet fingers on the board.
O, singing women, set it down in a book,
That love is all we need, even though it is
But the last drops we gather up like this;
And though the drops are all we have known of life,
For we have been most friendless – praise us for it,
And praise the double sunset, for naught's lacking
But a good end to the long, cloudy day.
NAOISE: Light torches there and drive the shadows out,
For day's grey end comes up.
(*A* MUSICIAN *lights a torch in the fire and then crosses*

before the chess-players, and slowly lights the torches in the sconces. The light is almost gone from the wood, but there is a clear evening light in the sky, increasing the sense of solitude and loneliness.)

DEIRDRE: Make no sad music.
   What is it but a king and queen at chess?
   They need a music that can mix itself
   Into imagination, but not break
   The steady thinking that the hard game needs.

(During the chess, the MUSICIANS *sing this song:)*
   Love is an immoderate thing
      And can never be content
   Till it dip an ageing wing
      Where some laughing element
   Leaps and Time's old lanthorn dims.
      What's the merit in love-play,
   In the tumult of the limbs
      That dies out before 'tis day,
   Heart on heart, or mouth on mouth,
      All that mingling of our breath,
   When love-longing is but drouth
      For the things come after death?

(During the last verses DEIRDRE *rises from the board and kneels at* NAOISE's *feet.)*

DEIRDRE: I cannot go on playing like that woman
   That had but the cold blood of the sea in her veins.

NAOISE: It is your move. Take up your man again.

DEIRDRE: Do you remember that first night in the woods
   We lay all night on leaves, and looking up,
   When the first grey of the dawn awoke the birds,
   Saw leaves above us? You thought that I still slept,
   And bending down to kiss me on the eyes,
   Found they were open. Bend and kiss me now,
   For it may be the last before our death.
   And when that's over, we'll be different;
   Imperishable things, a cloud or a fire.
   And I know nothing but this body, nothing

But that old vehement, bewildering kiss.
(CONCHUBAR *comes to the door.*)

FIRST MUSICIAN: Children, beware!

NAOISE: (*Laughing*)

> He has taken up my challenge;
> Whether I am a ghost or living man
> When day has broken, I'll forget the rest,
> And say that there is kingly stuff in him.

(*He turns to fetch spear and shield, and then sees that* CONCHUBAR *has gone.*)

FIRST MUSICIAN: He came to spy upon you, not to fight.

NAOISE: A prudent hunter, therefore, but no king.

> He'd find if what has fallen in the pit
> Were worth the hunting, but has come too near,
> And I turn hunter. You're not man, but beast.
> Go scurry in the bushes, now, beast, beast,
> For now it's topsy-turvy, I upon you.

(*He rushes out after* CONCHUBAR.)

DEIRDRE: You have a knife there, thrust into your girdle.

> I'd have you give it me.

FIRST MUSICIAN: No, but I dare not.

DEIRDRE: No, but you must.

FIRST MUSICIAN: If harm should come to you,

> They'd know I gave it.

DEIRDRE: (*Snatching knife*) There is no mark on this

> To make it different from any other
> Out of a common forge.

(*She goes to the door and looks out.*)

FIRST MUSICIAN: You have taken it,

> I did not give it you; but there are times
> When such a thing is all the friend one has.

DEIRDRE: The leaves hide all, and there's no way to find

> What path to follow. Why is there no sound?

(*She goes from door to window.*)

FIRST MUSICIAN: Where would you go?

DEIRDRE: To strike a blow for Naoise,

    If Conchubar call the Libyans to his aid.
    But why is there no clash? They have met by this!
FIRST MUSICIAN: Listen. I am called wise. If Conchubar win,
    You have a woman's wile that can do much,
    Even with men in pride of victory.
    He is in love and old. What were one knife
    Among a hundred?
DEIRDRE: (*Going towards them*) Women, if I die,
    If Naoise die this night, how will you praise?
    What words seek out? for that will stand to you;
    For being but dead we shall have many friends.
    All through your wanderings, the doors of kings
    Shall be thrown wider open, the poor man's hearth
    Heaped with new turf, because you are wearing this
(*She gives* MUSICIAN *a bracelet.*)
    To show that you have Deirdre's story right.
FIRST MUSICIAN: Have you not been paid servants in love's
      house
    To sweep the ashes out and keep the doors?
    And though you have suffered all for mere love's sake
    You'd live your lives again.
DEIRDRE: Even this last hour.
  (CONCHUBAR *enters with* DARK-FACED MEN.)
CONCHUBAR: One woman and two men; that is the quarrel
    That knows no mending. Bring in the man she chose
    Because of his beauty and the strength of his youth.
  (*The* DARK-FACED MEN *drag in* NAOISE *entangled in a net.*)
NAOISE: I have been taken like a bird or a fish.
CONCHUBAR: He cried 'Beast, beast!' and in a blind-beast rage
    He ran at me and fell into the nets,
    But we were careful for your sake, and took him
    With all the comeliness that woke desire
    Unbroken in him. I being old and lenient,
    I would not hurt a hair upon his head.
DEIRDRE: What do you say? Have you forgiven him?
NAOISE: He is but mocking us. What's left to say

Now that the seven years' hunt is at an end?

DEIRDRE: He never doubted you until I made him,
And therefore all the blame for what he says
Should fall on me.

CONCHUBAR: But his young blood is hot,
And if we're of one mind, he shall go free,
And I ask nothing for it, or, if something,
Nothing I could not take. There is no king
In the wide world that, being so greatly wronged,
Could copy me, and give all vengeance up.
Although her marriage day had all but come,
You carried her away; but I'll show mercy.
Because you had the insolent strength of youth
You carried her away; but I've had time
To think it out through all these seven years.
I will show mercy.

NAOISE: You have many words.

CONCHUBAR: I will not make a bargain; I but ask
What is already mine.

(DEIRDRE *moves slowly towards* CONCHUBAR *while he is speaking, her eyes fixed upon him.*)
You may go free
If Deirdre will but walk into my house
Before the people's eyes, that they may know,
When I have put the crown upon her head,
I have not taken her by force and guile.
The doors are open, and the floors are strewed
And in the bridal chamber curtains sewn
With all enchantments that give happiness
By races that are germane to the sun,
And nearest him, and have no blood in their veins –
For when they're wounded the wound drips with wine –
Nor speech but singing. At the bridal door
Two fair king's daughters carry in their hands
The crown and robe.

DEIDRE: O no! Not that, not that!
Ask any other thing but that one thing.

Leave me with Naoise. We will go away
Into some country at the ends of the earth.
We'll trouble you no more; and there is no one
That will not praise you if you pardon us.
'He is good, he is good,' they'll say to one another;
'There's nobody like him, for he forgave
Deirdre and Naoise.'

CONCHUBAR: Do you think that I
Shall let you go again, after seven years
Of longing and of planning here and there,
And trafficking with merchants for the stones
That make all sure, and watching my own face
That none might read it?

DEIRDRE: (*To* NAOISE) It's better to go with him.
Why should you die when one can bear it all?
My life is over; it's better to obey.
Why should you die? I will not live long, Naoise.
I'd not have you believe I'd long stay living;
O no, no, no! You will go far away.
You will forget me. Speak, speak, Naoise, speak,
And say that it is better that I go.
I will not ask it. Do not speak a word,
For I will take it all upon myself.
Conchubar, I will go.

NAOISE: And do you think
That, were I given life at such a price,
I would not cast it from me? O my eagle!
Why do you beat vain wings upon the rock
When hollow night's above?

DEIRDRE: It's better, Naoise.
It may be hard for you, but you'll forget.
For what am I, to be remembered always?
And there are other women. There was one,
The daughter of the King of Leodas;
I could not sleep because of her. Speak to him;
Tell it out plain, and make him understand.
And if it be he thinks I shall stay living,

Say that I will not.

NAOISE: Would I had lost life
Among those Scottish kings that sought it of me
Because you were my wife, or that the worst
Had taken you before this bargaining!
O eagle! If you were to do this thing,
And buy my life of Conchubar with your body,
Love's law being broken, I would stand alone
Upon the eternal summits, and call out,
And you could never come there, being banished.

DEIRDRE: (*Kneeling to* CONCHUBAR) I would obey, but cannot.
  Pardon us.
I know that you are good. I have heard you praised
For giving gifts; and you will pardon us,
Although I cannot go into your house.
It was my fault. I only should be punished.

(*Unseen by* DEIRDRE, NAOISE *is gagged.*)

The very moment these eyes fell on him,
I told him; I held out my hands to him;
How could he refuse? At first he would not –
I am not lying – he remembered you.
What do I say? My hands? – No, no, my lips –
For I had pressed my lips upon his lips –
I swear it is not false – my breast to his;

(CONCHUBAR *motions;* NAOISE, *unseen by* DEIRDRE, *is taken behind the curtain.*)

Until I woke the passion that's in all,
And how could he resist? I had my beauty.
You may have need of him, a brave, strong man,
Who is not foolish at the council-board,
Nor does he quarrel by the candle-light
And give hard blows to dogs. A cup of wine
Moves him to mirth, not madness.

(*She stands up.*)

                              What am I saying?
You may have need of him, for you have none

Who is so good a sword, or so well loved
Among the common people. You may need him,
And what king knows when the hour of need may come?
You dream that you have men enough. You laugh.
Yes; you are laughing to yourself. You say,
'I am Conchubar – I have no need of him.'
You will cry out for him some day and say,
'If Naoise were but living' –
(She misses Naoise.)

Where is he?
Where have you sent him? Where is the son of Usna?
Where is he, O, where is he?

(She staggers over to the MUSICIANS. *The* EXECUTIONER *has come out with a sword on which there is blood;* CONCHUBAR *points to it. The* MUSICIANS *give a wail.)*

CONCHUBAR: The traitor who has carried off my wife
No longer lives. Come to my house now, Deirdre,
For he that called himself your husband's dead.

DEIRDRE: O, do not touch me. Let me go to him.
(Pause.)
King Conchubar is right. My husband's dead.
A single woman is of no account,
Lacking array of servants, linen cupboards,
The bacon hanging – and King Conchubar's house
All ready, too – I'll to King Conchubar's house.
It is but wisdom to do willingly
What has to be.

CONCHUBAR: But why are you so calm?
I thought that you would curse me and cry out,
And fall upon the ground and tear your hair.

DEIRDRE: *(Laughing)* You know too much of women to think
so;
Though, if I were less worthy of desire,
I would pretend as much; but, being myself,
It is enough that you were master here.
Although we are so delicately made,

There's something brutal in us, and we are won
By those who can shed blood. It was some woman
That taught you how to woo: but do not touch me:
I shall do all you bid me, but not yet,
Because I have to do what's customary.
We lay the dead out, folding up the hands,
Closing the eyes, and stretching out the feet,
And push a pillow underneath the head,
Till all's in order; and all this I'll do
For Naoise, son of Usna.

CONCHUBAR: It is not fitting.
You are not now a wanderer, but a queen,
And there are plenty that can do these things.

DEIRDRE: (*Motioning* CONCHUBAR *away*) No, no. Not yet.
          I cannot be your queen
Till the past's finished, and its debts are paid.
When a man dies, and there are debts unpaid,
He wanders by the debtor's bed and cries,
'There's so much owing.'

CONCHUBAR: You are deceiving me.
You long to look upon his face again.
Why should I give you now to a dead man
That took you from a living?

(*He makes a step towards her.*)

DEIRDRE: In good time.
You'll stir me to more passion than he could,
And yet, if you are wise, you'll grant me this:
That I go look upon him that was once
So strong and comely and held his head so high
That women envied me. For I will see him
All blood-bedabbled and his beauty gone.
It's better, when you're beside me in your strength,
That the mind's eye should call up the soiled body,
And not the shape I loved. Look at him, women.
He heard me pleading to be given up,
Although my lover was still living, and yet

He doubts my purpose. I will have you tell him
How changeable all women are; how soon
Even the best of lovers is forgot
When his day's finished.

CONCHUBAR: No; but I will trust
The strength that you have praised, and not your purpose.

DEIRDRE: (*Almost with a caress*) It is so small a gift and you
    will grant it
Because it is the first that I have asked.
He has refused. There is no sap in him;
Nothing but empty veins. I thought as much.
He has refused me the first thing I have asked –
Me, me, his wife. I understand him now;
I know the sort of life I'll have with him;
But he must drag me to his house by force.
If he refuses (*laughs*), he shall be mocked of all.
They'll say to one another, 'Look at him
That is so jealous that he lured a man
From over sea, and murdered him, and yet
He trembled at the thought of a dead face!'
   (*She has her hand upon the curtain.*)

CONCHUBAR: How do I know that you have not some knife,
And go to die upon his body?

DEIRDRE: Have me searched,
If you would make so little of your queen.
It may be that I have a knife hid here
Under my dress. Bid one of these dark slaves
To search me for it.
   (*Pause.*)

CONCHUBAR: Go to your farewells, Queen.

DEIRDRE: Now strike the wire, and sing to it a while,
Knowing that all is happy, and that you know
Within what bride-bed I shall lie this night,
And by what man, and lie close up to him,
For the bed's narrow, and there outsleep the cockcrow.
   (*She goes behind the curtain.*)

FIRST MUSICIAN: They are gone, they are gone. The proud
      may lie by the proud.

SECOND MUSICIAN: Though we were bidden to sing, cry nothing
      loud.

FIRST MUSICIAN: They are gone, they are gone.

SECOND MUSICIAN: Whispering were enough.

FIRST MUSICIAN: Into the secret wilderness of their love.

SECOND MUSICIAN: A high, grey cairn. What more is to be said?

FIRST MUSICIAN: Eagles have gone into their cloudy bed.

(*Shouting outside.* FERGUS *enters. Many men with scythes
and sickles and torches gather about the doors. The house is lit
with the glare of their torches.*)

FERGUS: Where's Naoise, son of Usna, and his queen?
    I and a thousand reaping-hooks and scythes
    Demand him of you.

CONCHUBAR: You have come too late.
    I have accomplished all. Deirdre is mine;
    She is my queen, and no man now can rob me.
    I had to climb the topmost bough, and pull
    This apple among the winds. Open the curtain
    That Fergus learn my triumph from her lips.

(*The curtain is drawn back. The* MUSICIANS *begin to
keen with low voices.*)

    No, no; I'll not believe it. She is not dead –
    She cannot have escaped a second time!

FERGUS: King, she is dead; but lay no hand upon her.
    What's this but empty cage and tangled wire,
    Now the bird's gone? But I'll not have you touch it.

CONCHUBAR: You are all traitors, all against me – all.
    And she has deceived me for a second time;
    And every common man can keep his wife,
    But not the King.

(*Loud shouting outside:* 'Death to Conchubar!' 'Where
is Naoise?', *etc. The* DARK-FACED MEN *gather round*
CONCHUBAR *and draw their swords; but he motions them
away.*)

                  I have no need of weapons,

There's not a traitor that dare stop my way.
Howl, if you will; but I, being King, did right
In choosing her most fitting to be Queen,
And letting no boy lover take the sway.

THE PLAYER QUEEN

PERSONS IN THE PLAY

DECIMA
SEPTIMUS
NONA
THE QUEEN
THE PRIME MINISTER
THE BISHOP
THE STAGE MANAGER
THE TAPSTER
AN OLD BEGGAR
OLD MEN, OLD WOMEN, CITIZENS, COUNTRYMEN, PLAYERS, ETC.

SCENE 1

An open space at the meeting of three streets. One can see for some way down one of these streets, and at some little distance it turns, showing a bare piece of wall lighted by a hanging lamp. Against this lighted wall are silhouetted the heads and shoulders of two OLD MEN. *They are leaning from the upper windows, one on either side of the street. They wear grotesque masks. A little to one side of the stage is a great stone for mounting a horse from. The houses have knockers.*

FIRST OLD MAN: Can you see the Queen's castle? You have better sight than I.

SECOND OLD MAN: I can just see it rising over the tops of the houses yonder on its great rocky hill.

FIRST OLD MAN: Is the dawn breaking? Is it touching the tower?

SECOND OLD MAN: It is beginning to break upon the tower, but these narrow streets will be dark for a long while.
(*A pause.*)
Do you hear anything? You have better hearing than I.

FIRST OLD MAN: No, all is quiet.

SECOND OLD MAN: At least fifty passed by an hour since, a crowd of fifty men walking rapidly.

FIRST OLD MAN: Last night was very quiet, not a sound, not a breath.

SECOND OLD MAN: And not a thing to be seen till the Tapster's old dog came down the street upon this very hour from Cooper Malachi's ash-pit.

FIRST OLD MAN: Hush, I hear feet, many feet. Perhaps they

75

are coming this way. (*Pause.*) No, they are going the other way, they are gone now.

SECOND OLD MAN: The young are at some mischief, – the young and the middle-aged.

FIRST OLD MAN: Why can't they stay in their beds, and they can sleep too – seven hours, eight hours? I mind the time when I could sleep ten hours. They will know the value of sleep when they are near upon ninety years.

SECOND OLD MAN: They will never live so long. They have not the health and strength that we had. They wear themselves out. They are always in a passion about something or other.

FIRST OLD MAN: Hush! I hear a step now, and it is coming this way. We had best pull in our heads. The world has grown very wicked and there is no knowing what they might do to us or say to us.

SECOND OLD MAN: Yes, better shut the windows and pretend to be asleep.

(*They pull in their heads. One hears a knocker being struck in the distance, then a pause, and a knocker is struck close at hand. Another pause, and* SEPTIMUS, *a handsome man of thirty-five, staggers on to the stage. He is very drunk.*)

SEPTIMUS: An uncharitable place, an unchristian place. (*He begins banging at a knocker.*) Open there, open there. I want to come in and sleep.

(*A* THIRD OLD MAN *puts his head from an upper window.*)

THIRD OLD MAN: Who are you? What do you want?

SEPTIMUS: I am Septimus. I have a bad wife. I want to come in and sleep.

THIRD OLD MAN: You are drunk.

SEPTIMUS: Drunk! So would you be if you had as bad a wife.

THIRD OLD MAN: Go away.

(*He shuts the window.*)

SEPTIMUS: Is there not one Christian in this town?

(*He begins hammering the knocker of* FIRST OLD MAN, *but there is no answer.*)

No one there? All dead or drunk maybe – bad wives! There must be one Christian man.

(*He hammers a knocker at the other side of the stage. An* OLD WOMAN *puts her head out of the window above.*)

OLD WOMAN: (*In a shrill voice*) Who's there? What do you want? Has something happened?

SEPTIMUS: Yes, that's it. Something has happened. My wife has hid herself, has run away, or has drowned herself.

OLD WOMAN: What do I care about your wife? You are drunk.

SEPTIMUS: Not care about my wife! But I tell you that my wife has to play by order of the Prime Minister before all the people in the great hall of the Castle precisely at noon, and she cannot be found.

OLD WOMAN: Go away, go away! I tell you, go away.

(*She shuts the window.*)

SEPTIMUS: Treat Septimus, who has played before Kubla Khan, like this! Septimus, dramatist and poet!

(*The* OLD WOMAN *opens the window again and empties a jug of water over him.*)

Water! drenched to the skin – must sleep in the street. (*Lies down.*) Bad wife – others have had bad wives, but others were not left to lie down in the open street under the stars, drenched with cold water, a whole jug of cold water, shivering in the pale light of the dawn, to be run over, to be trampled upon, to be eaten by dogs, and all because their wives have hidden themselves.

(*Enter two* MEN *a little older than* SEPTIMUS. *They stand still and gaze into the sky.*)

FIRST MAN: Ah, my friend, the little fair-haired one is a minx.

SECOND MAN: Never trust fair hair – I will have nothing but brown hair.

FIRST MAN: They have kept us too long – brown or fair.

SECOND MAN: What are you staring at?

FIRST MAN: At the first streak of the dawn on the Castle tower.

SECOND MAN: I would not have my wife find out for the world.

SEPTIMUS: (*Sitting up*) Carry me, support me, drag me, roll me, pull me, or sidle me along, but bring me where

I may sleep in comfort. Bring me to a stable – my Saviour was content with a stable.

FIRST MAN: Who are you? I don't know your face.

SEPTIMUS: I am Septimus, a player, a playwright, and the most famous poet in the world.

SECOND MAN: That name, sir, is unknown to me.

SEPTIMUS: Unknown?

SECOND MAN: But my name will not be unknown to you. I am called Peter of the Purple Pelican, after the best known of my poems, and my friend is called Happy Tom. He also is a poet.

SEPTIMUS: Bad, popular poets.

SECOND MAN: You would be a popular poet if you could.

SEPTIMUS: Bad, popular poets.

FIRST MAN: Lie where you are if you can't be civil.

SEPTIMUS: What do I care for anyone now except Venus and Adonis and the other planets of heaven?

SECOND MAN: You can enjoy their company by yourself.

(*The two* MEN *go out.*)

SEPTIMUS: Robbed, so to speak; naked, so to speak – bleeding, so to speak – and they pass by on the other side of the street.

(*A crowd of* CITIZENS *and* COUNTRYMEN *enters. At first only a few, and then more and more till the stage is filled by an excited crowd.*)

FIRST CITIZEN: There is a man lying here.

SECOND CITIZEN: Roll him over.

FIRST CITIZEN: He is one of those players who are housed at the Castle. They arrived yesterday.

SECOND CITIZEN: Drunk, I suppose. He'll be killed or maimed by the first milk-cart.

THIRD CITIZEN: Better roll him into the corner. If we are in for a bloody day's business, there is no need for him to be killed – an unnecessary death might bring a curse upon us.

FIRST CITIZEN: Give me a hand here.

(*They begin rolling* SEPTIMUS.)

SEPTIMUS: (*Muttering*) Not allowed to sleep! Rolled off

the street! Shoved into a stony place! Unchristian town!

(*He is left lying at the foot of the wall to one side of the stage.*)

THIRD CITIZEN: Are we all friends here, are we all agreed?

FIRST CITIZEN: These men are from the country. They came in last night. They know little of the business. They won't be against the people, but they want to know more.

FIRST COUNTRYMAN: Yes, that is it. We are with the people, but we want to know more.

SECOND COUNTRYMAN: We want to know all, but we are with the people.

(*Other voices take up the words, 'We want to know all, but we are with the people', etc. There is a murmur of voices together.*)

THIRD CITIZEN: Have you ever seen the Queen, countryman?

FIRST COUNTRYMAN: No.

THIRD CITIZEN: Our Queen is a witch, a bad evil-living witch, and we will have her no longer for Queen.

THIRD COUNTRYMAN: I would be slow to believe her father's daughter a witch.

THIRD CITIZEN: Have you ever seen the Queen, countryman?

THIRD COUNTRYMAN: No.

THIRD CITIZEN: Nor has any one else. Not a man here has set eyes on her. For seven years she has been shut up in that great black house on the great rocky hill. From the day her father died she has been there with the doors shut on her, but we know now why she has hidden herself. She has no good companions in the dark night.

THIRD COUNTRYMAN: In my district they say that she is a holy woman and prays for us all.

THIRD CITIZEN: That story has been spread about by the Prime Minister. He has spies everywhere spreading stories. He is a crafty man.

FIRST COUNTRYMAN: It is true, they always deceive us country people. We are not educated like the people of the town.

A BIG COUNTRYMAN: The Bible says, 'Suffer not a witch to live.' Last Candlemas twelvemonth I strangled a witch with my own hands.

THIRD CITIZEN: When she is dead we will make the Prime Minister King.

SECOND CITIZEN: No, no, he is not a king's son.

SECOND COUNTRYMAN: I'd send a bellman through the world. There are many kings in Arabia, they say.

THIRD COUNTRYMAN: The people must be talking. If you and I were to hide ourselves, or to be someway hard to understand, maybe they would put some bad name on us. I am not against the people, but I want testimony.

THIRD CITIZEN: Come, Tapster, stand up there on the stone and tell what you know.

(*The* TAPSTER *climbs up on the mounting-stone.*)

TAPSTER: I live in the quarter where her Castle is. The garden of my house and the gardens of all the houses in my row run right up to the rocky hill that has her Castle on the top. There is a lad in my quarter that has a goat in his garden.

FIRST CITIZEN: That's Strolling Michael – I know him.

TAPSTER: That goat is always going astray. Strolling Michael got out of his bed early one morning to go snaring birds, and nowhere could he see that goat. So he began climbing up the rock, and up and up he went, till he was close under the wall, and there he found the goat and it shaking and sweating as though something had scared it. Presently he heard a thing neigh like a horse, and after that a something like a white horse ran by, but it was no horse, but a unicorn. He had his pistol, for he had thought to bring down a rabbit, and seeing it rushing at him as he imagined, he fired at the unicorn. It vanished all in a moment, but there was blood on a great stone.

THIRD CITIZEN: Seeing what company she keeps in the small hours, what wonder that she never sets foot out of doors!

THIRD COUNTRYMAN: I wouldn't believe all that night rambler says – boys are liars. All that we have against her for certain is that she won't put her foot out of doors. I knew a man once that when he was five-and-twenty refused to get out of his bed. He wasn't ill – no, not he, but he said life was a vale of tears, and for forty and four years till they carried him out to the churchyard he never left that bed. All tried him – parson tried him, priest tried him, doctor tried him, and all he'd say was, 'Life is a vale of tears.' It's too snug he was in his bed, and believe me, that ever since she has had no father to rout her out of a morning she has been in her bed, and small blame to her maybe.

THE BIG COUNTRYMAN: But that's the very sort that are witches. They know where to find their own friends in the lonely hours of the night. There was a witch in my own district that I strangled last Candlemas twelvemonth. She had an imp in the shape of a red cat, that sucked three drops of blood from her poll every night a little before the cock crew. It's with their blood they feed them; until they have been fed with the blood they are images and shadows; but when they have it drunk they can be for a while stronger than you or me.

THIRD COUNTRYMAN: The man I knew was no witch, he was no way active. 'Life is a vale of tears,' he said. Parson tried him, doctor tried him, priest tried him – but that was all he'd say.

FIRST CITIZEN: We'd have no man go beyond evidence and reason, but hear the Tapster out, and when you have you'll say that we cannot leave her alive this day – no, not for one day longer.

TAPSTER: It's not a story that I like to be telling, but you are all married men. Another night that boy climbed up after his goat, and it was an hour earlier by his clock and no light in the sky, and when he came to the Castle wall he clambered along the wall among the rocks and bushes till he saw a light from a little window over his head. It was an old wall full of holes, where mortar had fallen out, and he climbed up, putting his toes into the holes, till he could look in through the window; and when he looked in, what did he see but the Queen!

FIRST COUNTRYMAN: And did he say what she was like?

TAPSTER: He saw more than that. He saw her coupling with a great white unicorn.

(*Murmurs among the crowd.*)

SECOND COUNTRYMAN: I will not have the son of the unicorn

to reign over us, although you will tell me he would be no more than half a unicorn.

FIRST COUNTRYMAN: I'll not go against the people, but I'd let her live if the Prime Minister promised to rout her out of bed in the morning and to set a guard to drive off the unicorn.

THE BIG COUNTRYMAN: I have strangled an old witch with these two hands, and today I will strangle a young witch.

SEPTIMUS: (*Who has slowly got up and climbed up on to the mounting-stone which the* TAPSTER *has left*) Did I hear somebody say that the Unicorn is not chaste? It is a most noble beast, a most religious beast. It has a milk-white skin and a milk-white horn, and milk-white hoofs, but a mild blue eye, and it dances in the sun. I will have no one speak against it, not while I am still upon the earth. It is written in *The Great Beastery of Paris* that it is chaste, that it is the most chaste of all the beasts in the world.

THE BIG COUNTRYMAN: Pull him out of that, he's drunk.

SEPTIMUS: Yes, I am drunk, I am very drunk, but that is no reason why I should permit any one to speak against the Unicorn.

SECOND CITIZEN: Let's hear him out. We can do nothing till the sun's up.

SEPTIMUS: Nobody shall speak against the Unicorn. No, my friends and poets, nobody. I will hunt it if you will, though it is a dangerous and cross-grained beast. Much virtue has made it cross-grained. I will go with you to the high tablelands of Africa where it lives, and we will there shoot it through the head, but I will not speak against its character, and if any man declares it is not chaste I will fight him, for I affirm that its chastity is equal to its beauty.

THE BIG COUNTRYMAN: He is most monstrously drunk.

SEPTIMUS: No longer drunk, but inspired.

SECOND CITIZEN: Go on, go on, we'll never hear the like again.

THE BIG COUNTRYMAN: Come away. I've enough of this — we have work to do.

SEPTIMUS: Go away, did you say, and my breast-feathers thrust out and my white wings buoyed up with divinity?

Ah! but I can see it now – you are bent upon going to some lonely place where uninterrupted you can speak against the character of the Unicorn, but you shall not, I tell you that you shall not.

(*He comes down off the stone and squares up at the crowd which tries to pass him.*)

In the midst of this uncharitable town I will protect that noble, milk-white, flighty beast.

THE BIG COUNTRYMAN: Let me pass.

SEPTIMUS: No, I will not let you pass.

FIRST COUNTRYMAN: Leave him alone.

SECOND COUNTRYMAN: No violence – it might bring ill-luck upon us.

(*They try to hold back the* BIG COUNTRYMAN.)

SEPTIMUS: I will oppose your passing to the death. For I will not have it said that there is a smirch, or a blot, upon the most milky whiteness of an heroic brute that bathes by the sound of tabors at the rising of the sun and the rising of the moon, and the rising of the Great Bear, and above all, it shall not be said, whispered, or in any wise published abroad by you that stand there, so to speak, between two washings; for you were doubtless washed when you were born, and, it may be, shall be washed again after you are dead.

(*The* BIG COUNTRYMAN *knocks him down.*)

FIRST CITIZEN: You have killed him.

THE BIG COUNTRYMAN: Maybe I have, maybe I have not – let him lie there. A witch I strangled last Candlemas twelvemonth, a witch I will strangle today. What do I care for the likes of him?

THIRD CITIZEN: Come round to the east quarter of the town. The basket-makers and the sieve-makers will be out by this.

FOURTH CITIZEN: It is a short march from there to the Castle gate.

(*They go up one of the side streets, but return quickly in confusion and fear.*)

FIRST CITIZEN: Are you sure that you saw him?

SECOND CITIZEN: Who could mistake that horrible old man?

THIRD CITIZEN: I was standing by him when the ghost spoke out of him seven years ago.

FIRST COUNTRYMAN: I never saw him before. He has never been in my district. I don't rightly know what sort he is, but I have heard of him, many a time I have heard of him.

FIRST CITIZEN: His eyes become glassy, and that is the trance growing upon him, and when he is in the trance his soul slips away and a ghost takes its place and speaks out of him – a strange ghost.

THIRD CITIZEN: I was standing by him the last time. 'Get me straw,' said that old man, 'my back itches.' Then all of a sudden he lay down, with his eyes wide open and glassy, and he brayed like a donkey. At that moment the King died and the King's daughter was Queen.

FIRST COUNTRYMAN: They say it is the donkey that carried Christ into Jerusalem, and that is why it knows its rightful sovereign. He goes begging about the country and there is no man dare refuse him what he asks.

THE BIG COUNTRYMAN: Then it is certain nobody will take my hand off her throat. I will make my grip tighter. He will be lying down on the straw and he will bray, and when he brays she will be dead.

FIRST COUNTRYMAN: Look! There he is coming over the top of the hill, and the mad look upon him.

SECOND COUNTRYMAN: I wouldn't face him for the world this night. Come round to the market-place, we'll be less afraid in a big place.

THE BIG COUNTRYMAN: I'm not afraid, but I'll go with you till I get my hand on her throat.

(*They all go out but* SEPTIMUS. *Presently* SEPTIMUS *sits up; his head is bleeding. He rubs with his fingers his broken head and looks at the blood on his fingers.*)

SEPTIMUS: Unchristian town! First I am, so to speak, thrown out into the street, and then I am all but murdered; and I drunk, and therefore in need of protection. All creatures are in need of protection at some time or other. Even my wife was once a frail child in need of milk, of smiles, of love, as if in the midst of a flood, in danger of drowning, so to speak.

(*An* OLD BEGGAR *with long matted hair and beard and in ragged clothes comes in.*)

THE OLD BEGGAR: I want straw.

SEPTIMUS: Happy Tom and Peter of the Purple Pelican have done it all. They are bad, popular poets, and being jealous of my fame, they have stirred up the people. (*He catches sight of the* OLD BEGGAR.) There is a certain medicine which is made by distilling camphor, Peruvian bark, spurge and mandrake, and mixing all with twelve ounces of dissolved pearls and four ounces of the oil of gold; and this medicine is infallible to stop the flow of blood. Have you any of it, old man?

THE OLD BEGGAR: I want straw.

SEPTIMUS: I can see that you have not got it, but no matter, we shall be friends.

THE OLD BEGGAR: I want straw to lie down on.

SEPTIMUS: It is no doubt better that I should bleed to death. For that way, my friend, I shall disgrace Happy Tom and Peter of the Purple Pelican, but it is necessary that I shall die somewhere where my last words can be taken down. I am therefore in need of your support.

(*Having got up he now staggers over to the* OLD BEGGAR *and leans upon him.*)

THE OLD BEGGAR: Don't you know who I am – aren't you afraid? When something comes inside me, my back itches. Then I must lie down and roll, and then I bray and the crown changes.

SEPTIMUS: Ah! you are inspired. Then we are indeed brothers. Come, I will rest upon your shoulder and we will mount the hill side by side. I will sleep in the Castle of the Queen.

THE OLD BEGGAR: You will give me straw to lie upon?

SEPTIMUS: Asphodels! Yet, indeed, the asphodel is a flower much overrated by the classic authors. Still if a man has a preference, I say, for the asphodel –

(*They go out and one hears the voice of* SEPTIMUS *murmuring in the distance about asphodels. The* FIRST OLD MAN *opens his window and taps with his crutch at the opposite window. The* SECOND OLD MAN *opens his window.*)

FIRST OLD MAN: It is all right now. They are all gone. We can have our talk out.

SECOND OLD MAN: The whole Castle is lit by the dawn now, and it will begin to grow brighter in the street.

FIRST OLD MAN: It's time for the Tapster's old dog to come down the street.

SECOND OLD MAN: Yesterday he had a bone in his mouth.

SCENE 2

The Throne-Room in the Castle. Between pillars are gilded open-work doors, except at one side, where there is a large window. The morning light is slanting through the window, making dark shadows among the pillars. As the scene goes on, the light, at first feeble, becomes strong and suffused, and the shadows disappear. Through the openwork doors one can see down long passages, and one of these passages plainly leads into the open air. One can see daylight at the end of it. There is a throne in the centre of the room and a flight of steps that leads to it.

The PRIME MINISTER, *an elderly man with an impatient manner and voice, is talking to a group of* PLAYERS, *among whom is* NONA, *a fair, comely, comfortable-looking young woman of perhaps thirty-five; she seems to take the lead.*

PRIME MINISTER: I will not be trifled with. I chose the play myself; I chose *The Tragical History of Noah's Deluge* because when Noah beats his wife to make her go into the Ark everybody understands, everybody is pleased, everybody recognizes the mulish obstinacy of their own wives, sweethearts, sisters. And now, when it is of the greatest importance to the State that everybody should be pleased, the play cannot be given. The leading lady is lost, you say, and there is some unintelligible reason why nobody can take her place; but I know what you are all driving at – you object to the play I have chosen. You want some dull, poetical thing, full of long speeches. I will have that play and no other. The rehearsal must begin at once and the performance take place at noon punctually.

NONA: We have searched all night, sir, and we cannot find her anywhere. She was heard to say that she would drown rather than play a woman older than thirty. Seeing that Noah's wife is a very old woman, we are afraid that she has drowned herself indeed.

(DECIMA, *a very pretty woman, puts her head out from under the throne where she has been lying hidden*.)

PRIME MINISTER: Nonsense! It is all a conspiracy. Your manager should be here. He is responsible. You can tell him when he does come that if the play is not performed, I will clap him into gaol for a year and pitch the rest of you over the border.

NONA: O, sir, he couldn't help it. She does whatever she likes.

PRIME MINISTER: Does whatever she likes – I know her sort; would pull the world to pieces to spite her husband or her lover. I know her – a bladder full of dried peas for a brain, a brazen, bragging baggage. Of course he couldn't help it, but what do I care?

(DECIMA *pulls in her head*.)

To gaol he goes – somebody has got to go to gaol. Go and cry her name everywhere. Away with you! Let me hear you cry it out. Call the baggage. Louder. Louder.

(*The* PLAYERS *go out crying*, 'Where are you, Decima?')

O, Adam! why did you fall asleep in the garden? You might have known that, while you were lying there helpless, the Old Man in the Sky would play some prank upon you.

(*The* QUEEN, *who is young, with an ascetic timid face, enters in a badly fitting state dress*.)

Ah!

QUEEN: I will show myself to the angry people as you have bidden me. I am almost certain that I am ready for martyrdom. I have prayed all night. Yes, I am almost certain.

PRIME MINISTER: Ah!

QUEEN: I have now attained to the age of my patroness, Holy Saint Octema, when she was martyred at Antioch. You will remember that her unicorn was so pleased at the spectacle of her austerity that he caracoled in his excitement. Thereupon she dropped out of the saddle and was trampled to death under the feet of the mob. Indeed, but for the unicorn, the mob would have killed her long before.

PRIME MINISTER: No, you will not be martyred. I have a plan to settle that. I will stop their anger with a word. Who made that dress?

QUEEN: It was my mother's dress. She wore it at her coronation. I would not have a new one made. I do not deserve new clothes. I am always committing sin.

PRIME MINISTER: Is there sin in an egg that has never been hatched, that has never been warmed, in a chalk egg?

QUEEN: I wish I could resemble Holy Saint Octema in every thing.

PRIME MINISTER: What a dress! It is too late now. Nothing can be done. It may appear right to those on the edge of the crowd. The others must be conquered by charm, dignity, royal manner. As for the dress, I must think of some excuse, some explanation. Remember that they have never seen your face, and you will put them in a bad humour if you hang your head in that dumbfounded way.

QUEEN: I wish I could return to my prayers.

PRIME MINISTER: Walk! Permit me to see your Majesty walk. No, no, no. Be more majestic. Ah! If you had known the queens I have known – they had a way with them. Morals of a dragoon, but a way, a way! Put on a kind of eagle look, a vulture look.

QUEEN: There are cobble-stones – if I might go barefoot it

would be a blessed penance. It was especially the bleeding
feet of Saint Octema that gave pleasure to the unicorn.

PRIME MINISTER: Sleep of Adam! Barefoot – barefoot, did
you say? (*A pause.*) There is not time to take off your shoes
and stockings. If you were to look out of the window there,
you would see the crowd becoming wickeder every minute.
Come!

(*He gives his arm to the* QUEEN.)

QUEEN: You have a plan to stop their anger so that I shall
not be martyred?

PRIME MINISTER: My plan will be disclosed before the face
of the people and there alone.

(*They go out.* NONA *comes in with a bottle of wine and
a boiled lobster and lays them on the middle of the floor. She
puts her finger on her lip and stands in the doorway towards
the back of the stage.*

DECIMA: (*Comes cautiously out of her hiding-place singing:*)
    'He went away,' my mother sang,
    'When I was brought to bed.'
    And all the while her needle pulled
    The gold and silver thread.

    She pulled the thread and bit the thread
    And made a golden gown,
    She wept because she had dreamt that I
    Was born to wear a crown.

(*She is just reaching her hand for the lobster when* NONA
*comes forward holding out towards her the dress and mask of
Noah's wife which she has been carrying over her left arm.*)

NONA: Thank God you are found! (*Getting between her and
the lobster*) No, not until you have put on this dress and
mask. I have caught you now, and you are not going to
hide again.

DECIMA: Very well, when I have had my breakfast.

NONA: Not a mouthful till you are dressed ready for the
rehearsal.

DECIMA: Do you know what song I was singing just now?

NONA: It is that song you're always singing. Septimus made it up.

DECIMA: It is the song of the mad singing daughter of a harlot. The only song she had. Her father was a drunken sailor waiting for the full tide, and yet she thought her mother had foretold that she would marry a prince and become a great queen.

(*Singing*:) 'When she was got', my mother sang,
 'I heard a seamew cry,
 I saw a flake of yellow foam
 That dropped upon my thigh.'

 How therefore could she help but braid
 The gold upon my hair,
 And dream that I should carry
 The golden top of care?

The moment ago as I lay here I thought I could play a queen's part, a great queen's part; the only part in the world I can play is a great queen's part.

NONA: You play a queen's part? You that were born in a ditch between two towns and wrapped in a sheet that was stolen from a hedge.

DECIMA: The Queen cannot play at all, but I could play so well. I could bow with my whole body down to my ankles and could be stern when hard looks were in season. O, I would know how to put all summer in a look and after that all winter in a voice.

NONA: Low comedy is what you are fit for.

DECIMA: I understood all this in a wink of the eye, and then just when I am saying to myself that I was born to sit up there with soldiers and courtiers, you come shaking in front of me that mask and that dress. I am not to eat my breakfast unless I play an old peaky-chinned, drop-nosed harridan that a foul husband beats with a stick because she won't clamber among the other brutes into his cattle-boat.

(*She makes a dart at the lobster.*)

THE PLAYER QUEEN 91

NONA: No, no, not a drop, not a mouthful till you have put these on. Remember that if there is no play Septimus must go to prison.

DECIMA: Would they give him dry bread to eat?

NONA: They would.

DECIMA: And water to drink and nothing in the water?

NONA: They would.

DECIMA: And a straw bed?

NONA: They would, and only a little straw maybe.

DECIMA: And iron chains that clanked?

NONA: They would.

DECIMA: And keep him there for a whole week?

NONA: A month maybe.

DECIMA: And he would say to the turnkey, 'I am here because of my beautiful cruel wife, my beautiful flighty wife'?

NONA: He might not, he'd be sober.

DECIMA: But he'd think it, and every time he was hungry, every time he was thirsty, every time he felt the hardness of the stone floor, every time he heard the chains clank, he would think it, and every time he thought it I would become more beautiful in his eyes.

NONA: No, he would hate you.

DECIMA: Little do you know what the love of man is. If that Holy Image of the church where you put all those candles at Easter was pleasant and affable, why did you come home with the skin worn off your two knees?

NONA: (*In tears*) I understand – you cruel, bad woman! – you won't play the part at all, and all that Septimus may go to prison, and he a great genius that can't take care of himself.

(*Seeing* NONA *distracted with tears* DECIMA *makes a dart and almost gets the lobster.*)

No, no! Not a mouthful, not a drop. I will break the bottle if you go near it. There is not another woman in the world would treat a man like that, and you were sworn to him in church – yes, you were, there is no good denying it.

(DECIMA *makes another dart, but* NONA, *who is still in tears, puts the lobster in her pocket.*)
Leave the food alone; not one mouthful will you get. I have never sworn to a man in church, but if I did swear, I would not treat him like a tinker's donkey – before God I would not – I was properly brought up; my mother always told me it was no light thing to take a man in church.

DECIMA: You are in love with my husband.

NONA: Because I don't want to see him gaoled you say I am in love with him. Only a woman with no heart would think one can't be sorry for a man without being in love with him – a woman who has never been sorry for anybody! But I won't have him gaoled; if you won't play the part I'll play it myself.

DECIMA: When I married him, I made him swear never to play with anybody but me, and well you know it.

NONA: Only this once, and in a part nobody can do anything with.

DECIMA: That is the way it begins, and all the time you would be saying things the audience couldn't hear.

NONA: Septimus will break his oath, and I have learnt the part. Every line of it.

DECIMA: Septimus would not break his oath for anybody in the world.

NONA: There is one person in the world for whom he will break his oath.

DECIMA: What have you in your head now?

NONA: He will break it for me.

DECIMA: You are crazy.

NONA: Maybe I have my secrets.

DECIMA: What are you keeping back? Have you been sitting in corners with Septimus? giving him sympathy because of the bad wife he has, and all the while he has sat there to have the pleasure of talking about me?

NONA: You think that you have his every thought because you are a devil.

DECIMA: Because I am a devil I have his every thought.

You know how his own song runs. The man speaks first –
(*Singing*:) Put off that mask of burning gold
  With emerald eyes,
and then the woman answers –
  O no, my dear, you make so bold
  To find if hearts be wild and wise
  And yet not cold.

NONA: His every thought – that is a lie. He forgets
all about you the moment you're out of his sight.

DECIMA: Then look what I carry under my bodice.
This is a poem praising me, all my beauties one after the
other – eyes, hair, complexion, shape, disposition, mind –
everything. And there are a great many verses to it. And
here is a little one he gave me yesterday morning. I had
turned him out of bed and he had to lie alone by himself.

NONA: Alone by himself!

DECIMA: And as he lay there alone, unable to sleep, he
made it up, wishing that he were blind so as not to be
troubled by looking at my beauty. Hear how it goes!
(*Sings again*:) O would that I were an old beggar
  Without a friend on this earth
  But a thieving rascally cur,
  A beggar blind from his birth;
  Or anything else but a man
  Lying alone on a bed
  Remembering a woman's beauty,
  Alone with a crazy head.

NONA: Alone in his bed indeed. I know that long poem,
that one with all the verses; I know it to my hurt, though
I haven't read a word of it. Four lines in every verse, four
beats in every line, and fourteen verses – my curse upon it!

DECIMA: (*Taking out a manuscript from her bodice*) Yes,
fourteen verses. There are numbers to them.

NONA: You have another there – ten verses all in fours
and threes.

DECIMA: (*Looking at another manuscript*) Yes, the verses
are in fours and threes. But how do you know all this? I

carry them here. They are a secret between him and me, and nobody can see them till they have lain a long while upon my heart.

NONA: They have lain upon your heart, but they were made upon my shoulder. Ay, and down along my spine in the small hours of the morning; so many beats a line, and for every beat a tap of the fingers.

DECIMA: My God!

NONA: That one with the fourteen verses kept me from my sleep two hours, and when the lines were finished he lay upon his back another hour waving one arm in the air, making up the music. I liked him well enough to seem to be asleep through it all, and many another poem too – but when he made up that short one you sang he was so pleased that he muttered the words all about his lying alone in his bed thinking of you, and that made me mad. So I said to him, 'Am I not beautiful? Turn round and look.' O, I cut it short, for even I can please a man when there is but one candle. (*She takes a pair of scissors that are hanging round her neck and begins snipping at the dress for Noah's wife.*) And now you know why I can play the part in spite of you and not be driven out. Work upon Septimus if you have a mind for it. Little need I care. I will clip this a trifle and re-stitch it again – I have a needle and thread ready.

(*The* STAGE MANAGER *comes in ringing a bell. He is followed by various players all dressed up in the likeness of various beasts.*)

STAGE MANAGER: Put on that mask – get into your clothes. Why are you standing there as if in a trance?

NONA: Decima and I have talked the matter over and we have settled that I am to play the part.

STAGE MANAGER: Do as you please. Thank God it's a part that anybody can play. All you have got to do is to copy an old woman's squeaky voice. We are all here now but Septimus, and we cannot wait for him. I will read the part of Noah. He will be here before we are finished, I dare say. We will suppose that the audience is upon this side, and that the Ark is over there with a gangway for the beasts to climb. All you beasts are to crowd up on the prompt side. Lay down Noah's hat and cloak there till Septimus comes. As the first scene is between Noah and the beasts, you can go on with your sewing.

DECIMA: No, I must first be heard. My husband has been spending his nights with Nona, and that is why she sits clipping and stitching with that vainglorious air.

NONA: She made him miserable, she knows every trick of breaking a man's heart – he came to me with his troubles – I seemed to be a comfort to him, and now – why should I deny it? – he is my lover.

DECIMA: I will take the vainglory out of her. I have been a plague to him. O, I have been a badger and a weasel and a hedgehog and pole-cat, and all because I was dead sick of him. And, thank God!, she has got him and I am free. I threw away a part and I threw away a man – she has picked both up.

STAGE MANAGER: It seems to me that it all concerns you two. It's your business and not ours. I don't see why we should delay the rehearsal.

DECIMA: I will have no rehearsal yet. I'm too happy now that I am free. I must find somebody who will dance with me for a while. Come, we must have music. (*She picks up a lute which has been laid down amongst some properties*.) You can't all be claws and hoofs.

STAGE MANAGER: We've only an hour and the whole play to go through.

NONA: O, she has taken my scissors, she is only pretending not to care. Look at her! She is mad! Take them away from her! Hold her hand! She is going to kill me or to kill herself. (*To* STAGE MANAGER) Why don't you interfere? My God! She is going to kill me.

DECIMA: Here, Peter.

(*She begins cutting through the breast feathers of the Swan.*)

NONA: She is doing it all to stop the rehearsal, out of vengeance; and you stand there and do nothing.

STAGE MANAGER: If you have taken her husband, why didn't

you keep the news till the play was over? She is going to make them all mad now, I can see that much in her eyes.

DECIMA: Now that I have thrown Septimus into her lap, I will choose a new man. Shall it be you, Turkey-cock? or you, Bullhead?

STAGE MANAGER: There is nothing to be done. It is all your fault. If Septimus can't manage his wife, it's certain that I can't.

(*He sits down helplessly.*)

DECIMA: Dance, Bullhead, dance – no – no – stop. I will not have you for my man, slow on the feet and heavy of build, and that means jealousy, and there is a sort of melancholy in your voice. What a folly that I should find love nothing, and yet through sympathy with that voice should stretch and yawn as if I loved! Dance, Turkey-cock, dance – no, stop. I cannot have you, for my man must be lively on his feet and have a quick eye. I will not have that round eye fixed upon me now that I have sent my mind asleep. Yet what do I care who it is, so that I choose and get done with it? Dance, all dance, and I will choose the best dancer among you. Quick, quick, begin to dance.

(*All dance round* DECIMA.)

(*Singing:*) Shall I fancy beast or fowl?
   Queen Pasiphae chose a bull,
   While a passion for a swan
   Made Queen Leda stretch and yawn,
   Wherefore spin ye, whirl ye, dance ye,
   Till Queen Decima's found her fancy.

CHORUS: Wherefore spin ye, whirl ye, dance ye,
   Till Queen Decima's found her fancy.

DECIMA: Spring and straddle, stride and strut,
   Shall I chose a bird or brute?
   Name the feather or the fur
   For my single comforter?

CHORUS: Wherefore spin ye, whirl ye, dance ye,
   Till Queen Decima's found her fancy.

DECIMA: None has found, that found out love,

Single bird or brute enough;
Any bird or brute may rest
An empty head upon my breast.

CHORUS: Wherefore spin ye, whirl ye, dance ye,
Till Queen Decima's found her fancy.

STAGE MANAGER: Stop, stop, here is Septimus.

SEPTIMUS: (*The blood still upon his face, and but little soberer*) Gather about me, for I announce the end of the Christian Era, the coming of a New Dispensation, that of the New Adam, that of the Unicorn; but alas, he is chaste, he hesitates, he hesitates.

STAGE MANAGER: This is not a time for making up speeches for your new play.

SEPTIMUS: His unborn children are but images; we merely play with images.

STAGE MANAGER: Let us get on with the rehearsal.

SEPTIMUS: No; let us prepare to die. The mob is climbing up the hill with pitchforks to stick into our vitals and burning wisps to set the roof on fire.

FIRST PLAYER: (*Who has gone to the window*) My God, it's true. There is a great crowd at the bottom of the hill.

SECOND PLAYER: But why should they attack us?

SEPTIMUS: Because we are the servants of the Unicorn.

THIRD PLAYER: (*At window*) My God, they have dung-forks and scythes set on poles and they are coming this way.

(*Many* PLAYERS *gather round the window.*)

SEPTIMUS: (*Who has found the bottle and is drinking*) Some will die like Cato, some like Cicero, some like Demosthenes, triumphing over death in sonorous eloquence, or, like Petronius Arbiter, will tell witty, scandalous tales; but I will speak, no, I will sing, as if the mob did not exist. I will rail upon the Unicorn for his chastity. I will bid him trample mankind to death and beget a new race. I will even put my railing into rhyme, and all shall run sweetly, sweetly, for, even if they blow up the floor with gunpowder, they are merely the mob.

Upon the round blue eye I rail,

Damnation on the milk-white horn.

A telling sound, a sound to linger in the ear – hale, tale, bale, gale – my God, I am even too sober to find a rhyme! (*He drinks and then picks up a lute*.) – a tune that my murderers may remember my last words and croon them to their grandchildren.

(*For the next few speeches he is busy making his tune*.)

FIRST PLAYER: The players of this town are jealous. Have we not been chosen before them all, because we are the most famous players in the world? It is they who have stirred up the mob.

SECOND PLAYER: It is of me they are jealous. They know what happened at Xanadu. At the end of that old play *The Fall of Troy* Kubla Khan sent for me and said that he would give his kingdom for such a voice, and for such a presence. I stood before him dressed as Agamemnon just as when in a great scene at the end I had reproached Helen for all the misery she had wrought.

FIRST PLAYER: My God, listen to him! Is it not always the comedian who draws the crowd? Am I dreaming, or was it not I who was called six times before the curtain? Answer me that –

SECOND PLAYER: What if you were called six dozen times? The players of this town are not jealous because of the crowd's applause. They have that themselves. The unendurable thought, the thought that wrenches their hearts, the thought that puts murder into their minds is that I alone, alone of all the world's players, have looked as an equal into the eyes of Kubla Khan.

STAGE MANAGER: Stop quarrelling with one another and listen to what is happening out there. There is a man making a speech, and the crowd is getting angrier and angrier, and which of you they are jealous of I don't know, but they are all coming this way and maybe they will burn the place down as if it were Troy, and if you will do what I say you will get out of this.

FIRST PLAYER: Must we go dressed like this?

SECOND PLAYER: There is not time to change, and besides, should the hill be surrounded, we can gather in some cleft of the rocks where we can be seen only from a distance. They will suppose we are a drove of cattle or a flock of birds.

(*All go out except* SEPTIMUS, DECIMA, *and* NONA. NONA *is making a bundle of Noah's hat and cloak and other properties.* DECIMA *is watching* SEPTIMUS.)

SEPTIMUS: (*While the* PLAYERS *are going out*) Leave me to die alone? I do not blame you. There is courage in red wine, in white wine, in beer, even in thin beer sold by a blear-eyed pot-boy in a bankrupt tavern, but there is none in the human heart. When my master the Unicorn bathes by the light of the Great Bear, and to the sound of tabors, even the sweet river-water makes him drunk; but it is cold, it is cold, alas! it is cold.

NONA: I'll pile these upon your back. I shall carry the rest myself and so we shall save all.

(*She begins tying a great bundle of properties on* SEPTIMUS' *back.*)

SEPTIMUS: You are right. I accept the reproach. It is necessary that we who are the last artists – all the rest have gone over to the mob – shall save the images and implements of our art. We must carry into safety the cloak of Noah, the high-crowned hat of Noah, and the mask of the sister of Noah. She was drowned because she thought her brother was telling lies; certainly we must save her rosy cheeks and rosy mouth, that drowned, wicked mouth.

NONA: Thank God you can still stand upright on your legs.

SEPTIMUS: Tie all upon my back and I will tell you the great secret that came to me at the second mouthful of the bottle. Man is nothing till he is united to an image. Now the Unicorn is both an image and beast; that is why he alone can be the new Adam. When we have put all in safety we will go to the high tablelands of Africa and find where the Unicorn is stabled and sing a marriage song. I will stand before the terrible blue eye.

NONA: There, now, I have tied them on.

(*She begins making another bundle for herself, but forgets the mask of the sister of Noah. It lies near the throne.*)

SEPTIMUS: You will make Ionian music – music with its eyes upon that voluptuous Asia – the Dorian scale would but confirm him in his chastity. One Dorian note might undo us, and above all we must be careful not to speak of Delphi. The oracle is chaste.

NONA: Come, let us go.

SEPTIMUS: If we cannot fill him with desire he will deserve death. Even unicorns can be killed. What they dread most in the world is a blow from a knife that has been dipped in the blood of a serpent that died gazing upon an emerald.

(NONA *and* SEPTIMUS *are about to go out,* NONA *leading* SEPTIMUS.)

DECIMA: Stand back, do not dare to move a step.

SEPTIMUS: Beautiful as the Unicorn, but fierce.

DECIMA: I have locked the gates that we may have a talk.

(NONA *lets the hat of Noah fall in her alarm.*)

SEPTIMUS: That is well, very well. You would talk with me because today I am extraordinarily wise.

DECIMA: I will not unlock the gate till I have a promise that you will drive her from the company.

NONA: Do not listen to her; take the key from her.

SEPTIMUS: If I were not her husband I would take the key, but because I am her husband she is terrible. The Unicorn will be terrible when it loves.

NONA: You are afraid.

SEPTIMUS: Could not you yourself take it? She does not love you, therefore she will not be terrible.

NONA: If you are a man at all you will take it.

SEPTIMUS: I am more than a man, I am extraordinarily wise. I will take the key.

DECIMA: If you come a step nearer I will shove the key through the grating of the door.

NONA: (*Pulling him back*) Don't go near her; if she shoves it through the door we shall not be able to escape. The crowd will find us and murder us.

DECIMA: I will unlock this gate when you have taken an oath to drive her from the company, an oath never to speak with her or look at her again, a terrible oath.

SEPTIMUS: You are jealous; it is very wrong to be jealous. An ordinary man would be lost – even I am not yet wise enough. (*Drinks again.*) Now all is plain.

DECIMA: You have been unfaithful to me.

SEPTIMUS: I am only unfaithful when I am sober. Never trust a sober man. All the world over they are unfaithful. Never trust a man who has not bathed by the light of the Great Bear. I warn you against all sober men from the bottom of my heart. I am extraordinarily wise.

NONA: Promise, if it is only an oath she wants. Take whatever oath she bids you. If you delay we shall all be murdered.

SEPTIMUS: I can see your meaning. You would explain to me that an oath can be broken, more especially an oath under compulsion, but no, I say to you, no, I say to you, certainly not. Am I a rascally sober man, such a man as I have warned you against? Shall I be forsworn before the very eyes of Delphi, so to speak, before the very eyes of that cold, rocky oracle? What I promise I perform, therefore, my little darling, I will not promise anything at all.

DECIMA: Then we shall wait here. They will come in through this door, they will carry dung-forks with burning wisps. They will put the burning wisps into the roof and we shall be burnt.

SEPTIMUS: I shall die railing upon that beast. The Christian Era has come to an end, but because of the machinations of Delphi he will not become the new Adam.

DECIMA: I shall be avenged. She starved me, but I shall have killed her.

NONA: (*Who has crept behind* DECIMA *and snatched the key*) I have it, I have it!

(DECIMA *tries to take the key again, but* SEPTIMUS *holds her.*)

SEPTIMUS: Because I am an unforsworn man I am strong: a violent virginal creature, that is how it is put in *The Great Beastery of Paris*.

DECIMA: Go, then, I shall stay here and die.

NONA: Let us go. A half-hour since she offered herself to every man in the company.

DECIMA: If you would be faithful to me, Septimus, I would not let a man of them touch me.

SEPTIMUS: Flighty, but beautiful.

NONA: She is a bad woman.

(NONA *runs out*.)

SEPTIMUS: A beautiful, bad, flighty woman I will follow, but follow slowly. I will take with me this noble hat. (*He picks up Noah's hat with difficulty*.) No, it may lie there, what have I to do with that drowned, wicked mouth – beautiful, drowned, flighty mouth? I will have nothing to do with it, but I will save the noble, high-crowned hat of Noah. I will carry it thus with dignity. I will go slowly that they may see I am not afraid.

(*Singing*:) Upon the round blue eye I rail,
   Damnation on the milk-white horn.

But not one word of Delphi. I am extraordinarily wise.

(*He goes*.)

DECIMA: Betrayed, betrayed, and for a nobody. For a woman that a man can shake and twist like so much tallow. A woman that till now never looked higher than a prompter or a property man.

(*The* OLD BEGGAR *comes in*.)

Have you come to kill me, old man?

OLD BEGGAR: I am looking for straw. I must soon lie down and roll, and where will I get straw to roll on? I went round to the kitchen, and 'Go away,' they said. They made the sign of the cross as if it were a devil that puts me rolling.

DECIMA: When will the mob come to kill me?

OLD BEGGAR: Kill you? It is not you they are going to kill. It's the itching in my back that drags them hither, for when I bray like a donkey, the crown changes.

DECIMA: The crown? So it is the Queen they are going to kill.

OLD BEGGAR: But, my dear, she can't die till I roll and bray, and I will whisper to you what it is that rolls. It is the donkey that carried Christ into Jerusalem, and that is why he is so proud; and that is why he knows the hour when there is to be a new King or a new Queen.

DECIMA: Are you weary of the world, old man?

OLD BEGGAR: Yes, yes, because when I roll and bray I am asleep. I know nothing about it, and that is a great pity. I remember nothing but the itching in my back. But I must stop talking and find some straw.

DECIMA: (*Picking up the scissors*) Old man, I am going to drive this into my heart.

OLD BEGGAR: No, no; don't do that. You don't know what you will be put to when you are dead, into whose gullet you will be put to sing or to bray. You have a look of a foretelling sort. Who knows but you might be put to foretell the death of kings; and bear in mind I will have no rivals, I could not endure a rival.

DECIMA: I have been betrayed by a man, I have been made a mockery of. Do those who are dead, old man, make love and do they find good lovers?

OLD BEGGAR: I will whisper you another secret. People talk, but I have never known of anything to come from there but an old jackass. Maybe there is nothing else. Who knows but he has the whole place to himself? But there, my back is beginning to itch, and I have not yet found any straw.

(*He goes out.* DECIMA *leans the scissors upon the arm of the throne and is about to press herself upon them when the* QUEEN *enters.*)

QUEEN: (*Stopping her*) No, no – that would be a great sin.

DECIMA: Your Majesty!

QUEEN: I thought I would like to die a martyr, but that would be different, that would be to die for God's glory. The Holy Saint Octema was a martyr.

DECIMA: I am very unhappy.

QUEEN: I, too, am very unhappy. When I saw the great angry crowd and knew that they wished to kill me, though I had wanted to be a martyr, I was afraid and ran away.

DECIMA: I would not have run away, O no; but it is hard to drive a knife into one's own flesh.

QUEEN: In a moment they will have come and they will beat in the door, and how shall I escape them?

DECIMA: If they could mistake me for you, you would escape.

QUEEN: I could not let another die instead of me. That would be very wrong.

DECIMA: O, your Majesty, I shall die whatever you do, and if only I could wear that gold brocade and those gold slippers for one moment, it would not be so hard to die.

QUEEN: They say that those who die to save a rightful sovereign show great virtue.

DECIMA: Quick! the dress.

QUEEN: If you killed yourself your soul would be lost, and now you will be sure of Heaven.

DECIMA: Quick, I hear them coming.

(DECIMA *puts on the* QUEEN's *robe of state and her slippers. Underneath her robe of state the* QUEEN *wears some kind of nun-like dress. The following speech is spoken by the* QUEEN *while she is helping* DECIMA *to fasten the dress and the slippers.*)

QUEEN: Was it love?

(DECIMA *nods.*)

O, that is a great sin. I have never known love. Of all things, that is what I have had most fear of. Saint Octema shut herself up in a tower on a mountain because she was loved by a beautiful prince. I was afraid it would come in at the eye and seize upon me in a moment. I am not naturally good, and they say people will do anything for love, there is so much sweetness in it. Even Saint Octema was afraid of it. But you will escape all that and go up to God as a pure virgin.

(*The change is now complete.*)

Goodbye, I know how I can slip away. There is a convent that will take me in. It is not a tower, it is only a convent, but I have long wanted to go there to lose my name and disappear. Sit down upon the throne and turn your face away. If you do not turn your face away, you will be afraid.

(*The* QUEEN *goes out.* DECIMA *is seated upon the throne. A great crowd gathers outside the gates. A* BISHOP *enters.*)

BISHOP: Your loyal people, your Majesty, offer you their homage. I bow before you in their name. Your royal will has spoken by the mouth of the Prime Minister – has filled them with gratitude. All misunderstandings are at an end, all has been settled by your condescension in bestowing your royal hand upon the Prime Minister. (*To crowd*) Her Majesty, who has hitherto shut herself away from all men's eyes that she might pray for this kingdom undisturbed, will henceforth show herself to her people. (*To* PLAYER QUEEN) So beautiful a Queen need never fear the disobedience of her people. (*Shouts from crowd of* 'Never.')

PRIME MINISTER: (*Entering hurriedly*) I will explain all, your Majesty – there was nothing else to be done – this Bishop has been summoned to unite us; (*seeing the* QUEEN) but, sleep of Adam! – this – who is this?

DECIMA: Your emotion is too great for words. Do not try to speak.

PRIME MINISTER: This – this . . . !

DECIMA: (*Standing up*) I am Queen. I know what it is to be Queen. If I were to say to you I had an enemy you would kill him – you would tear him in pieces, would you not? (*Shouts*: 'We would kill him', 'We would tear him in pieces', *etc.*)

But I do not bid you kill anyone – I bid you obey my husband when I have raised him to the throne. He is not of royal blood, but I choose to raise him to the throne. That is my will. Show me that you will obey him so long as I bid you to obey.

(*Great cheering.* SEPTIMUS, *who has been standing among*

the crowd, comes forward and takes the PRIME MINISTER
by the sleeve. Various persons kiss the hand of the supposed
QUEEN.)

SEPTIMUS: My lord, that is not the Queen; that is my bad
wife.

(DECIMA *looks at them.*)

PRIME MINISTER: Did you see that? Did you see the devil in
her eye? They are mad after her pretty face, and she knows
it. They would not believe a word I say; there is nothing to
be done till they cool.

DECIMA: Are all here my faithful servants?

BISHOP: All, your Majesty.

DECIMA: All?

PRIME MINISTER: (*Bowing low*) All, your Majesty.

DECIMA: (*Singing:*) She pulled the thread, and bit the thread
    And made a golden gown.

Hand me that plate. While I am eating I will have a good
look at my new man.

(*The plate and a bottle of wine are handed to her. The bray
of a donkey is heard and the* OLD BEGGAR *is dragged in.*)

BISHOP: At last we have found this impostor out. He has
been accepted by the whole nation as if he were the Voice
of God. As if the crown could not be settled firmly on any
head without his help. It's plain that he has been in league
with the conspirators, and believed that your Majesty had
been killed. He is keeping it up still. Look at his glassy eye.
But his madman airs won't help him now.

PRIME MINISTER: Carry him to prison, we will hang him in
the morning. (*Shaking* SEPTIMUS) Do you understand that
there has been a miracle, that God or the Fiend has spoken,
and that the crown is on her head for good, that fate has
brayed on that man's lips? (*Aloud*) We will hang him in
the morning.

SEPTIMUS: She is my wife.

PRIME MINISTER: The crown has changed and there is no help
for it. Sleep of Adam, I must have that woman for wife. The
Oracle has settled that.

SEPTIMUS: She is my wife, she is my bad, flighty wife.

PRIME MINISTER: Seize this man. He has been whispering slanders against Her Majesty. Cast him beyond the borders of the kingdom, and his players after him.

DECIMA: He must not return upon pain of death. He has wronged me, and I will never look upon his face again.

PRIME MINISTER: Away with him.

DECIMA: My good name is dearer than my life, but I will see the players before they go.

PRIME MINISTER: Sleep of Adam! What has she got into her head? Fetch the players.

DECIMA: (*Picking up the mask of the sister of Noah*) My loyal subjects must forgive me if I hide my face – it is not yet used to the light of day, it is a modest face. I will be much happier if His Holiness will help me to tie the mask.

PRIME MINISTER: The players come.

(*Enter* PLAYERS, *who all bow to the new* QUEEN.)

DECIMA: They had some play they were to perform, but I will make them dance instead, and after that they must be richly rewarded.

PRIME MINISTER: It shall be as you will.

DECIMA: You are banished and must not return upon pain of death, and yet not one of you shall be poorer because banished. That I promise. But you have lost one thing that I will not restore. A woman player has left you. Do not mourn her. She was a bad, headstrong, cruel woman, and seeks destruction somewhere and with some man she knows nothing of; such a woman they tell me that this mask would well become, this foolish, smiling face! Come, dance.

(*They dance, and at certain moments she cries* 'Goodbye, goodbye' *or else* 'Farewell'. *And she throws them money.*)

THE DREAMING OF THE BONES

PERSONS IN THE PLAY

THREE MUSICIANS, *their faces made up to resemble masks*
A YOUNG MAN
A STRANGER, *wearing a mask*
A YOUNG GIRL, *wearing a mask*

Time — 1916. The stage is any bare place in a room close to the wall. A screen, with a pattern of mountain and sky, can stand against the wall, or a curtain with a like pattern hang upon it, but the pattern must only symbolize or suggest. One MUSICIAN *enters and then two others; the first stands singing, while the others take their places. Then all three sit down against the wall by their instruments, which are already there — a drum, a zither, and a flute. Or they unfold a cloth while the instruments are carried in.*

Song for the folding and unfolding of the cloth:

FIRST MUSICIAN: (*or all three* MUSICIANS, *singing:*)
Why does my heart beat so?
Did not a shadow pass?
It passed but a moment ago.
Who can have trod in the grass?
What rogue is night-wandering?
Have not old writers said
That dizzy dreams can spring
From the dry bones of the dead?
And many a night it seems
That all the valley fills
With those fantastic dreams.
They overflow the hills,
So passionate is a shade,
Like wine that fills to the top
A grey-green cup of jade,
Or maybe an agate cup.
(*The three* MUSICIANS *are now seated by the drum, flute, and zither at the back of the stage.*)

111

FIRST MUSICIAN: The hour before dawn and the moon covered
    up;

    The little village of Abbey is covered up;
    The little narrow trodden way that runs
    From the white road to the Abbey of Corcomroe
    Is covered up; and all about the hills
    Are like a circle of agate or of jade.
    Somewhere among great rocks on the scarce grass
    Birds cry, they cry their loneliness.
    Even the sunlight can be lonely here,
    Even hot noon is lonely. I hear a footfall –
    A young man with a lantern comes this way.
    He seems an Aran fisher, for he wears
    The flannel bawneen and the cow-hide shoe.
    He stumbles wearily, and stumbling prays.

    (*A* YOUNG MAN *enters, praying in Irish.*)

    Once more the birds cry in their loneliness,
    But now they wheel about our heads; and now
    They have dropped on the grey stone to the north-east.

    (*A* STRANGER *and a* YOUNG GIRL, *in the costume of a past
    time, come in. They wear heroic masks.*)

YOUNG MAN: (*Raising his lantern*) Who is there? I cannot
    see what you are like.

    Come to the light.

STRANGER: But what have you to fear?

YOUNG MAN: And why have you come creeping through the
    dark?

    (*The* GIRL *blows out the lantern.*)

    The wind has blown my lantern out. Where are you?
    I saw a pair of heads against the sky
    And lost them after; but you are in the right,
    I should not be afraid in County Clare;
    And should be, or should not be, have no choice,
    I have to put myself into your hands,
    Now that my candle's out.

STRANGER: You have fought in Dublin?

YOUNG MAN: I was in the Post Office, and if taken

I shall be put against a wall and shot.

STRANGER: You know some place of refuge, have some plan
    Or friend who will come to meet you?

YOUNG MAN: I am to lie
    At daybreak on the mountain and keep watch
    Until an Aran coracle puts in
    At Muckanish or at the rocky shore
    Under Finvara, but would break my neck
    If I went stumbling there alone in the dark.

STRANGER: We know the pathways that the sheep tread out,
    And all the hiding-places of the hills,
    And that they had better hiding-places once.

YOUNG MAN: You'd say they had better before English robbers
    Cut down the trees or set them upon fire
    For fear their owners might find shelter there.
    What is that sound?

STRANGER: An old horse gone astray.
    He has been wandering on the road all night.

YOUNG MAN: I took him for a man and horse. Police
    Are out upon the roads. In the late Rising
    I think there was no man of us but hated
    To fire at soldiers who but did their duty
    And were not of our race, but when a man
    Is born in Ireland and of Irish stock,
    When he takes part against us –

STRANGER: I will put you safe,
    No living man shall set his eyes upon you;
    I will not answer for the dead.

YOUNG MAN: The dead?

STRANGER: For certain days the stones where you must lie
    Have in the hour before the break of day
    Been haunted.

YOUNG MAN: But I was not born at midnight.

STRANGER: Many a man that was born in the full daylight
    Can see them plain, will pass them on the high road
    Or in the crowded market-place of the town,
    And never know that they have passed.

YOUNG MAN: My Grandam
    Would have it they did penance everywhere;
    Some lived through their old lives again.
STRANGER: In a dream;
    And some for an old scruple must hang spitted
    Upon the swaying tops of lofty trees;
    Some are consumed in fire, some withered up
    By hail and sleet out of the wintry North,
    And some but live through their old lives again.
YOUNG MAN: Well, let them dream into what shape they please
    And fill waste mountains with the invisible tumult
    Of the fantastic conscience. I have no dread;
    They cannot put me into gaol or shoot me;
    And seeing that their blood has returned to fields
    That have grown red from drinking blood like mine,
    They would not if they could betray.
STRANGER: This pathway
    Runs to the ruined Abbey of Corcomroe;
    The Abbey passed, we are soon among the stone
    And shall be at the ridge before the cocks
    Of Aughanish or Bailevelehan
    Or grey Aughtmana shake their wings and cry.
    (*They go round the stage once.*)
FIRST MUSICIAN: (*Speaking:*) They've passed the shallow well
    and the flat stone
    Fouled by the drinking cattle, the narrow lane
    Where mourners for five centuries have carried
    Noble or peasant to his burial;
    An owl is crying out above their heads.
    (*Singing:*) Why should the heart take fright?
    What sets it beating so?
    The bitter sweetness of the night
    Has made it but a lonely thing.
    Red bird of March, begin to crow!
    Up with the neck and clap the wing,
    Red cock, and crow!
    (*They go round the stage once.*)

(*Speaking*:) And now they have climbed through the long
    grassy field
  And passed the ragged thorn-trees and the gap
  In the ancient hedge; and the tomb-nested owl
  At the foot's level beats with a vague wing.
(*Singing*:) My head is in a cloud;
  I'd let the whole world go;
  My rascal heart is proud
  Remembering and remembering.
  Red bird of March, begin to crow!
  Up with the neck and clap the wing,
  Red cock, and crow!
(*They go round the stage once*.)
(*Speaking*:) They are among the stones above the ash,
  Above the briar and thorn and the scarce grass;
  Hidden amid the shadow far below them
  The cat-headed bird is crying out.
(*Singing*:) The dreaming bones cry out
  Because the night winds blow
  And heaven's a cloudy blot.
  Calamity can have its fling.
  Red bird of March, begin to crow!
  Up with the neck and clap the wing,
  Red cock, and crow!

STRANGER: We're almost at the summit and can rest.
  The road is a faint shadow there; and there
  The Abbey lies amid its broken tombs.
  In the old days we should have heard a bell
  Calling the monks before day broke to pray;
  And when the day had broken on the ridge,
  The crowing of its cocks.

YOUNG MAN: Is there no house
  Famous for sanctity or architectural beauty
  In Clare or Kerry, or in all wide Connacht,
  The enemy has not unroofed?

STRANGER: Close to the altar
  Broken by wind and frost and worn by time

Donough O'Brien has a tomb, a name in Latin.
He wore fine clothes and knew the secrets of women,
But he rebelled against the King of Thomond
And died in his youth.

YOUNG MAN: And why should he rebel?
The King of Thomond was his rightful master.
It was men like Donough who made Ireland weak –
My curse on all that troop, and when I die
I'll leave my body, if I have any choice,
Far from his ivy-tod and his owl. Have those
Who, if your tale is true, work out a penance
Upon the mountain-top where I am to hide,
Come from the Abbey graveyard?

YOUNG GIRL: They have not that luck,
But are more lonely; those that are buried there
Warred in the heat of the blood; if they were rebels
Some momentary impulse made them rebels,
Or the commandment of some petty king
Who hated Thomond. Being but common sinners,
No callers-in of the alien from oversea,
They and their enemies of Thomond's party
Mix in a brief dream-battle above their bones;
Or make one drove; or drift in amity;
Or in the hurry of the heavenly round
Forget their earthly names. These are alone,
Being accursed.

YOUNG MAN: But if what seems is true
And there are more upon the other side
Than on this side of death, many a ghost
Must meet them face to face and pass the word
Even upon this grey and desolate hill.

YOUNG GIRL: Until this hour no ghost or living man
Has spoken, though seven centuries have run
Since they, weary of life and of men's eyes,
Flung down their bones in some forgotten place,
Being accursed.

YOUNG MAN: I have heard that there are souls

Who, having sinned after a monstrous fashion,
Take on them, being dead, a monstrous image
To drive the living, should they meet its face,
Crazy, and be a terror to the dead.

YOUNG GIRL: But these
Were comely even in their middle life
And carry, now that they are dead, the image
Of their first youth, for it was in that youth
Their sin began.

YOUNG MAN: I have heard of angry ghosts
Who wander in a wilful solitude.

YOUNG GIRL: These have no thought but love; nor any joy
But that upon the instant when their penance
Draws to its height, and when two hearts are wrung
Nearest to breaking, if hearts of shadows break,
His eyes can mix with hers; nor any pang
That is so bitter as that double glance,
Being accursed.

YOUNG MAN: But what is this strange penance –
That when their eyes have met can wring them most?

YOUNG GIRL: Though eyes can meet, their lips can never meet.

YOUNG MAN: And yet it seems they wander side by side.
But doubtless you would say that when lips meet
And have not living nerves, it is no meeting.

YOUNG GIRL: Although they have no blood, or living nerves,
Who once lay warm and live the live-long night
In one another's arms, and know their part
In life, being now but of the people of dreams,
Is a dream's part; although they are but shadows,
Hovering between a thorn-tree and a stone,
Who have heaped up night on wingèd night; although
No shade however harried and consumed
Would change his own calamity for theirs,
Their manner of life were blessed could their lips
A moment meet; but when he has bent his head
Close to her head, or hand would slip in hand,
The memory of their crime flows up between

And drives them apart.

YOUNG MAN: The memory of a crime –
He took her from a husband's house, it may be,
But does the penance for a passionate sin
Last for so many centuries?

YOUNG GIRL: No, no;
The man she chose, the man she was chosen by,
Cared little and cares little from whose house
They fled towards dawn amid the flights of arrows,
Or that it was a husband's and a king's;
And how, if that were all, could she lack friends,
On crowded roads or on the unpeopled hill?
Helen herself had opened wide the door
Where night by night she dreams herself awake
And gathers to her breast a dreaming man.

YOUNG MAN: What crime can stay so in the memory?
What crime can keep apart the lips of lovers
Wandering and alone?

YOUNG GIRL: Her king and lover
Was overthrown in battle by her husband,
And for her sake and for his own, being blind
And bitter and bitterly in love, he brought
A foreign army from across the sea.

YOUNG MAN: You speak of Diarmuid and Dervorgilla
Who brought the Norman in?

YOUNG GIRL: Yes, yes, I spoke
Of that most miserable, most accursed pair
Who sold their country into slavery; and yet
They were not wholly miserable and accursed
If somebody of their race at last would say,
'I have forgiven them.'

YOUNG MAN: O, never, never
Shall Diarmuid and Dervorgilla be forgiven.

YOUNG GIRL: If some one of their race forgave at last
Lip would be pressed on lip.

YOUNG MAN: O, never, never
Shall Diarmuid and Dervorgilla be forgiven.
You have told your story well, so well indeed

I could not help but fall into the mood
And for a while believe that it was true,
Or half believe; but better push on now.
The horizon to the east is growing bright.
    (*They go round stage once. The* MUSICIANS *play.*)
So here we're on the summit. I can see
The Aran Islands, Connemara Hills,
And Galway in the breaking light; there too
The enemy has toppled roof and gable,
And torn the panelling from ancient rooms;
What generations of old men had known
Like their own hands, and children wondered at,
Has boiled a trooper's porridge. That town had lain,
But for the pair that you would have me pardon,
Amid its gables and its battlements
Like any old admired Italian town;
For though we have neither coal, nor iron ore,
To make us wealthy and corrupt the air,
Our country, if that crime were uncommitted,
Had been most beautiful. Why do you dance?
Why do you gaze, and with so passionate eyes,
One on the other; and then turn away,
Covering your eyes, and weave it in a dance?
Who are you? what are you? you are not natural.

YOUNG GIRL: Seven hundred years our lips have never met.

YOUNG MAN: Why do you look so strangely at one another,
    So strangely and so sweetly?

YOUNG GIRL: Seven hundred years.

YOUNG MAN: So strangely and so sweetly. All the ruin,
    All, all their handiwork is blown away
    As though the mountain air had blown it away
    Because their eyes have met. They cannot hear,
    Being folded up and hidden in their dance.
    The dance is changing now. They have dropped their eyes,
    They have covered up their eyes as though their hearts
    Had suddenly been broken – never, never
    Shall Diarmuid and Dervorgilla be forgiven.
    They have drifted in the dance from rock to rock.

They have raised their hands as though to snatch the
  sleep
That lingers always in the abyss of the sky
Though they can never reach it. A cloud floats up
And covers all the mountain-head in a moment;
And now it lifts and they are swept away.

(*The* STRANGER *and the* YOUNG GIRL *go out.*)

I had almost yielded and forgiven it all –
Terrible the temptation and the place!

(*The* MUSICIANS *begin unfolding and folding a black cloth.
The* FIRST MUSICIAN *comes forward to the front of the stage,
at the centre. He holds the cloth before him. The other two come
one on either side and unfold it. They afterwards fold it up in
the same way. While it is unfolded, the* YOUNG MAN *leaves
the stage.*)

Songs for the unfolding and folding of the cloth:
THE MUSICIANS: (*Singing*:) At the grey round of the hill
      Music of a lost kingdom
    Runs, runs and is suddenly still.
    The winds out of Clare-Galway
    Carry it: suddenly it is still.

    I have heard in the night air
    A wandering airy music;
    And moidered in that snare
    A man is lost of a sudden,
    In that sweet wandering snare.

    What finger first began
    Music of a lost kingdom?
    They dream that laughed in the sun.
    Dry bones that dream are bitter,
    They dream and darken our sun.

    Those crazy fingers play
    A wandering airy music;

Our luck is withered away,
And wheat in the wheat-ear withered,
And the wind blows it away.

*

My heart ran wild when it heard
The curlew cry before dawn
And the eddying cat-headed bird;
But now the night is gone.
I have heard from far below
The strong March birds a-crow.
Stretch neck and clap the wing,
Red cocks, and crow!

THE ONLY JEALOUSY OF EMER

PERSONS IN THE PLAY

THREE MUSICIANS, *their faces made up to resemble masks*
THE GHOST OF CUCHULAIN, *wearing a mask*
THE FIGURE OF CUCHULAIN, *wearing a mask*
EMER \} *masked, or their faces*
EITHNE INGUBA \} *made up to resemble masks*
WOMAN OF THE SIDHE, *wearing a mask*

Enter the MUSICIANS. *Their musical instruments — string, flute and drum — can either be already upon the stage or be brought in by the* FIRST MUSICIAN *before he stands in the centre with the black cloth between his hands, or by a player when the cloth has been unfolded. The stage can be against the wall of any room.*

Song for the folding and unfolding of the cloth:

FIRST MUSICIAN: A woman's beauty is like a white
    Frail bird, like a white sea-bird alone
    At daybreak after stormy night
    Between two furrows upon the ploughed land:
    A sudden storm, and it was thrown
    Between dark furrows upon the ploughed land.
    How many centuries spent
    The sedentary soul
    In toils of measurement
    Beyond eagle or mole,
    Beyond hearing or seeing,
    Or Archimedes' guess,
    To raise into being
    That loveliness?

    A strange, unserviceable thing,
    A fragile, exquisite, pale shell,
    That the vast troubled waters bring
    To the loud sands before day has broken.
    The storm arose and suddenly fell
    Amid the dark before day had broken.
    What death? what discipline?
    What bonds no man could unbind,

125

Being imagined within
The labyrinth of the mind,
What pursuing or fleeing,
What wounds, what bloody press,
Dragged into being
This loveliness?

(*When the cloth is folded again the* MUSICIANS *take their place against the wall. The folding of the cloth shows on one side of the stage the curtained bed or litter on which lies a* MAN *in his grave-clothes. He wears an heroic mask. Another man with exactly similar clothes and mask crouches near the front.* EMER *is sitting beside the bed.*)

(*Speaking*) I call before the eyes a roof
  With cross-beams darkened by smoke;
  A fisher's net hangs from a beam,
  A long oar lies against the wall.
  I call up a poor fisher's house;
  A man lies dead or swooning,
  That amorous man,
  That amorous, violent man, renowned Cuchulain,
  Queen Emer at his side.
  At her own bidding all the rest have gone;
  But now one comes on hesitating feet,
  Young Eithne Inguba, Cuchulain's mistress.
  She stands a moment in the open door.
  Beyond the open door the bitter sea,
  The shining, bitter sea, is crying out,

(*Singing*) White shell, white wing!
  I will not choose for my friend
  A frail, unserviceable thing
  That drifts and dreams, and but knows
  That waters are without end
  And that wind blows.

EMER: (*Speaking*) Come hither, come sit down beside the
      bed;
    You need not be afraid, for I myself
    Sent for you, Eithne Inguba.

EITHNE INGUBA: No, Madam,
 I have too deeply wronged you to sit there.
EMER: Of all the people in the world we two,
 And we alone, may watch together here,
 Because we have loved him best.
EITHNE INGUBA: And is he dead?
EMER: Although they have dressed him out in his grave-
  clothes
 And stretched his limbs, Cuchulain is not dead;
 The very heavens when that day's at hand,
 So that his death may not lack ceremony,
 Will throw out fires, and the earth grow red with blood.
 There shall not be a scullion but foreknows it
 Like the world's end.
EITHNE INGUBA: How did he come to this?
EMER: Towards noon in the assembly of the kings
 He met with one who seemed a while most dear.
 The kings stood round; some quarrel was blown up;
 He drove him out and killed him on the shore
 At Baile's tree, and he who was so killed
 Was his own son begot on some wild woman
 When he was young, or so I have heard it said;
 And thereupon, knowing what man he had killed,
 And being mad with sorrow, he ran out;
 And after, to his middle in the foam,
 With shield before him and with sword in hand,
 He fought the deathless sea. The kings looked on
 And not a king dared stretch an arm, or even
 Dared call his name, but all stood wondering
 In that dumb stupor like cattle in a gale,
 Until at last, as though he had fixed his eyes
 On a new enemy, he waded out
 Until the water had swept over him;
 But the waves washed his senseless image up
 And laid it at this door.
EITHNE INGUBA: How pale he looks!
EMER: He is not dead.

EITHNE INGUBA: You have not kissed his lips
    Nor laid his head upon your breast.
EMER: It may be
    An image has been put into his place,
    A sea-borne log bewitched into his likeness,
    Or some stark horseman grown too old to ride
    Among the troops of Manannan, Son of the Sea,
    Now that his joints are stiff.
EITHNE INGUBA: Cry out his name.
    All that are taken from our sight, they say,
    Loiter amid the scenery of their lives
    For certain hours or days, and should he hear
    He might, being angry, drive the changeling out.
EMER: It is hard to make them hear amid their darkness.
    And it is long since I could call him home;
    I am but his wife, but if you cry aloud
    With the sweet voice that is so dear to him
    He cannot help but listen.
EITHNE INGUBA: He loves me best,
    Being his newest love, but in the end
    Will love the woman best who loved him first
    And loved him through the years when love seemed lost.
EMER: I have that hope, the hope that some day somewhere
    We'll sit together at the hearth again.
EITHNE INGUBA: Women like me, the violent hour passed over,
    Are flung into some corner like old nut-shells.
    Cuchulain, listen.
EMER: No, not yet, for first
    I'll cover up his face to hide the sea;
    And throw new logs upon the hearth and stir
    The half-burnt logs until they break in flame.
    Old Manannan's unbridled horses come
    Out of the sea, and on their backs his horsemen;
    But all the enchantments of the dreaming foam
    Dread the hearth-fire.

(*She pulls the curtains of the bed so as to hide the sick* MAN'S *face, that the actor may change his mask unseen. She goes to one side of the platform and moves her hand as though putting logs on a fire and stirring it into a blaze. While she makes these movements the* MUSICIANS *play, marking the movements with drum and flute perhaps. Having finished she stands beside the imaginary fire at a distance from* CUCHULAIN *and* EITHNE INGUBA.)

                            Call on Cuchulain now.

EITHNE INGUBA: Can you not hear my voice?

EMER: Bend over him;
    Call out dear secrets till you have touched his heart,
    If he lies there; and if he is not there,
    Till you have made him jealous.

EITHNE INGUBA: Cuchulain, listen.

EMER: Those words sound timidly; to be afraid
    Because his wife is but three paces off,
    When there is so great need, were but to prove
    The man that chose you made but a poor choice:
    We're but two women struggling with the sea.

EITHNE INGUBA: O my beloved, pardon me, that I
    Have been ashamed. I thrust my shame away.
    I have never sent a message or called out,
    Scarce had a longing for your company
    But you have known and come; and if indeed
    You are lying there, stretch out your arms and speak;
    Open your mouth and speak, for to this hour
    My company has made you talkative.
    What ails your tongue, or what has closed your ears?
    Our passion had not chilled when we were parted
    On the pale shore under the breaking dawn.
    He cannot speak: or else his ears are closed
    And no sound reaches him.

EMER: Then kiss that image;
    The pressure of your mouth upon his mouth
    May reach him where he is.

EITHNE INGUBA: (*Starting back*)   It is no man.
    I felt some evil thing that dried my heart

When my lips touched it.

EMER: No, his body stirs;
The pressure of your mouth has called him home;
He has thrown the changeling out.

EITHNE INGUBA: (*Going further off*)   Look at that arm;
That arm is withered to the very socket.

EMER: (*Going up to the bed*) What do you come for; and
from where?

FIGURE OF CUCHULAIN: I have come
From Manannan's court upon a bridleless horse.

EMER: What one among the Sidhe has dared to lie
Upon Cuchulain's bed and take his image?

FIGURE OF CUCHULAIN: I am named Bricriu – not the man
– that Bricriu,
Maker of discord among gods and men,
Called Bricriu of the Sidhe.

EMER: Come for what purpose?

FIGURE OF CUCHULAIN: (*Sitting up, parting curtain and showing
its distorted face, as* EITHNE INGUBA *goes out*) I show my face,
and everything he loves
Must fly away.

EMER: You people of the wind
Are full of lying speech and mockery:
I have not fled your face.

FIGURE OF CUCHULAIN: You are not loved.

EMER: And therefore have no dread to meet your eyes
And to demand him of you.

FIGURE OF CUCHULAIN: For that I have come.
You have but to pay the price and he is free.

EMER: Do the Sidhe bargain?

FIGURE OF CUCHULAIN: When they would free a captive
They take in ransom a less valued thing.
The fisher, when some knowledgeable man
Restores to him his wife, or son, or daughter,
Knows he must lose a boat or a net, or it may be
The cow that gives his children milk; and some
Have offered their own lives. I do not ask

Your life, or any valuable thing;
You spoke but now of the mere chance that some day
You'd be the apple of his eye again
When old and ailing, but renounce that chance
And he shall live again.

EMER: I do not question
But you have brought ill-luck on all he loves;
And now, because I am thrown beyond your power
Unless your words are lies, you come to bargain.

FIGURE OF CUCHULAIN: You loved your mastery, when but
    newly married,
And I love mine for all my withered arm;
You have but to put yourself into that power
And he shall live again.

EMER: No, never, never.

FIGURE OF CUCHULAIN: You dare not be accursed, yet he has
    dared.

EMER: I have but two joyous thoughts, two things I prize,
A hope, a memory, and now you claim that hope.

FIGURE OF CUCHULAIN: He'll never sit beside you at the hearth
Or make old bones, but die of wounds and toil
On some far shore or mountain, a strange woman
Beside his mattress.

EMER: You ask for my one hope
That you may bring your curse on all about him.

FIGURE OF CUCHULAIN: You've watched his loves and you
    have not been jealous,
Knowing that he would tire, but do those tire
That love the Sidhe? Come closer to the bed
That I may touch your eyes and give them sight.

(*He touches her eyes with his left hand, the right being withered.*)

EMER: (*Seeing the crouching* GHOST OF CUCHULAIN) My husband
    is there.

FIGURE OF CUCHULAIN: I have dissolved the dark
That hid him from your eyes, but not that other
That's hidden you from his.

EMER: O husband, husband!

FIGURE OF CUCHULAIN: He cannot hear – being shut off,
  a phantom
 That can neither touch, nor hear, nor see;
 The longing and the cries have drawn him hither.
 He heard no sound, heard no articulate sound;
 They could but banish rest, and make him dream,
 And in that dream, as do all dreaming shades
 Before they are accustomed to their freedom,
 He has taken his familiar form; and yet
 He crouches there not knowing where he is
 Or at whose side he is crouched.

 (*A* WOMAN OF THE SIDHE *has entered and stands a little
 inside the door.*)

EMER: Who is this woman?

FIGURE OF CUCHULAIN: She has hurried from the Country-
  under-Wave
 And dreamed herself into that shape that he
 May glitter in her basket; for the Sidhe
 Are dexterous fishers and they fish for men
 With dreams upon the hook.

EMER: And so that woman
 Has hid herself in this disguise and made
 Herself into a lie.

FIGURE OF CUCHULAIN: A dream is body;
 The dead move ever towards a dreamless youth
 And when they dream no more return no more;
 And those more holy shades that never lived
 But visit you in dreams.

EMER: I know her sort.
 They find our men asleep, weary with war,
 Lap them in cloudy hair or kiss their lips;
 Our men awake in ignorance of it all,
 But when we take them in our arms at night
 We cannot break their solitude.

 (*She draws a knife from her girdle.*)

FIGURE OF CUCHULAIN: No knife
 Can wound that body of air. Be silent; listen;

I have not given you eyes and ears for nothing.

(*The* WOMAN OF THE SIDHE *moves round the crouching* GHOST OF CUCHULAIN *at front of stage in a dance that grows gradually quicker, as he slowly awakes. At moments she may drop her hair upon his head, but she does not kiss him. She is accompanied by string and flute and drum. Her mask and clothes must suggest gold or bronze or brass or silver, so that she seems more an idol than a human being. This suggestion may be repeated in her movements. Her hair, too, must keep the metallic suggestion.*)

GHOST OF CUCHULAIN: Who is it stands before me there
    Shedding such light from limb and hair
    As when the moon, complete at last
    With every labouring crescent past,
    And lonely with extreme delight,
    Flings out upon the fifteenth night?

WOMAN OF THE SIDHE: Because I long I am not complete.
    What pulled your hands about your feet,
    Pulled down your head upon your knees,
    And hid your face?

GHOST OF CUCHULAIN: Old memories:
    A woman in her happy youth
    Before her man had broken troth,
    Dead men and women. Memories
    Have pulled my head upon my knees.

WOMAN OF THE SIDHE: Could you that have loved many a
      woman
    That did not reach beyond the human,
    Lacking a day to be complete,
    Love one that, though her heart can beat,
    Lacks it but by an hour or so?

GHOST OF CUCHULAIN: I know you now, for long ago
    I met you on a cloudy hill
    Beside old thorn-trees and a well.
    A woman danced and a hawk flew,
    I held out arms and hands; but you,
    That now seem friendly, fled away,

Half woman and half bird of prey.

WOMAN OF THE SIDHE: Hold out your arms and hands again;
You were not so dumbfounded when
I was that bird of prey, and yet
I am all woman now.

GHOST OF CUCHULAIN: I am not
The young and passionate man I was,
And though that brilliant light surpass
All crescent forms, my memories
Weigh down my hands, abash my eyes.

WOMAN OF THE SIDHE: Then kiss my mouth. Though memory
Be beauty's bitterest enemy
I have no dread, for at my kiss
Memory on the moment vanishes:
Nothing but beauty can remain.

GHOST OF CUCHULAIN: And shall I never know again
Intricacies of blind remorse?

WOMAN OF THE SIDHE: Time shall seem to stay his course;
When your mouth and my mouth meet
All my round shall be complete
Imagining all its circles run;
And there shall be oblivion
Even to quench Cuchulain's drouth,
Even to still that heart.

GHOST OF CUCHULAIN: Your mouth!
(*They are about to kiss; he turns away.*)
O, Emer, Emer!

WOMAN OF THE SIDHE: So then it is she
Made you impure with memory.

GHOST OF CUCHULAIN: O Emer, Emer, there we stand;
Side by side and hand in hand
Tread the threshold of the house
As when our parents married us.

WOMAN OF THE SIDHE: Being among the dead you love her
That valued every slut above her
While you still lived.

GHOST OF CUCHULAIN: O my lost Emer!

WOMAN OF THE SIDHE: And there is not a loose-tongued schemer
But could draw you, if not dead,
From her table and her bed.
But what could make you fit to wive
With flesh and blood, being born to live
Where no one speaks of broken troth,
For all have washed out of their eyes
Wind-blown dirt of their memories
To improve their sight?

GHOST OF CUCHULAIN: Your mouth, your mouth!

(*She goes out followed by the* GHOST OF CUCHULAIN.)

FIGURE OF CUCHULAIN: Cry out that you renounce his love; make haste
And cry that you renounce his love for ever.

EMER: No, never will I give that cry.

FIGURE OF CUCHULAIN: Fool, fool!
I am Fand's enemy come to thwart her will,
And you stand gaping there. There is still time.
Hear how the horses trample on the shore,
Hear how they trample! She has mounted up.
Cuchulain's not beside her in the chariot.
There is still a moment left; cry out, cry out!
Renounce him, and her power is at an end.
Cuchulain's foot is on the chariot-step.
Cry –

EMER: I renounce Cuchulain's love for ever.

(*The* FIGURE OF CUCHULAIN *sinks back upon the bed, half-drawing the curtain.* EITHNE INGUBA *comes in and kneels by the bed.*)

EITHNE INGUBA: Come to me, my beloved, it is I.
I, Eithne Inguba. Look! He is there.
He has come back and moved upon the bed.
And it is I that won him from the sea,
That brought him back to life.

EMER: Cuchulain wakes.

(*The figure turns round. It once more wears the heroic mask.*)

CUCHULAIN: Your arms, your arms! O Eithne Inguba,
   I have been in some strange place and am afraid.

(*The* FIRST MUSICIAN *comes to the front of stage, the others
from each side, and unfold the cloth singing. Song for the
unfolding and folding of the cloth:*)

THE MUSICIANS: Why does your heart beat thus?
   Plain to be understood,
   I have met in a man's house
   A statue of solitude,
   Moving there and walking;
   Its strange heart beating fast
   For all our talking.
   O still that heart at last.

   O bitter reward
   Of many a tragic tomb!
   And we though astonished are dumb
   Or give but a sigh and a word,
   A passing word.

   Although the door be shut
   And all seem well enough,
   Although wide world hold not
   A man but will give you his love
   The moment he has looked at you,
   He that has loved the best
   May turn from a statue
   His too human breast.

   O bitter reward
   Of many a tragic tomb!
   And we though astonished are dumb
   Or give but a sigh and a word,
   A passing word.

What makes your heart so beat?
What man is at your side?
When beauty is complete
Your own thought will have died
And danger not be diminished;
Dimmed at three-quarter light,
When moon's round is finished
The stars are out of sight.

O bitter reward
Of many a tragic tomb!
And we though astonished are dumb
Or give but a sigh and a word,
A passing word.
(*When the cloth is folded again the stage is bare.*)

THE RESURRECTION

TO

JUNZO SATO

PERSONS IN THE PLAY

THE HEBREW
THE GREEK
THE SYRIAN
CHRIST
THREE MUSICIANS

Before I had finished this play I saw that its subject-matter might make it unsuited for the public stage in England or in Ireland. I had begun it with an ordinary stage scene in the mind's eye, curtained walls, a window and door at back, a curtained door at left. I now changed the stage directions and wrote songs for the unfolding and folding of the curtain that it might be played in a studio or a drawing room like my dance plays, or at the Peacock Theatre before a specially chosen audience. If it is played at the Peacock Theatre the MUSICIANS *may sing the opening and closing songs, as they pull apart or pull together the proscenium curtain; the whole stage may be hung with curtains with an opening at the left. While the play is in progress the* MUSICIANS *will sit towards the right of the audience; if at the Peacock, on the step which separates the stage from the audience, or one on either side of the proscenium.*

Song for the unfolding and folding of the curtain:

I saw a staring virgin stand
Where holy Dionysus died,
And tear the heart out of his side,
And lay the heart upon her hand
And bear that beating heart away;
And then did all the Muses sing
Of Magnus Annus at the spring,
As though God's death were but a play.

*

Another Troy must rise and set,
Another lineage feed the crow,
Another Argo's painted prow

141

Drive to a flashier bauble yet.
The Roman Empire stood appalled:
It dropped the reins of peace and war
When that fierce virgin and her Star
Out of the fabulous darkness called.

(*The* HEBREW *is discovered alone upon the stage; he has a sword or spear. The* MUSICIANS *make faint drum-taps, or sound a rattle; the* GREEK *enters through the audience from the left.*)

THE HEBREW: Did you find out what the noise was?

THE GREEK: Yes, I asked a Rabbi.

THE HEBREW: Were you not afraid?

THE GREEK: How could he know that I am called a Christian? I wore the cap I brought from Alexandria. He said the followers of Dionysus were parading the streets with rattles and drums; that such a thing had never happened in this city before; that the Roman authorities were afraid to interfere. The followers of Dionysus have been out among the fields tearing a goat to pieces and drinking its blood, and are now wandering through the streets like a pack of wolves. The mob was so terrified of their frenzy that it left them alone, or, as seemed more likely, so busy hunting Christians it had time for nothing else. I turned to go, but he called me back and asked where I lived. When I said outside the gates, he asked if it was true that the dead had broken out of the cemeteries.

THE HEBREW: We can keep the mob off for some minutes, long enough for the Eleven to escape over the roofs. I shall defend the narrow stair between this and the street until I am killed, then you will take my place. Why is not the Syrian here?

THE GREEK: I met him at the door and sent him on a message; he will be back before long.

THE HEBREW: The three of us will be few enough for the work in hand.

THE GREEK: (*Glancing towards the opening at the left*) What are they doing now?

THE HEBREW: While you were down below, James brought

a loaf out of a bag, and Nathanael found a skin of wine. They put them on the table. It was a long time since they had eaten anything. Then they began to speak in low voices, and John spoke of the last time they had eaten in that room.

THE GREEK: They were thirteen then.

THE HEBREW: He said that Jesus divided bread and wine among them. When John had spoken they sat still, nobody eating or drinking. If you stand here you will see them. That is Peter close to the window. He has been quite motionless for a long time, his head upon his breast.

THE GREEK: Is it true that when the soldier asked him if he were a follower of Jesus he denied it?

THE HEBREW: Yes, it is true. James told me. Peter told the others what he had done. But when the moment came they were all afraid. I must not blame. I might have been no braver. What are we all but dogs who have lost their master?

THE GREEK: Yet you and I if the mob come will die rather than let it up that stair.

THE HEBREW: Ah! That is different. I am going to draw that curtain; they must not hear what I am going to say. (*He draws curtain.*)

THE GREEK: I know what is in your mind.

THE HEBREW: They are afraid because they do not know what to think. When Jesus was taken they could no longer believe him the Messiah. We can find consolation, but for the Eleven it was always complete light or complete darkness.

THE GREEK: Because they are so much older.

THE HEBREW: No, no. You have only to look into their faces to see they were intended to be saints. They are unfitted for anything else. What makes you laugh?

THE GREEK: Something I can see through the window. There, where I am pointing. There, at the end of the street. (*They stand together looking out over the heads of the audience.*)

THE HEBREW: I cannot see anything.

THE GREEK: The hill.

THE HEBREW: That is Calvary.

THE GREEK: And the three crosses on the top of it.

(*He laughs again.*)

THE HEBREW: Be quiet. You do not know what you are doing. You have gone out of your mind. You are laughing at Calvary.

THE GREEK: No, no. I am laughing because they thought they were nailing the hands of a living man upon the Cross, and all the time there was nothing there but a phantom.

THE HEBREW: I saw him buried.

THE GREEK: We Greeks understand these things. No god has ever been buried; no god has ever suffered. Christ only seemed to be born, only seemed to eat, seemed to sleep, seemed to walk, seemed to die. I did not mean to tell you until I had proof.

THE HEBREW: Proof?

THE GREEK: I shall have proof before nightfall.

THE HEBREW: You talk wildly, but a masterless dog can bay the moon.

THE GREEK: No Jew can understand these things.

THE HEBREW: It is you who do not understand. It is I and those men in there, perhaps, who begin to understand at last. He was nothing more than a man, the best man who ever lived. Nobody before him had so pitied human misery. He preached the coming of the Messiah because he thought the Messiah would take it all upon himself. Then some day when he was very tired, after a long journey perhaps, he thought that he himself was the Messiah. He thought it because of all destinies it seemed the most terrible.

THE GREEK: How could a man think himself the Messiah?

THE HEBREW: It was always foretold that he would be born of a woman.

THE GREEK: To say that a god can be born of a woman, carried in her womb, fed upon her breast, washed as children are washed, is the most terrible blasphemy.

THE HEBREW: If the Messiah were not born of a woman he could not take away the sins of man. Every sin starts a stream of suffering, but the Messiah takes it all away.

THE GREEK: Every man's sins are his property. Nobody else has a right to them.

THE HEBREW: The Messiah is able to exhaust human suffering as though it were all gathered together in the spot of a burning-glass.

THE GREEK: That makes me shudder. The utmost possible suffering as an object of worship! You are morbid because your nation has no statues.

THE HEBREW: What I have described is what I thought until three days ago.

THE GREEK: I say that there is nothing in the tomb.

THE HEBREW: I saw him carried up the mountain and the tomb shut upon him.

THE GREEK: I have sent the Syrian to the tomb to prove that there is nothing there.

THE HEBREW: You knew the danger we were all in and yet you weakened our guard?

THE GREEK: I have risked the apostles' lives and our own. What I have sent the Syrian to find out is more important.

THE HEBREW: None of us are in our right mind today. I have got something in my own head that shocks me.

THE GREEK: Something you do not want to speak about?

THE HEBREW: I am glad that he was not the Messiah; we might all have been deceived to our lives' end, or learnt the truth too late. One had to sacrifice everything that the divine suffering might, as it were, descend into one's mind and soul and make them pure.

(*A sound of rattles and drums, at first in short bursts that come between sentences, but gradually growing continuous.*)

One had to give up all worldly knowledge, all ambition, do nothing of one's own will. Only the divine could have any reality. God had to take complete possession. It must be a terrible thing when one is old, and the tomb round the corner, to think of all the ambitions one has put aside; to think, perhaps, a great deal about women. I want to marry and have children.

THE GREEK: (*Who is standing facing the audience, and looking*

out over their heads) It is the worshippers of Dionysus. They
are under the window now. There is a group of women who
carry upon their shoulders a bier with an image of the dead
god upon it. No, they are not women. They are men dressed
as women. I have seen something like it in Alexandria. They
are all silent, as if something were going to happen. My God!
What a spectacle! In Alexandria a few men paint their lips ver-
milion. They imitate women that they may attain in worship a
woman's self-abandonment. No great harm comes of it – but
here! Come and look for yourself.

THE HEBREW: I will not look at such madmen.

THE GREEK: Though the music has stopped, some men
are still dancing, and some of the dancers have gashed
themselves with knives, imagining themselves, I suppose,
at once the god and the Titans that murdered him. A little
further off a man and woman are coupling in the middle of
the street. She thinks the surrender to some man the dance
threw into her arms may bring her god back to life. All are
from the foreign quarter, to judge by face and costume, and
are the most ignorant and excitable class of Asiatic Greeks,
the dregs of the population. Such people suffer terribly and
seek forgetfulness in monstrous ceremonies. Ah, that is what
they were waiting for. The crowd has parted to make way for
a singer. It is a girl. No, not a girl; a boy from the theatre. I
know him. He acts girls' parts. He is dressed as a girl, but his
fingernails are gilded and his wig is made of gilded cords. He
looks like a statue out of some temple. I remember something
of the kind in Alexandria. Three days after the full moon, a
full moon in March, they sing the death of the god and pray
for his resurrection.

(*One of the* MUSICIANS *sings the following song*:)

MUSICIAN: Astrea's holy child!

  A rattle in the wood
  Where a Titan strode!
  His rattle drew the child
  Into that solitude.
  Barrum, barrum, barrum.

(*Drum-taps accompany and follow the words.*)

We wandering women,
Wives for all that come,
Tried to draw him home;
And every wandering woman
Beat upon a drum.
Barrum, barrum, barrum.
(*Drum-taps as before.*)

But the murderous Titans
Where the woods grow dim
Stood and waited him.
The great hands of those Titans
Tore limb from limb.
Barrum, barrum, barrum.
(*Drum-taps as before.*)

On virgin Astrea
That can succour all
Wandering women call;
Call out to Astrea
That the moon stood at the full.
Barrum, barrum, barrum.
(*Drum-taps as before.*)

THE GREEK: I cannot think all that self-surrender and self-abasement is Greek, despite the Greek name of its god. When the goddess came to Achilles in the battle she did not interfere with his soul, she took him by his yellow hair. Lucretius thinks that the gods appear in the visions of the day and night but are indifferent to human fate; that, however, is the exaggeration of a Roman rhetorician. They can be discovered by contemplation, in their faces a high keen joy like the cry of a bat, and the man who lives heroically gives them the only earthly body that they covet. He, as it were, copies their gestures and their acts. What seems their indifference is but their eternal possession of themselves. Man, too, remains separate. He does not surrender his soul. He keeps his privacy.

(*Drum-taps to represent knocking at the door.*)

THE HEBREW: There is someone at the door, but I dare not open with that crowd in the street.

THE GREEK: You need not be afraid. The crowd has begun to move away.

(*The* HEBREW *goes down into the audience towards the left.*)

I deduce from our great philosophers that a god can overwhelm man with disaster, take health and wealth away, but man keeps his privacy. If that is the Syrian he may bring such confirmation that mankind will never forget his words.

THE HEBREW: (*From amongst the audience*) It is the Syrian. There is something wrong. He is ill or drunk.

(*He helps the* SYRIAN *on to the stage.*)

THE SYRIAN: I am like a drunken man. I can hardly stand upon my feet. Something incredible has happened. I have run all the way.

THE HEBREW: Well?

THE SYRIAN: I must tell the Eleven at once. Are they still in there? Everybody must be told.

THE HEBREW: What is it? Get your breath and speak.

THE SYRIAN: I was on my way to the tomb. I met the Galilean women, Mary the mother of Jesus, Mary the mother of James, and the other women. The younger women were pale with excitement and began to speak all together. I did not know what they were saying; but Mary the mother of James said that they had been to the tomb at daybreak and found that it was empty.

THE GREEK: Ah!

THE HEBREW: The tomb cannot be empty. I will not believe it.

THE SYRIAN: At the door stood a man all shining, and cried out that Christ had risen.

(*Faint drum-taps and the faint sound of a rattle.*)

As they came down the mountain a man stood suddenly at their side; that man was Christ himself. They stooped down and kissed his feet. Now stand out of my way that I may tell Peter and James and John.

THE HEBREW: (*Standing before the curtained entrance of the inner room*) I will not stand out of the way.

THE SYRIAN: Did you hear what I said? Our master has arisen.

THE HEBREW: I will not have the Eleven disturbed for the dreams of women.

THE GREEK: The women were not dreaming. They told you the truth, and yet this man is in the right. He is in charge here. We must all be convinced before we speak to the Eleven.

THE SYRIAN: The Eleven will be able to judge better than we.

THE GREEK: Though we are so much younger we know more of the world than they do.

THE HEBREW: If you told your story they would no more believe it than I do, but Peter's misery would be increased. I know him longer than you do and I know what would happen. Peter would remember that the women did not flinch; that not one among them denied her master; that the dream proved their love and faith. Then he would remember that he had lacked both, and imagine that John was looking at him. He would turn away and bury his head in his hands.

THE GREEK: I said that we must all be convinced, but there is another reason why you must not tell them anything. Somebody else is coming. I am certain that Jesus never had a human body; that he is a phantom and can pass through that wall; that he will so pass; that he will pass through this room; that he himself will speak to the apostles.

THE SYRIAN: He is no phantom. We put a great stone over the mouth of the tomb, and the women say that it has been rolled back.

THE HEBREW: The Romans heard yesterday that some of our people planned to steal the body, and to put abroad a story that Christ had arisen; and so escape the shame of our defeat. They probably stole it in the night.

THE SYRIAN: The Romans put sentries at the tomb. The women found the sentries asleep. Christ had put them asleep that they might not see him move the stone.

THE GREEK: A hand without bones, without sinews, cannot move a stone.

THE SYRIAN: What matter if it contradicts all human knowledge? – another Argo seeks another fleece, another Troy is sacked.

THE GREEK: Why are you laughing?

THE SYRIAN: What is human knowledge?

THE GREEK: The knowledge that keeps the road from here to Persia free from robbers, that has built the beautiful humane cities, that has made the modern world, that stands between us and the barbarian.

THE SYRIAN: But what if there is something it cannot explain, something more important than anything else?

THE GREEK: You talk as if you wanted the barbarian back.

THE SYRIAN: What if there is always something that lies outside knowledge, outside order? What if at the moment when knowledge and order seem complete that something appears?

(*He has begun to laugh.*)

THE HEBREW: Stop laughing.

THE SYRIAN: What if the irrational return? What if the circle begin again?

THE HEBREW: Stop! He laughed when he saw Calvary through the window, and now you laugh.

THE GREEK: He too has lost control of himself.

THE HEBREW: Stop, I tell you.

(*Drums and rattles.*)

THE SYRIAN: But I am not laughing. It is the people out there who are laughing.

THE HEBREW: No, they are shaking rattles and beating drums.

THE SYRIAN: I thought they were laughing. How horrible!

THE GREEK: (*Looking out over the heads of the audience*) The worshippers of Dionysus are coming this way again. They have hidden their image of the dead god, and have begun their lunatic cry, 'God has arisen! God has arisen!'

(*The* MUSICIANS *who have been saying* 'God has arisen!' *fall silent.*)

They will cry 'God has arisen!' through all the streets of the city. They can make their god live and die at their pleasure;

but why are they silent? They are dancing silently. They are coming nearer and nearer, dancing all the while, using some kind of ancient step unlike anything I have seen in Alexandria. They are almost under the window now.

THE HEBREW: They have come back to mock us, because their god arises every year, whereas our god is dead for ever.

THE GREEK: How they roll their painted eyes as the dance grows quicker and quicker! They are under the window. Why are they all suddenly motionless? Why are all those unseeing eyes turned upon this house? Is there anything strange about this house?

THE HEBREW: Somebody has come into the room.

THE GREEK: Where?

THE HEBREW: I do not know; but I thought I heard a step.

THE GREEK: I knew that he would come.

THE HEBREW: There is no one here. I shut the door at the foot of the steps.

THE GREEK: The curtain over there is moving.

THE HEBREW: No, it is quite still, and besides there is nothing behind it but a blank wall.

THE GREEK: Look, look!

THE HEBREW: Yes, it has begun to move.

(*During what follows he backs in terror towards the left-hand corner of the stage.*)

THE GREEK: There is someone coming through it.

(*The* FIGURE OF CHRIST *wearing a recognizable but stylistic mask enters through the curtain. The* SYRIAN *slowly draws back the curtain that shuts off the inner room where the apostles are. The three young* MEN *are towards the left of the stage, the* FIGURE OF CHRIST *is at the back towards the right.*)

THE GREEK: It is the phantom of our master. Why are you afraid? He has been crucified and buried, but only in semblance, and is among us once more.

(*The* HEBREW *kneels.*)

There is nothing here but a phantom, it has no flesh and blood. Because I know the truth I am not afraid. Look, I will touch it. It may be hard under my hand like a statue –

I have heard of such things – or my hand may pass through it – but there is no flesh and blood. (*He goes slowly up to the figure and passes his hand over its side.*) The heart of a phantom is beating! The heart of a phantom is beating!
(*He screams. The* FIGURE OF CHRIST *crosses the stage and passes into the inner room.*)

THE SYRIAN: He is standing in the midst of them. Some are afraid. He looks at Peter and James and John. He smiles. He has parted the clothes at his side. He shows them his side. There is a great wound there. Thomas has put his hand into the wound. He has put his hand where the heart is.

THE GREEK: O Athens, Alexandria, Rome, something has come to destroy you. The heart of a phantom is beating. Man has begun to die. Your words are clear at last, O Heraclitus. God and man die each other's life, live each other's death.
(*The* MUSICIANS *rise, one or more singing the following words. If the performance is in a private room or studio, they unfold and fold a curtain; if at the Peacock Theatre, they draw the proscenium curtain across.*)

In pity for man's darkening thought
He walked that room and issued thence
In Galilean turbulence;
The Babylonian starlight brought
A fabulous, formless darkness in;
Odour of blood when Christ was slain
Made all Platonic tolerance vain
And vain all Doric discipline.

*

Everything that man esteems
Endures a moment or a day:
Love's pleasure drives his love away,
The painter's brush consumes his dreams;
The herald's cry, the soldier's tread
Exhaust his glory and his might:
Whatever flames upon the night
Man's own resinous heart has fed.

THE WORDS UPON THE
WINDOW-PANE

IN MEMORY OF

LADY GREGORY

IN WHOSE HOUSE IT WAS WRITTEN

PERSONS IN THE PLAY

DR TRENCH
MISS MACKENNA
JOHN CORBET
CORNELIUS PATTERSON
ABRAHAM JOHNSON
MRS MALLET
MRS HENDERSON

A lodging-house room, an armchair, a little table in front of it, chairs on either side. A fireplace and window. A kettle on the hob and some tea-things on a dresser. A door to back and towards the right. Through the door one can see an entrance hall. The sound of a knocker. MISS MACKENNA *passes through and then she re-enters hall together with* JOHN CORBET, *a man of twenty-two or twenty-three, and* DR TRENCH, *a man of between sixty and seventy.*

DR TRENCH: (*In hall*) May I introduce John Corbet, one of the Corbets of Ballymoney, but at present a Cambridge student? This is Miss Mackenna, our energetic secretary.

(*They come into room, take off their coats.*)

MISS MACKENNA: I thought it better to let you in myself. This country is still sufficiently medieval to make spiritualism an undesirable theme for gossip. Give me your coats and hats. I will put them in my own room. It is just across the hall. Better sit down; your watches must be fast. Mrs Henderson is lying down, as she always does before a seance. We won't begin for ten minutes yet.

(*She goes out with hats and coats.*)

DR TRENCH: Miss Mackenna does all the real work of the Dublin Spiritualists' Association. She did all the correspondence with Mrs Henderson, and persuaded the landlady to let her this big room and a small room upstairs. We are a poor society and could not guarantee anything in advance. Mrs Henderson has come from London at her own risk. She was born in Dublin and wants to spread the movement here. She lives very economically and does not expect a great deal. We all give what we can. A poor woman with the soul of an apostle.

155

JOHN CORBET: Have there been many seances?

DR TRENCH: Only three so far.

JOHN CORBET: I hope she will not mind my scepticism. I have looked into Myers' *Human Personality* and a wild book by Conan Doyle, but am unconvinced.

DR TRENCH: We all have to find the truth for ourselves. Lord Dunraven, then Lord Adare, introduced my father to the famous David Home. My father often told me that he saw David Home floating in the air in broad daylight, but I did not believe a word of it. I had to investigate for myself, and I was very hard to convince. Mrs Piper, an American trance-medium, not unlike Mrs Henderson, convinced me.

JOHN CORBET: A state of somnambulism and voices coming through her lips that purport to be those of dead persons?

DR TRENCH: Exactly: quite the best kind of mediumship if you want to establish the identity of a spirit. But do not expect too much. There has been a hostile influence.

JOHN CORBET: You mean an evil spirit?

DR TRENCH: The poet Blake said that he never knew a bad man that had not something very good about him. I say a hostile influence, an influence that disturbed the last seance very seriously. I cannot tell you what happened, for I have not been at any of Mrs Henderson's seances. Trance mediumship has nothing new to show me – I told the young people when they made me their President that I would probably stay at home, that I could get more out of Emanuel Swedenborg than out of any seance.

(*A knock.*)

That is probably old Cornelius Patterson; he thinks they race horses and whippets in the other world, and is, so they tell me, so anxious to find out if he is right that he is always punctual. Miss Mackenna will keep him to herself for some minutes. He gives her tips for Harold's Cross.

(MISS MACKENNA *crosses to hall door and admits* CORNELIUS PATTERSON. *She brings him to her room across the hall.*)

JOHN CORBET: (*Who has been wandering about*) This is a wonderful room for a lodging house.

DR TRENCH: It was a private house until about fifty years ago. It was not so near the town in those days, and there are large stables at the back. Quite a number of notable people lived here. Grattan was born upstairs; no, not Grattan, Curran perhaps – I forget – but I do know that this house in the early part of the eighteenth century belonged to friends of Jonathan Swift, or rather of Stella. Swift chaffed her in the *Journal to Stella* because of certain small sums of money she lost at cards probably in this very room. That was before Vanessa appeared upon the scene. It was a country house in those days, surrounded by trees and gardens. Somebody cut some lines from a poem of hers upon the window-pane – tradition says Stella herself.

(*A knock.*)

Here they are, but you will hardly make them out in this light.

(*They stand in the window.* CORBET *stoops down to see better.* MISS MACKENNA *and* ABRAHAM JOHNSON *enter and stand near door.*)

ABRAHAM JOHNSON: Where is Mrs Henderson?

MISS MACKENNA: She is upstairs; she always rests before a seance.

ABRAHAM JOHNSON: I must see her before the seance. I know exactly what to do to get rid of this evil influence.

MISS MACKENNA: If you go up to see her there will be no seance at all. She says it is dangerous even to think, much less to speak, of an evil influence.

ABRAHAM JOHNSON: Then I shall speak to the President.

MISS MACKENNA: Better talk the whole thing over first in my room. Mrs Henderson says that there must be perfect harmony.

ABRAHAM JOHNSON: Something must be done. The last seance was completely spoiled.

(*A knock.*)

MISS MACKENNA: That may be Mrs Mallet; she is a very experienced spirtualist. Come to my room, old Patterson and some others are there already.

(*She brings him to the other room and later crosses to hall door to admit* MRS MALLET.)

JOHN CORBET: I know those lines well – they are part of a poem Stella wrote for Swift's fifty-fourth birthday. Only three poems of hers – and some lines she added to a poem of Swift's – have come down to us, but they are enough to prove her a better poet than Swift. Even those few words on the window make me think of a seventeenth-century poet, Donne or Crashaw. (*He quotes:*)

'You taught how I might youth prolong
By knowing what is right and wrong,
How from my heart to bring supplies
Of lustre to my fading eyes.'

How strange that a celibate scholar, well on in life, should keep the love of two such women! He met Vanessa in London at the height of his political power. She followed him to Dublin. She loved him for nine years, perhaps died of love, but Stella loved him all her life.

DR TRENCH: I have shown that writing to several persons, and you are the first who has recognized the lines.

JOHN CORBET: I am writing an essay on Swift and Stella for my doctorate at Cambridge. I hope to prove that in Swift's day men of intellect reached the height of their power – the greatest position they ever attained in society and the State, that everything great in Ireland and in our character, in what remains of our architecture, comes from that day; that we have kept its seal longer than England.

DR TRENCH: A tragic life: Bolingbroke, Harley, Ormonde, all those great Ministers that were his friends, banished and broken.

JOHN CORBET: I do not think you can explain him in that way – his tragedy had deeper foundations. His ideal order was the Roman Senate, his ideal men Brutus and Cato. Such an order and such men had seemed possible once more, but the movement passed and he foresaw the ruin to come, Democracy, Rousseau, the French Revolution; that is why he hated the common run of men – 'I hate lawyers, I hate doctors,' he said, 'though I love Dr So-and-so and Judge So-and-so' – that is why he wrote *Gulliver*, that is why he wore out his brain, that is why he felt *saeva indignatio*, that is why he sleeps under the greatest epitaph in history. You remember how it goes? It is almost finer in English than in Latin: 'He has gone where fierce indignation can lacerate his heart no more.'

(ABRAHAM JOHNSON *comes in, followed by* MRS MALLET *and* CORNELIUS PATTERSON.)

ABRAHAM JOHNSON: Something must be done, Dr Trench, to drive away the influence that has destroyed our seances. I have come here week after week at considerable expense. I am from Belfast. I am by profession a minister of the Gospel, I do a great deal of work among the poor and ignorant. I produce considerable effect by singing and preaching, but I know that my effect should be much greater than it is. My hope is that I shall be able to communicate with the great Evangelist Moody. I want to ask him to stand invisible beside me when I speak or sing, and lay his hands upon my head and give me such a portion of his power that my work may be blessed as the work of Moody and Sankey was blessed.

MRS MALLET: What Mr Johnson says about the hostile influence is quite true. The last two seances were completely spoilt. I am thinking of starting a tea shop in Folkestone. I followed Mrs Henderson to Dublin to get my husband's advice, but two spirits kept talking and would not let any other spirit say a word.

DR TRENCH: Did the spirits say the same thing and go through the same drama at both seances?

MRS MALLET: Yes – just as if they were characters in some kind of horrible play.

DR TRENCH: That is what I was afraid of.

MRS MALLET: My husband was drowned at sea ten years ago,

but constantly speaks to me through Mrs Henderson as if he were still alive. He advises me about everything I do, and I am utterly lost if I cannot question him.

CORNELIUS PATTERSON: I never did like the Heaven they talk about in churches: but when somebody told me that Mrs Mallet's husband ate and drank and went about with his favourite dog, I said to myself, 'That is the place for Corney Patterson.' I came here to find out if it was true, and I declare to God I have not heard one word about it.

ABRAHAM JOHNSON: I ask you, Dr Trench, as President of the Dublin Spiritualists' Association, to permit me to read the ritual of exorcism appointed for such occasions. After the last seance I copied it out of an old book in the library of Belfast University. I have it here.

(*He takes paper out of his pocket.*)

DR TRENCH: The spirits are people like ourselves, we treat them as our guests and protect them from discourtesy and violence, and every exorcism is a curse or a threatened curse. We do not admit that there are evil spirits. Some spirits are earth-bound – they think they are still living and go over and over some action of their past lives, just as we go over and over some painful thought, except that where they are thought is reality. For instance, when a spirit which has died a violent death comes to a medium for the first time, it relives all the pains of death.

MRS MALLET: When my husband came for the first time the medium gasped and struggled as if she was drowning. It was terrible to watch.

DR TRENCH: Sometimes a spirit relives not the pain of death but some passionate or tragic moment of life. Swedenborg describes this and gives the reason for it. There is an incident of the kind in the *Odyssey*, and many in Eastern literature; the murderer repeats his murder, the robber his robbery, the lover his serenade, the soldier hears the trumpet once again. If I were a Catholic I would say that such spirits were in Purgatory. In vain do we write *requiescat in pace* upon the tomb, for they must suffer, and we in our turn must suffer until God gives peace. Such spirits do not often come to seances unless those seances are held in houses where those spirits lived, or where the event took place. This spirit which speaks those incomprehensible words and does not answer when spoken to is of such a nature. The more patient we are, the more quickly will it pass out of its passion and its remorse.

ABRAHAM JOHNSON: I am still convinced that the spirit which disturbed the last seance is evil. If I may not exorcise it I will certainly pray for protection.

DR TRENCH: Mrs Henderson's control, Lulu, is able and experienced and can protect both medium and sitters, but it may help Lulu if you pray that the spirit find rest.

(ABRAHAM JOHNSON *sits down and prays silently, moving his lips.* MRS HENDERSON *comes in with* MISS MACKENNA *and others.* MISS MACKENNA *shuts the door.*)

DR TRENCH: Mrs Henderson, may I introduce to you Mr Corbet, a young man from Cambridge and a sceptic, who hopes that you will be able to convince him?

MRS HENDERSON: We were all sceptics once. He must not expect too much from a first seance. He must persevere.

(*She sits in the armchair, and the others begin to seat themselves.* MISS MACKENNA *goes to* JOHN CORBET *and they remain standing.*)

MISS MACKENNA: I am glad that you are a sceptic.

JOHN CORBET: I thought you were a spiritualist.

MISS MACKENNA: I have seen a good many seances, and sometimes think it is all coincidence and thought-transference. (*She says this in a low voice.*) Then at other times I think as Dr Trench does, and then I feel like Job – you know the quotation – the hair of my head stands up. A spirit passes before my face.

MRS MALLET: Turn the key, Dr Trench, we don't want anybody blundering in here.

(DR TRENCH *locks door.*)

Come and sit here, Miss Mackenna.

MISS MACKENNA: No, I am going to sit beside Mr Corbet.

(CORBET *and* MISS MACKENNA *sit down.*)

JOHN CORBET: You feel like Job tonight?

MISS MACKENNA: I feel that something is going to happen, that is why I am glad that you are a sceptic.

JOHN CORBET: You feel safer?

MISS MACKENNA: Yes, safer.

MRS HENDERSON: I am glad to meet all my dear friends again and to welcome Mr Corbet among us. As he is a stranger I must explain that we do not call up spirits, we make the right conditions and they come. I do not know who is going to come; sometimes there are a great many and the guides choose between them. The guides try to send somebody for everybody but do not always succeed. If you want to speak to some dear friend who has passed over, do not be discouraged. If your friend cannot come this time, maybe he can next time. My control is a dear little girl called Lulu who died when she was five or six years old. She describes the spirits present and tells us what spirit wants to speak. Miss Mackenna, a verse of a hymn, please, the same we had last time, and will everyone join in the singing.

(*They sing the following lines from Hymn 564*, Irish Church Hymnal:)

'Sun of my soul, Thou Saviour dear,

It is not night if Thou be near:

O may no earth-born cloud arise

To hide Thee from Thy servant's eyes.'

(MRS HENDERSON *is leaning back in her chair asleep.*)

MISS MACKENNA: (*to* JOHN CORBET) She always snores like that when she is going off.

MRS HENDERSON: (*In a child's voice*) Lulu so glad to see all her friends.

MRS MALLET: And we are glad you have come, Lulu.

MRS HENDERSON: (*In a child's voice*) Lulu glad to see new friend.

MISS MACKENNA: (*to* JOHN CORBET) She is speaking to you.

JOHN CORBET: Thank you, Lulu.

MRS HENDERSON: (*In a child's voice*) You mustn't laugh at the way I talk.

JOHN CORBET: I am not laughing, Lulu.

MRS HENDERSON: (*In a child's voice*) Nobody must laugh. Lulu does her best but can't say big long words. Lulu sees a tall man here, lots of hair on face (MRS HENDERSON *passes her hands over her cheeks and chin*), not much on the top of his head (MRS HENDERSON *passes her hand over the top of her head*), red necktie, and such a funny sort of pin.

MRS MALLET: Yes . . . Yes . . .

MRS HENDERSON: (*In a child's voice*) Pin like a horseshoe.

MRS MALLET: It's my husband.

MRS HENDERSON: (*In a child's voice*) He has a message.

MRS MALLET: Yes.

MRS HENDERSON: (*In a child's voice*) Lulu cannot hear. He is too far off. He has come near. Lulu can hear now. He says . . . he says, 'Drive that man away!' He is pointing to somebody in the corner, that corner over there. He says it is the bad man who spoilt everything last time. If they won't drive him away, Lulu will scream.

MISS MACKENNA: That horrible spirit again.

ABRAHAM JOHNSON: Last time he monopolized the seance.

MRS MALLET: He would not let anybody speak but himself.

MRS HENDERSON: (*In a child's voice*) They have driven that bad man away. Lulu sees a young lady.

MRS MALLET: Is not my husband here?

MRS HENDERSON: (*In a child's voice*) Man with funny pin gone away. Young lady here – Lulu thinks she must be at a fancy-dress party, such funny clothes, hair all in curls – all bent down on floor near that old man with glasses.

DR TRENCH: No, I do not recognize her.

MRS HENDERSON: (*In a child's voice*) That bad man, that bad old man in the corner, they have let him come back. Lulu is going to scream. O . . . O . . . (*In a man's voice*) How dare you write to her? How dare you ask if we were married? How dare you question her?

DR TRENCH: A soul in its agony – it cannot see us or hear us.

MRS HENDERSON: (*Upright and rigid, only her lips moving,*

and still in a man's voice) You sit crouching there. Did you not hear what I said? How dared you question her? I found you an ignorant little girl without intellect, without moral ambition. How many times did I not stay away from great men's houses, how many times forsake the Lord Treasurer, how many times neglect the business of the State that we might read Plutarch together!

(ABRAHAM JOHNSON *half rises.* DR TRENCH *motions him to remain seated.*)

DR TRENCH: Silence!

ABRAHAM JOHNSON: But, Dr Trench . . .

DR TRENCH: Hush – we can do nothing.

MRS HENDERSON: (*Speaking as before*) I taught you to think in every situation of life not as Hester Vanhomrigh would think in that situation, but as Cato or Brutus would, and now you behave like some common slut with her ear against the keyhole.

JOHN CORBET: (*To* MISS MACKENNA) It is Swift, Jonathan Swift, talking to the woman he called Vanessa. She was christened Hester Vanhomrigh.

MRS HENDERSON: (*In Vanessa's voice*) I questioned her, Jonathan, because I love. Why have you let me spend hours in your company if you did not want me to love you? (*In Swift's voice*) When I rebuilt Rome in your mind it was as though I walked its streets. (*In Vanessa's voice*) Was that all, Jonathan? Was I nothing but a painter's canvas? (*In Swift's voice*) My God, do you think it was easy? I was a man of strong passions and I had sworn never to marry. (*In Vanessa's voice*) If you and she are not married, why should we not marry like other men and women? I loved you from the first moment when you came to my mother's house and began to teach me. I thought it would be enough to look at you, to speak to you, to hear you speak. I followed you to Ireland five years ago and I can bear it no longer. It is not enough to look, to speak, to hear. Jonathan, Jonathan, I am a woman, the women Brutus and Cato loved were not different. (*In Swift's voice*) I have something in my blood that no child must inherit. I have constant attacks of dizziness; I pretend they come from a surfeit of fruit when I was a child. I had them in London . . . There was a great doctor there, Dr Arbuthnot; I told him of those attacks of dizziness, I told him of worse things. It was he who explained. There is a line of Dryden's . . . (*In Vanessa's voice*) O, I know – 'Great wits are sure to madness near allied.' If you had children, Jonathan, my blood would make them healthy. I will take your hand, I will lay it upon my heart – upon the Vanhomrigh blood that has been healthy for generations. (MRS HENDERSON *slowly raises her left hand.*) That is the first time you have touched my body, Jonathan. (MRS HENDERSON *stands up and remains rigid. In Swift's voice*) What do I care if it be healthy? What do I care if it could make mine healthy? Am I to add another to the healthy rascaldom and knavery of the world? (*In Vanessa's voice*) Look at me, Jonathan. Your arrogant intellect separates us. Give me both your hands. I will put them upon my breast. (MRS HENDERSON *raises her right hand to the level of her left and then raises both to her breast.*) O, it is white – white as the gambler's dice – white ivory dice. Think of the uncertainty. Perhaps a mad child – perhaps a rascal – perhaps a knave – perhaps not, Jonathan. The dice of the intellect are loaded, but I am the common ivory dice. (*Her hands are stretched out as though drawing somebody towards her.*) It is not my hands that draw you back. My hands are weak, they could not draw you back if you did not love as I love. You said that you have strong passions; that is true, Jonathan – no man in Ireland is so passionate. That is why you need me, that is why you need children, nobody has greater need. You are growing old. An old man without children is very solitary. Even his friends, men as old as he, turn away, they turn towards the young, their children or their children's children. They cannot endure an old man like themselves. (MRS HENDERSON *moves away from the chair, her movements gradually growing convulsive.*) You are not too old for the dice, Jonathan, but a few years if you turn away will make you an old miserable childless man. (*In*

Swift's voice) O God, hear the prayer of Jonathan Swift, that afflicted man, and grant that he may leave to posterity nothing but his intellect that came to him from Heaven. (*In Vanessa's voice*) Can you face solitude with that mind, Jonathan? (MRS HENDERSON *goes to the door, finds that it is closed.*) Dice, white ivory dice. (*In Swift's voice*) My God, I am left alone with my enemy. Who locked the door, who locked me in with my enemy? (MRS HENDERSON *beats upon the door, sinks to the floor and then speaks as Lulu.*) Bad old man! Do not let him come back. Bad old man does not know he is dead. Lulu cannot find fathers, mothers, sons that have passed over. Power almost gone.

(MRS MALLET *leads* MRS HENDERSON, *who seems very exhausted, back to her chair. She is still asleep. She speaks again as Lulu.*)

Another verse of hymn. Everybody sing. Hymn will bring good influence.

(*They sing:*)

'If some poor wandering child of Thine
Have spurned today the voice divine,
Now, Lord, the gracious work begin;
Let him no more lie down in sin.'

(*During the hymn* MRS HENDERSON *has been murmuring 'Stella', but the singing has almost drowned her voice. The singers draw one another's attention to the fact that she is speaking. The singing stops.*)

DR TRENCH: I thought she was speaking.

MRS MALLET: I saw her lips move.

DR TRENCH: She would be more comfortable with a cushion, but we might wake her.

MRS MALLET: Nothing can wake her out of a trance like that until she wakes up herself.

(*She brings a cushion and she and* DR TRENCH *put* MRS HENDERSON *into a more comfortable position.*)

MRS HENDERSON: (*In Swift's voice*) Stella.

MISS MACKENNA: (*To* JOHN CORBET) Did you hear that? She said 'Stella'.

JOHN CORBET: Vanessa has gone, Stella has taken her place.

MISS MACKENNA: Did you notice the change while we were singing? The new influence in the room?

JOHN CORBET: I thought I did, but it must have been fancy.

MRS MALLET: Hush!

MRS HENDERSON: (*In Swift's voice*) Have I wronged you, beloved Stella? Are you unhappy? You have no children, you have no lover, and you have no husband. A cross and ageing man for friend – nothing but that. But no, do not answer – you have answered already in that poem you wrote for my last birthday. With what scorn you speak of the common lot of women 'with no endowments but a face – '

'Before the thirtieth year of life
A maid forlorn or hated wife.'

It is the thought of the great Chrysostom who wrote in a famous passage that women loved according to the soul, loved as saints can love, keep their beauty longer, have greater happiness than women loved according to the flesh. That thought has comforted me, but it is a terrible thing to be responsible for another's happiness. There are moments when I doubt, when I think Chrysostom may have been wrong. But now I have your poem to drive doubt away. You have addressed me in these noble words:

'You taught how I might youth prolong
By knowing what is right and wrong;
How from my heart to bring supplies
Of lustre to my fading eyes;
How soon a beauteous mind repairs
The loss of chang'd or falling hairs;
How wit and virtue from within
Can spread a smoothness o'er the skin.'

JOHN CORBET: The words upon the window-pane!

MRS HENDERSON: (*In Swift's voice*) Then, because you understand that I am afraid of solitude, afraid of outliving my friends – and myself – you comfort me in that last verse – you overpraise my moral nature when you attribute to it a

rich mantle, but O how touching those words which describe
your love:

'Late dying may you cast a shred
Of that rich mantle o'er my head;
To bear with dignity my sorrow,
One day alone, then die tomorrow.'

Yes, you will close my eyes, Stella. O, you will live long
after me, dear Stella, for you are still a young woman, but
you will close my eyes. (MRS HENDERSON *sinks back in
chair and speaks as Lulu.*) Bad old man gone. Power all
used up. Lulu can do no more. Goodbye, friends. (MRS
HENDERSON, *speaking in her own voice*) Go away, go
away! (*She wakes.*) I saw him a moment ago, has he spoilt
the seance again?

MRS MALLET: Yes, Mrs Henderson, my husband came, but
he was driven away.

DR TRENCH: Mrs Henderson is very tired. We must leave
her to rest. (*To* MRS HENDERSON) You did your best
and nobody can do more than that.

(*He takes out money.*)

MRS HENDERSON: No . . . No . . . I cannot take any money,
not after a seance like that.

DR TRENCH: Of course you must take it, Mrs Henderson.

(*He puts money on table, and* MRS HENDERSON *gives a furtive
glance to see how much it is. She does the same as each sitter
lays down his or her money.*)

MRS MALLET: A bad seance is just as exhausting as a good
seance, and you must be paid.

MRS HENDERSON: No . . . No . . . Please don't. It is very
wrong to take money for such a failure.

(MRS MALLET *lays down money.*)

CORNELIUS PATTERSON: A jockey is paid whether he wins
or not.

(*He lays down money.*)

MISS MACKENNA: That spirit rather thrilled me.

(*She lays down money.*)

MRS HENDERSON: If you insist, I must take it.

ABRAHAM JOHNSON: I shall pray for you tonight. I shall ask God to bless and protect your seances.

(*He lays down money. All go out except* JOHN CORBET *and* MRS HENDERSON.)

JOHN CORBET: I know you are tired, Mrs Henderson, but I must speak to you. I have been deeply moved by what I have heard. This is my contribution to prove that I am satisfied, completely satisfied.

(*He puts a note on the table.*)

MRS HENDERSON: A pound note – nobody ever gives me more than ten shillings, and yet the seance was a failure.

JOHN CORBET: (*Sitting down near* MRS HENDERSON) When I say I am satisfied I do not mean that I am convinced it was the work of spirits. I prefer to think that you created it all, that you are an accomplished actress and scholar. In my essay for my Cambridge doctorate I examine all the explanations of Swift's celibacy offered by his biographers and prove that the explanation you selected was the only plausible one. But there is something I must ask you. Swift was the chief representative of the intellect of his epoch, that arrogant intellect free at last from superstition. He foresaw its collapse. He foresaw Democracy, he must have dreaded the future. Did he refuse to beget children because of that dread? Was Swift mad? Or was it the intellect itself that was mad?

MRS HENDERSON: Who are you talking of, sir?

JOHN CORBET: Swift, of course.

MRS HENDERSON: Swift? I do not know anybody called Swift.

JOHN CORBET: Jonathan Swift, whose spirit seemed to be present tonight.

MRS HENDERSON: What? That dirty old man?

JOHN CORBET: He was neither old nor dirty when Stella and Vanessa loved him.

MRS HENDERSON: I saw him very clearly just as I woke up. His clothes were dirty, his face covered with boils. Some disease had made one of his eyes swell up, it stood out from his face like a hen's egg.

JOHN CORBET: He looked like that in his old age. Stella had been dead a long time. His brain had gone, his friends had deserted him. The man appointed to take care of him beat him to keep him quiet.

MRS HENDERSON: Now they are old, now they are young. They change all in a moment as their thought changes. It is sometimes a terrible thing to be out of the body, God help us all.

DR TRENCH: (*At doorway*) Come along, Corbet, Mrs Henderson is tired out.

JOHN CORBET: Goodbye, Mrs Henderson.

(*He goes out with* DR TRENCH. *All the sitters except* MISS MACKENNA, *who has returned to her room, pass along the passage on their way to the front door.* MRS HENDERSON *counts the money, finds her purse, which is in a vase on the mantelpiece, and puts the money in it.*)

MRS HENDERSON: How tired I am! I'd be the better of a cup of tea. (*She finds the teapot and puts kettle on fire, and then as she crouches down by the hearth suddenly lifts up her hands and counts her fingers, speaking in Swift's voice.*) Five great Ministers that were my friends are gone, ten great Ministers that were my friends are gone. I have not fingers enough to count the great Ministers that were my friends and that are gone. (*She wakes with a start and speaks in her own voice.*) Where did I put that tea-caddy? Ah! there it is. And there should be a cup and saucer. (*She finds the saucer.*) But where's the cup? (*She moves aimlessly about the stage and then, letting the saucer fall and break, speaks in Swift's voice.*) Perish the day on which I was born!

A FULL MOON IN MARCH

PERSONS IN THE PLAY

FIRST ATTENDANT
SECOND ATTENDANT
THE QUEEN
THE SWINEHERD

The SWINEHERD *wears a half-savage mask covering the upper part of his face. He is bearded. When the inner curtain rises for the second time the player who has hitherto taken the part of the* QUEEN *is replaced by a dancer.*

When the stage curtain rises, two ATTENDANTS, *an elderly woman and a young man, are discovered standing before an inner curtain.*

FIRST ATTENDANT: What do we do?
  What part do we take?
  What did he say?
SECOND ATTENDANT: Join when we like,
  Singing or speaking.
FIRST ATTENDANT: Before the curtain rises on the play?
SECOND ATTENDANT: Before it rises.
FIRST ATTENDANT: What do we sing?
SECOND ATTENDANT: 'Sing anything, sing any old thing,' said
  he.
FIRST ATTENDANT: Come then and sing about the dung of
  swine.

(They slowly part the inner curtain. The SECOND ATTENDANT *sings – the* FIRST ATTENDANT *may join in the singing at the end of the first or second verse. The* FIRST ATTENDANT *has a soprano, the* SECOND *a bass voice.)*

SECOND ATTENDANT: Every loutish lad in love
  Thinks his wisdom great enough,
  What cares love for this and that?
  To make all his parish stare,
  As though Pythagoras wandered there.
  Crown of gold or dung of swine.

173

Should old Pythagoras fall in love
Little may he boast thereof.
What cares love for this and that?
Days go by in foolishness.
O how great their sweetness is!
Crown of gold or dung of swine.

Open wide those gleaming eyes,
That can make the loutish wise.
What cares love for this and that?
Make a leader of the schools
Thank the Lord, all men are fools.
Crown of gold or dung of swine.

(*They sit at one side of stage near audience. If they are
musicians, they have beside them drum, flute, and zither.
The* QUEEN *is discovered seated and veiled.*)

THE QUEEN: (*Stretching and yawning*) What man is at the door?

SECOND ATTENDANT: Nobody, Queen.

THE QUEEN: Some man has come, some terrifying man,
    For I have yawned and stretched myself three times.
    Admit him, Captain of the Guard . . .

SECOND ATTENDANT: (*Speaking as Captain of the Guard*) He
    comes.

(*Enter the* SWINEHERD)

THE SWINEHERD: The beggars of my country say that he
    That sings you best shall take you for a wife.

THE QUEEN: He that best sings his passion.

THE SWINEHERD: And they say
    The kingdom is added to the gift.

THE QUEEN: I swore it.

THE SWINEHERD: But what if some blind aged cripple sing
    Better than wholesome men?

THE QUEEN: Some I reject.
    Some I have punished for their impudence.
    None I abhor can sing.

THE SWINEHERD: So that's the catch.
    Queen, look at me, look long at these foul rags,

At hair more foul and ragged than my rags;
Look on my scratched foul flesh. Have I not come
Through dust and mire? There in the dust and mire
Beasts scratched my flesh; my memory too is gone,
Because great solitudes have driven me mad.
But when I look into a stream, the face
That trembles upon the surface makes me think
My origin more foul than rag or flesh.

THE QUEEN: But you have passed through perils for my sake;
Come a great distance. I permit the song.

THE SWINEHERD: Kingdom and lady, if I sing the best?
But who decides?

THE QUEEN: I and my heart decide.
We say that song is best that moves us most.
No song has moved us yet.

THE SWINEHERD: You must be won
At a full moon in March, those beggars say.
That moon has come, but I am here alone.

THE QUEEN: No other man has come.

THE SWINEHERD: The moon is full.

THE QUEEN: Remember through what perils you have come;
That I am crueller than solitude,
Forest or beast. Some I have killed or maimed
Because their singing put me in a rage,
And some because they came at all. Men hold
That woman's beauty is a kindly thing,
But they that call me cruel speak the truth,
Cruel as the winter of virginity.
But for a reason that I cannot guess
I would not harm you. Go before I change.
Why do you stand, your chin upon your breast?

THE SWINEHERD: My mind is running on our marriage night,
Imagining all from the first touch and kiss.

THE QUEEN: What gives you that strange confidence? What
    makes
You think that you can move my heart and me?

THE SWINEHERD: Because I look upon you without fear.

THE QUEEN: A lover in railing or in flattery said
    God only looks upon me without fear.
THE SWINEHERD: Desiring cruelty, he made you cruel.
    I shall embrace body and cruelty,
    Desiring both as though I had made both.
THE QUEEN: One question more. You bring like all the rest
    Some novel simile, some wild hyperbole
    Praising my beauty?
THE SWINEHERD: My memory has returned.
    I tended swine, when I first heard your name.
    I rolled among the dung of swine and laughed.
    What do I know of beauty?
THE QUEEN: Sing the best
    And you are not a swineherd, but a king.
THE SWINEHERD: What do I know of kingdoms?
  (*Snapping his fingers*)   That for kingdoms.
THE QUEEN: If trembling of my limbs or sudden tears
    Proclaim your song beyond denial best,
    I leave these corridors, this ancient house,
    A famous throne, the reverence of servants –
    What do I gain?
THE SWINEHERD: A song – the night of love,
    An ignorant forest and the dung of swine.
  (*The* QUEEN *leaves throne and comes downstage.*)
THE QUEEN: All here have heard the man and all have judged.
    I led him, that I might not seem unjust,
    From point to point, established in all eyes
    That he came hither not to sing but to heap
    Complexities of insult upon my head.
THE SWINEHERD: She shall bring forth her farrow in the dung.
    But first my song – what nonsense shall I sing?
THE QUEEN: Send for the headsman, Captain of the Guard.
SECOND ATTENDANT: (*Speaking as Captain of the Guard*) I
    have already sent. He stands without.
THE QUEEN: I owe my thanks to God that this foul wretch,
    Foul in his rags, his origin, his speech,
    In spite of all his daring has not dared

Ask me to drop my veil. Insulted ears
Have heard and shuddered, but my face is pure.
Had it but known the insult of his eyes
I had torn it with these nails.

THE SWINEHERD: (*Going upstage*) Why should I ask?
What do these features matter? When I set out
I picked a number on the roulette wheel.
I trust the wheel, as every lover must.

THE QUEEN: Pray, if your savagery has learnt to pray,
For in a moment they will lead you out
Then bring your severed head.

THE SWINEHERD: My severed head.
   (*Laughs.*)
There is a story in my country of a woman
That stood all bathed in blood – a drop of blood
Entered her womb and there begat a child.

THE QUEEN: A severed head! She took it in her hands;
She stood all bathed in blood; the blood begat.
O foul, foul, foul!

THE SWINEHERD: She sank in bridal sleep.

THE QUEEN: Her body in that sleep conceived a child.
Begone! I shall not see your face again.
   (*She turns towards him, her back to the audience, and
   slowly drops her veil. The* ATTENDANTS *close the inner
   curtain.*)

SECOND ATTENDANT: What do we sing?

FIRST ATTENDANT: An ancient Irish Queen
That stuck a head upon a stake.

SECOND ATTENDANT: Her lover's head;
But that's a different queen, a different story.

FIRST ATTENDANT: He had famished in a wilderness,
Braved lions for my sake,
And all men lie that say that I
Bade that swordsman take
His head from off his body
And set it on a stake.

                  *

He swore to sing my beauty
Though death itself forbade.
They lie that say, in mockery
Of all that lovers said,
Or in mere woman's cruelty
I bade them fetch his head.

(*They begin to part the inner curtain.*)

O what innkeeper's daughter
Shared the Byzantine crown?
Girls that have governed cities,
Or burned great cities down,
Have bedded with their fancy-man
Whether a king or clown;

Gave their bodies, emptied purses
For praise of clown or king,
Gave all the love that women know!
O they had their fling,
But never stood before a stake
And heard the dead lips sing.

(*The* QUEEN *is discovered standing exactly as before, the dropped veil at her side, but she holds above her head the severed head of the Swineherd. Her hands are red. There are red blotches upon her dress, not realistically represented: red gloves, some pattern of red cloth.*)

FIRST ATTENDANT: Her lips are moving.

SECOND ATTENDANT: She has begun to sing.

FIRST ATTENDANT: I cannot hear what she is singing.

Ah, now I can hear.

(*Singing as the* QUEEN) Child and darling, hear my song,
Never cry I did you wrong;
Cry that wrong came not from me
But my virgin cruelty.
Great my love before you came,
Greater when I loved in shame,
Greatest when there broke from me
Storm of virgin cruelty.

(*The* QUEEN *dances to drum-taps and in the dance lays the head upon the throne.*)

SECOND ATTENDANT: She is waiting.

FIRST ATTENDANT: She is waiting for his song.

The song he has come so many miles to sing.

She has forgotten that no dead man sings.

SECOND ATTENDANT: (*Laughs softly as* HEAD) He has begun to laugh.

FIRST ATTENDANT: No; he has begun to sing.

SECOND ATTENDANT: (*Singing as* HEAD) I sing a song of Jack and Jill.

Jill had murdered Jack;
The moon shone brightly;
Ran up the hill, and round the hill,
Round the hill and back.
A full moon in March.

Jack had a hollow heart, for Jill
Had hung his heart on high;
The moon shone brightly;
Had hung his heart beyond the hill,
A-twinkle in the sky.
A full moon in March.

(*The* QUEEN *in her dance moves away from the head, alluring and refusing. The* FIRST ATTENDANT *laughs as the* QUEEN.)

She is laughing. How can she laugh,
Loving the dead?

FIRST ATTENDANT: She is crazy. That is why she is laughing.

(*She laughs again as the* QUEEN. *The* QUEEN *takes up the* HEAD *and lays it upon the ground. She dances before it – a dance of adoration. She takes the head up and dances with it to drum-taps, which grow quicker and quicker. As the drum-taps approach their climax, she presses her lips to the lips of the head. Her body shivers to very rapid drum-taps. The drum-taps cease. She sinks slowly down, holding the head to her breast. The* ATTENDANTS *close inner curtain, singing,*

*and then stand one on either side while the stage curtain
descends.*)

SECOND ATTENDANT: Why must those holy, haughty feet
    descend
  From emblematic niches, and what hand
  Ran that delicate raddle through their white?
  My heart is broken, yet must understand.
  What do they seek for? Why must they descend?
FIRST ATTENDANT: For desecration and the lover's night.
SECOND ATTENDANT: I cannot face that emblem of the moon
  Nor eyelids that the unmixed heavens dart,
  Nor stand upon my feet, so great a fright
  Descends upon my savage, sunlit heart.
  What can she lack whose emblem is the moon?
FIRST ATTENDANT: But desecration and the lover's night.
SECOND ATTENDANT: Delight my heart with sound; speak
    yet again.
  But look and look with understanding eyes
  Upon the pitchers that they carry; tight
  Therein all time's completed treasure is:
  What do they lack? O cry it out again.
FIRST ATTENDANT: Their desecration and the lover's night.

THE HERNE'S EGG

PERSONS IN THE PLAY

CONGAL, *King of Connacht*
AEDH, *King of Tara*
CORNEY, *Attracta's servant*
MIKE, PAT, MALACHI, MATHIAS, PETER, JOHN, *Connacht soldiers*
ATTRACTA, *a priestess*
KATE, AGNES, MARY, *friends of Attracta*
A FOOL
SOLDIERS OF TARA

SCENE 1

Mist and rocks; high up on backcloth a rock, its base hidden in mist; on this rock stands a great herne. All should be suggested, not painted realistically. Many MEN *fighting with swords and shields, but sword and sword, shield and sword, never meet. The* MEN *move rhythmically as if in a dance; when swords approach one another cymbals clash; when swords and shields approach drums boom. The battle flows out at one side; two* KINGS *are left fighting in the centre of the stage; the battle returns and flows out at the other side. The two* KINGS *remain, but are now face to face and motionless. They are* CONGAL, *King of Connacht, and* AEDH, *King of Tara.*

CONGAL: How many men have you lost?

AEDH: Some five-and-twenty men.

CONGAL: No need to ask my losses.

AEDH: Your losses equal mine.

CONGAL: They always have and must.

AEDH: Skill, strength, arms matched.

CONGAL: Where is the wound this time?

AEDH: There, left shoulder-blade.

CONGAL: Here, right shoulder-blade.

AEDH: Yet we have fought all day.

CONGAL: This is our fiftieth battle.

AEDH: And all were perfect battles.

CONGAL: Come, sit upon this stone.
    Come and take breath awhile.

AEDH: From daybreak until noon,

183

Hopping among these rocks.

CONGAL: Nothing to eat or drink.

AEDH: A story is running round
Concerning two rich fleas.

CONGAL: We hop like fleas, but war
Has taken all our riches.

AEDH: Rich, and rich, so rich that they
Retired and bought a dog.

CONGAL: Finish the tale and say
What kind of dog they bought.

AEDH: Heaven knows.

CONGAL: You must have thought
What kind of dog they bought.

AEDH: Heaven knows.

CONGAL: Unless you say,
I'll up and fight all day.

AEDH: A fat, square, lazy dog,
No sort of scratching dog.

SCENE 2

The same place as in previous scene. CORNEY *enters, leading a
donkey, a donkey on wheels like a child's toy, but life-size.*

CORNEY: A tough, rough mane, a tougher skin,
Strong legs though somewhat thin,
A strong body, a level line
Up to the neck along the spine.
All good points, and all are spoilt
By that rapscallion Clareman's eye!
What if before your present shape
You could slit purses and break hearts,
You are a donkey now, a chattel,
A taker of blows, not a giver of blows.
No tricks, you're not in County Clare,

No, not one kick upon the shin.

(CONGAL, PAT, MIKE, JAMES, MATHIAS, PETER, JOHN, *enter, in the dress and arms of the previous scene but without shields.*)

CONGAL: I have learned of a great hernery
    Among these rocks, and that a woman,
    Prophetess or priestess, named Attracta,
    Owns it – take this donkey and man,
    Look for the creels, pack them with eggs.

MIKE: Manners!

CONGAL: This man is in the right.
    I will ask Attracta for the eggs
    If you will tell how to summon her.

CORNEY: A flute lies there upon the rock
    Carved out of a herne's thigh.
    Go pick it up and play the tune
    My mother calls 'The Great Herne's Feather'.
    If she has a mind to come, she will come.

CONGAL: That's a queer way of summoning.

CORNEY: This is a holy place and queer;
    But if you do not know that tune,
    Custom permits that I should play it,
    But you must cross my hand with silver.

(CONGAL *gives money, and* CORNEY *plays flute.*)

CONGAL: Go pack the donkey creels with eggs.

(*All go out except* CONGAL *and* MIKE. ATTRACTA *enters.*)

ATTRACTA: For a thousand or ten thousand years,
    For who can count so many years,
    Some woman has lived among these rocks,
    The Great Herne's bride, or promised bride,
    And when a visitor has played the flute
    Has come or not. What would you ask?

CONGAL: Tara and I have made a peace;
    Our fiftieth battle fought, there is need
    Of preparation for the next;
    He and all his principal men,
    I and all my principal men,
    Take supper at his principal house

This night, in his principal city, Tara,
And we have set our minds upon
A certain novelty or relish.

MIKE: Herne's eggs.

CONGAL: This man declares our need;
A donkey, both creels packed with eggs,
Somebody that knows the mind of a donkey
For donkey-boy.

ATTRACTA: Custom forbids:
Only the women of these rocks,
Betrothed or married to the Herne,
The god or ancestor of hernes,
Can eat, handle, or look upon those eggs.

CONGAL: Refused! Must old campaigners lack
The one sole dish that takes their fancy,
My cooks what might have proved their skill,
Because a woman thinks that she
Is promised or married to a bird?

MIKE: Mad!

CONGAL: Mad! This man is right,
But you are not to blame for that.
Women thrown into despair
By the winter of their virginity
Take its abominable snow,
As boys take common snow, and make
An image of god or bird or beast
To feed their sensuality:
Ovid had a literal mind,
And though he sang it neither knew
What lonely lust dragged down the gold
That crept on Danae's lap, nor knew
What rose against the moony feathers
When Leda lay upon the grass.

ATTRACTA: There is no reality but the Great Herne.

MIKE: The cure.

CONGAL: Why, that is easy said;
An old campaigner is the cure

For everything that woman dreams –
Even I myself, had I but time.

MIKE: Seven men.

CONGAL: This man of learning means
That not a weather-stained, war-battered
Old campaigner such as I –
But seven men packed into a day
Or dawdled out through seven years –
Are needed to melt down the snow
That's fallen among these wintry rocks.

ATTRACTA: There is no happiness but the Great Herne.

CONGAL: It may be that life is suffering,
But youth that has not yet known pleasure
Has not the right to say so; pick,
Or be picked by seven men,
And we shall talk it out again.

ATTRACTA: Being betrothed to the Great Herne
I know what may be known: I burn
Not in the flesh but in the mind;
Chosen out of all my kind
That I may lie in a blazing bed
And a bird take my maidenhead,
To the unbegotten I return,
All a womb and a funeral urn.

(*Enter* CORNEY, PAT, JAMES, MATHIAS, *etc., with donkey.
A creel packed with eggs is painted upon the side of the
donkey.*)

CORNEY: Think of yourself; think of the songs:
Bride of the Herne, and the Great Herne's bride,
Grow terrible: go into a trance.

ATTRACTA: Stop!

CORNEY: Bring the god out of your gut;
Stand there asleep until the rascals
Wriggle upon his beak like eels.

ATTRACTA: Stop!

CORNEY: The country calls them rascals,
I, sacrilegious rascals that have taken

Every new-laid egg in the hernery.
ATTRACTA: Stop! When have I permitted you
    To say what I may, or may not do?
    But you and your donkey must obey
    All big men who can say their say.
CONGAL: And bid him keep a civil tongue.
ATTRACTA: Those eggs are stolen from the god.
    It is but right that you hear said
    A curse so ancient that no man
    Can say who made it, or any thing at all
    But that it was nailed upon a post
    Before a herne had stood on one leg.
CORNEY: Hernes must stand on one leg when they fish
    In honour of the bird who made it.

    'This they nailed upon a post,
    On the night my leg was lost,'
    Said the old, old herne that had but one leg.

    'He that a herne's egg dare steal
    Shall be changed into a fool,'
    Said the old, old herne that had but one leg.

    'And to end his fool breath
    At a fool's hand meet his death,'
    Said the old, old herne that had but one leg.

    I think it was the Great Herne made it,
    Pretending that he had but the one leg
    To fool us all; but Great Herne or another
    It has not failed these thousand years.
CONGAL: That I shall live and die a fool,
    And die upon some battlefield
    At some fool's hand, is but natural,
    And needs no curse to bring it.
MIKE: Pickled!

CONGAL: He says that I am an old campaigner,
    Robber of sheepfolds and cattle trucks,
    So cursed from morning until midnight
    There is not a quarter of an inch
    To plaster a new curse upon.
CORNEY: Luck!
CONGAL: Adds that your luck begins when you
    Recall that though we took those eggs
    We paid with good advice; and then
    Take to your bosom seven men.

    (CONGAL, MIKE, CORNEY, MATHIAS, JAMES, *and donkey go
    out. Enter timidly three girls*, KATE, AGNES, MARY.)

MARY: Have all those fierce men gone?
ATTRACTA: All those fierce men have gone.
AGNES: But they will come again?
ATTRACTA: No, never again.
KATE: We bring three presents.

    (*All except* ATTRACTA *kneel.*)

MARY: This is a jug of cream.
AGNES: This is a bowl of butter.
KATE: This is a basket of eggs.

    (*They lay jug, bowl, and basket on the ground.*)

ATTRACTA: I know what you would ask.
    Sit round upon these stones.
    Children, why do you fear
    A woman but little older,
    A child yesterday?
    All, when I am married,
    Shall have good husbands. Kate
    Shall marry a black-headed lad.
AGNES: She swore but yesterday
    That she would marry black.
ATTRACTA: But Agnes there shall marry
    A honey-coloured lad.
AGNES: O!
ATTRACTA: Mary shall be married
    When I myself am married

To the lad that is in her mind.

MARY: Are you not married yet?

ATTRACTA: No. But it is almost come,
    May come this very night.

MARY: And must he be all feathers?

AGNES: Have a terrible beak?

KATE: Great terrible claws?

ATTRACTA: Whatever shape he choose,
    Though that be terrible,
    Will best express his love.

AGNES: When he comes – will he? –

ATTRACTA: Child, ask what you please.

AGNES: Do all that a man does?

ATTRACTA: Strong sinew and soft flesh
    Are foliage round the shaft
    Before the arrowsmith
    Has stripped it, and I pray
    That I, all foliage gone,
    May shoot into my joy –

(*Sound of a flute, playing 'The Great Herne's Feather'*.)

MARY: Who plays upon that flute?

AGNES: Her god is calling her.

KATE: Look, look, she takes
    An egg out of the basket.
    My white hen laid it,
    My favourite white hen.

MARY: Her eyes grow glassy, she moves
    According to the notes of the flute.

AGNES: Her limbs grow rigid, she seems
    A doll upon a wire.

MARY: Her human life is gone
    And that is why she seems
    A doll upon a wire.

AGNES: You mean that when she looks so
    She is but a puppet?

MARY: How do I know? And yet
    Twice have I seen her so,

She will move for certain minutes
As though her god were there
Thinking how best to move
A doll upon a wire.
Then she will move away
In long leaps as though
He had remembered his skill.
She has still my little egg.

AGNES: Who knows but your little egg
Comes into some mystery?

KATE: Some mystery to make
Love-loneliness more sweet.

AGNES: She has moved. She has moved away.

KATE: Travelling fast asleep
In long loops like a dancer.

MARY: Like a dancer, like a hare.

AGNES: The last time she went away
The moon was full – she returned
Before its side had flattened.

KATE: This time she will not return.

AGNES: Because she is called to her marriage?

KATE: Those leaps may carry her where
No woman has gone, and he
Extinguish sun, moon, star.
No bridal torch can burn
When his black midnight is there.

AGNES: I have heard her claim that they couple
In the blazing heart of the sun.

KATE: But you have heard it wrong!
In blue-black midnight they couple.

AGNES: No, in the sun.

KATE: Blue-black!

AGNES: In the sun!

KATE: Blue-black, blue-black!

MARY: All I know is that she
Shall lie there in his bed.
Nor shall it end until

She lies there full of his might,
His thunderbolts in her hand.

SCENE 3

Before the gates of Tara, CONGAL, MIKE, PAT, PETER, JAMES, MATHIAS, *etc.,* SOLDIERS OF CONGAL, CORNEY, *and the donkey.*

CONGAL: This is Tara; in a moment
    Men must come out of the gate
    With a great basket between them
    And we give up our arms;
    No armed man can enter.
CORNEY: And here is that great bird
    Over our heads again.
PAT: The Great Herne himself
    And he in a red rage.
MIKE: Stones.
CONGAL: This man is right.
    Beat him to death with stones.
    (*All go through the motion of picking up and throwing stones. There are no stones except in so far as their gestures can suggest them.*)
PAT: All those stones fell wide.
CORNEY: He has come down so low
    His legs are sweeping the grass.
MIKE: Swords.
CONGAL: This man is right.
    Cut him up with swords.
PAT: I have him within my reach.
CONGAL: No, no, he is here at my side.
CORNEY: His wing has touched my shoulder.
CONGAL: We missed him again and he
    Rises again and sinks
    Behind the wall of Tara.

(*Two* MEN *come in carrying a large basket slung between two poles. One is whistling. All except* CORNEY, *who is unarmed, drop their swords and helmets into the basket. Each soldier when he takes off his helmet shows that he wears a skull-cap of soft cloth.*)

CONGAL: Where have I heard that tune?

MIKE: This morning.

CONGAL: I know it now,
    The tune of 'The Great Herne's Feather'.
    It puts my teeth on edge.

SCENE 4

Banqueting hall. A throne painted on the backcloth. Enter CONGAL, *alone, drunk, and shouting.*

CONGAL: To arms, to arms! Connacht to arms!
    Insulted and betrayed, betrayed and insulted.
    Who has insulted me? Tara has insulted.
    To arms, to arms! Connacht to arms!
    To arms – but if you have not got any
    Take a table-leg or a candlestick,
    A boot or a stool or any odd thing.
    Who has betrayed me? Tara has betrayed!
    To arms, to arms! Connacht to arms!

(*He goes out to one side. Music, perhaps drum and concertina, to suggest breaking of wood. Enter, at the other side, the* KING OF TARA, *drunk.*)

AEDH: Where is that beastly drunken liar
    That says I have insulted him?

(CONGAL *enters with two table-legs.*)

CONGAL: I say it!

AEDH: What insult?

CONGAL: How dare you ask?
    When I have had a common egg,
    A common hen's egg put before me,

An egg dropped in the dirty straw
And crowed for by a cross-bred gangling cock,
And every other man at the table
A herne's egg.

(*Throws a table-leg on the floor.*)

There is your weapon. Take it!
Take it up, defend yourself.
An egg that some half-witted slattern
Spat upon and wiped on her apron!

AEDH: A servant put the wrong egg there.

CONGAL: But at whose orders?

AEDH: At your own.
A murderous drunken plot, a plot
To put a weapon that I do not know
Into my hands.

CONGAL: Take up that weapon.
If I am as drunken as you say,
And you as sober as you think,
A coward and a drunkard are well matched.

(AEDH *takes up the table-leg.* CONNACHT *and* TARA SOLDIERS *come in, they fight, and the fight sways to and fro. The weapons, table-legs, candlesticks, etc., do not touch. Drum-taps represent blows. All go out fighting. Enter* PAT, *drunk, with bottle.*)

PAT: Herne's egg, hen's egg, great difference.
There's insult in that difference.
What do hens eat? Hens live upon mash,
Upon slop, upon kitchen odds and ends.
What do hernes eat? Hernes live on eels,
On things that must always run about.
Man's a high animal and runs about,
But mash is low, O, very low.
Or, to speak like a philosopher,
When a man expects the movable
But gets the immovable, he is insulted.

(*Enter* CONGAL, PETER, MALACHI, MATHIAS, *etc.*)

CONGAL: Tara knew that he was overmatched;

Knew from the start he had no chance;
Died of a broken head; died drunk;
Accused me with his dying breath
Of secretly practising with a table-leg,
Practising at midnight until I
Became a perfect master with the weapon.
But that is all lies.

PAT: Let all men know
He was a noble character
And I must weep at his funeral.

CONGAL: He insulted me with a hen's egg,
Said I had practised with a table-leg,
But I have taken kingdom and throne
And that has made all level again
And I can weep at his funeral.
I would not have had him die that way
Or die at all, he should have been immortal.
Our fifty battles had made us friends;
And there are fifty more to come.
New weapons, a new leader will be found
And everything begin again.

MIKE: Much bloodier.

CONGAL: They had, we had
Forgotten what we fought about,
So fought like gentlemen, but now
Knowing the truth must fight like the beasts.
Maybe the Great Herne's curse has done it.
Why not? Answer me that; why not?

MIKE: Horror henceforth.

CONGAL: This wise man means
We fought so long like gentlemen
That we grew blind.

(ATTRACTA enters, walking in her sleep, a herne's egg in her hand. She stands near the throne and holds her egg towards it for a moment.)

MATHIAS: Look! Look!
She offers that egg. Who is to take it?

CONGAL: She walks with open eyes but in her sleep.

MATHIAS: I can see it all in a flash.
    She found that herne's egg on the table
    And left the hen's egg there instead.

JAMES: She brought the hen's egg on purpose
    Walking in her wicked sleep.

CONGAL: And if I take that egg, she wakes,
    Completes her task, her circle;
    We all complete a task or circle,
    Want a woman, then all goes – pff.
    (*He goes to take the egg.*)

MIKE: Not now.

CONGAL: This wise man says 'not now'.
    There must be something to consider first.

JAMES: By changing one egg for another
    She has brought bloodshed on us all.

PAT: He was a noble character,
    And I must weep at his funeral.

JAMES: I say that she must die, I say;
    According to what my mother said,
    All that have done what she did must die,
    But, in a manner of speaking, pleasantly,
    Because legally, certainly not
    By beating with a table-leg
    As though she were a mere Tara man,
    Nor yet by beating with a stone
    As though she were the Great Herne himself.

MIKE: The Great Herne's bride.

CONGAL: I had forgotten
    That all she does he makes her do,
    But he is god and out of reach;
    Nor stone can bruise, nor a sword pierce him,
    And yet through his betrothed, his bride,
    I have the power to make him suffer;
    His curse has given me the right,
    I am to play the fool and die
    At a fool's hands.

MIKE: Seven men.
    (*He begins to count, seeming to strike the table with the table-
    leg, but table and table-leg must not meet, the blow is represented
    by the sound of the drum.*)
    One, two, three, four,
    Five, six, seven men.
PAT: Seven that are present in this room,
    Seven that must weep at his funeral.
CONGAL: This man who struck those seven blows
    Means that we seven in the name of the law
    Must handle, penetrate, and possess her,
    And do her a great good by that action,
    Melting out the virgin snow,
    And that snow image, the Great Herne;
    For nothing less than seven men
    Can melt that snow, but when it melts
    She may, being free from all obsession,
    Live as every woman should.
    I am the Court; judgment has been given.
    I name the seven: Congal of Tara,
    Patrick, Malachi, Mike, John, James,
    And that coarse hulk of clay, Mathias.
MATHIAS: I dare not lay a hand upon that woman.
    The people say that she is holy
    And carries a great devil in her gut.
PAT: What mischief can a Munster devil
    Do to a man that was born in Connacht?
MALACHI: I made a promise to my mother
    When we set out on this campaign
    To keep from women.
JOHN: I have a wife that's jealous
    If I but look the moon in the face.
JAMES: I am promised to an educated girl.
    Her family are most particular,
    What would they say – O my God!
CONGAL: Whoever disobeys the Court
    Is an unmannerly, disloyal lout,

And no good citizen.

PAT: Here is my bottle.
Pass it along, a long, long pull;
Although it's round like a woman carrying,
No unmannerly, disloyal bottle,
An affable, most loyal bottle.
(*All drink*.)

MATHIAS: I first.

CONGAL: That's for the Court to say.
A Court of Law is a blessed thing,
Logic, Mathematics, ground in one,
And everything out of balance accursed.
When the Court decides on a decree
Men carry it out with dignity.
Here where I put down my hand
I will put a mark, then all must stand
Over there in a level row.
And all take off their caps and throw.
The nearest cap shall take her first,
The next shall take her next, so on
Till all is in good order done.
I need a mark and so must take
The herne's egg, and let her wake.

(*He takes egg and lays it upon the ground.* ATTRACTA
*stands motionless, looking straight in front of her. She sings.
The seven standing in a row throw their caps one after another.*)

ATTRACTA: When I take a beast to my joyful breast,
Though beak and claw I must endure,
Sang the bride of the Herne, and the Great Herne's bride,
No lesser life, man, bird or beast,
Can make unblessed what a beast made blessed,
Can make impure what a beast made pure.

Where is he gone, where is that other,
He that shall take my maidenhead?
Sang the bride of the Herne, and the Great Herne's bride,
Out of the moon came my pale brother,

The blue-black midnight is my mother.
Who will turn down the sheets of the bed?

When beak and claw their work begin
Shall horror stir in the roots of my hair?
Sang the bride of the Herne, and the Great Herne's bride,
And who lie there in the cold dawn
When all that terror has come and gone?
Shall I be the woman lying there?

SCENE 5

Before the Gate of Tara. CORNEY *enters with donkey.*

CORNEY: You thought to go on sleeping though dawn was up,
    Rapscallion of a beast, old highwayman.
    That light in the eastern sky is dawn,
    You cannot deny it; many a time
    You looked upon it following your trade.
    Cheer up, we shall be home before sunset.
    (ATTRACTA *comes in.*)
ATTRACTA: I have packed all the uneaten or unbroken eggs
    Into the creels. Help carry them
    And hang them on the donkey's back.
CORNEY: We could boil them hard and keep them in the larder,
    But Congal has had them all boiled soft.
ATTRACTA: Such eggs are holy. Many pure souls,
    Especially among the country-people,
    Would shudder if herne's eggs were left
    For foul-tongued, bloody-minded men.
    (CONGAL, MALACHI, MIKE, *etc., enter.*)
CONGAL: A sensible woman; you gather up what's left,
    Your thoughts upon the cupboard and the larder.
    No more a herne's bride – a crazed loony
    Waiting to be trodden by a bird –
    But all woman, all sensible woman.

MIKE: Manners.

CONGAL: This man who is always right
        Desires that I should add these words,
        The seven that held you in their arms last night
        Wish you good luck.

ATTRACTA: What do you say?
        My husband came to me in the night.

CONGAL: Seven men lay with you in the night.
        Go home desiring and desirable,
        And look for a man.

ATTRACTA: The Herne is my husband.
        I lay beside him, his pure bride.

CONGAL: Pure in the embrace of seven men?

MIKE: She slept.

CONGAL: You say that though I thought,
        Because I took the egg out of her hand,
        That she awoke, she did not wake
        Until day broke upon her sleep –
        Her sleep and ours – did she wake pure?
        Seven men can answer that.

CORNEY: King though you are, I will not hear
        The bride of the Great Herne defamed –
        A king, a king but a Mayo man.
        A Mayo man's lying tongue can beat
        A Clare highwayman's rapscallion eye,
        Seven times a liar.

MIKE: Seven men.

CONGAL: I, Congal, lay with her last night.

MATHIAS: And I, Mathias.

MIKE: And I.

JAMES: And I.

PETER: And I.

JOHN: And I.

PAT: And I; swear it;
        And not a drop of drink since dawn.

CORNEY: One plain liar, six men bribed to lie.

ATTRACTA: Great Herne, Great Herne, Great Herne,
    Your darling is crying out,
    Great Herne, declare her pure,
    Pure as that beak and claw,
    Great Herne, Great Herne, Great Herne,
    Let the round heaven declare it.
    (*Silence. Then low thunder growing louder. All except* ATTRACTA
    and CONGAL *kneel.*)
JAMES: Great Herne, I swear that she is pure;
    I never laid a hand upon her.
MATHIAS: I was a fool to believe myself
    When everybody knows that I am a liar.
PAT: Even when it seemed that I covered her
    I swear that I knew it was the drink.
ATTRACTA: I lay in the bride-bed,
    His thunderbolts in my hand,
    But gave them back, for he,
    My lover, the Great Herne,
    Knows everything that is said
    And every man's intent,
    And every man's deed; and he
    Shall give these seven that say
    That they upon me lay
    A most memorable punishment.
    (*It thunders. All prostrate themselves except* ATTRACTA *and*
CONGAL. CONGAL *had half knelt, but he has stood up again.*)
    I share his knowledge, and I know
    Every punishment decreed.
    He will come when you are dead,
    Push you down a step or two
    Into cat or rat or bat,
    Into dog or wolf or goose.
    Everybody in his new shape I can see,
    But Congal there stands in a cloud
    Because his fate is not yet settled.
    Speak out, Great Herne, and make it known

That everything I have said is true.

(*Thunder. All now, except* ATTRACTA, *have prostrated them-selves.*)

What has made you kneel?

CONGAL: This man
   That's prostrate at my side would say,
   Could he say anything at all,
   That I am terrified by thunder.

ATTRACTA: Why did you stand up so long?

CONGAL: I held you in my arms last night,
   We seven held you in our arms.

ATTRACTA: You were under the curse, in all
   You did, in all you seemed to do.

CONGAL: If I must die at a fool's hand,
   When must I die?

ATTRACTA: When the moon is full.

CONGAL: And where?

ATTRACTA: Upon the holy mountain,
   Upon Slieve Fuadh, there we meet again
   Just as the moon comes round the hill.
   There all the gods must visit me,
   Acknowledging my marriage to a god;
   One man will I have among the gods.

CONGAL: I know the place and I will come,
   Although it be my death, I will come.
   Because I am terrified, I will come.

SCENE 6

A mountain-top, the moon has just risen; the moon of comic tradition, a round smiling face. A cauldron lid, a cooking-pot, and a spit lie together at one side of the stage. The FOOL, *a man in ragged clothes, enters carrying a large stone; he lays it down at one side and goes out.* CONGAL *enters carrying a wineskin and stands at the other side of the stage. The* FOOL *re-enters with a second large stone which he places beside the first.*

CONGAL: What is your name, boy?

FOOL: Poor Tom Fool.
    Everybody knows Tom Fool.

CONGAL: I saw something in the mist,
    There lower down upon the slope,
    I went up close to it and saw
    A donkey, somebody's stray donkey.
    A donkey and a Fool – I don't like it at all.

FOOL: I won't be Tom the Fool after tonight.
    I have made a level patch out there,
    Clearing away the stones, and there
    I shall fight a man and kill a man
    And get great glory.

CONGAL: Where did you get
    The cauldron lid, the pot and the spit?

FOOL: I sat in Widow Rooney's kitchen,
    Somebody said, 'King Congal's on the mountain
    Cursed to die at the hands of a fool.'
    Somebody else said 'Kill him, Tom.'
    And everybody began to laugh
    And said I should kill him at the full moon,
    And that is tonight.

CONGAL: I too have heard
    That Congal is to die tonight.
    Take a drink.

FOOL: I took this lid,
    And all the women screamed at me.
    I took the spit, and all screamed worse.
    A shoulder of lamb stood ready for the roasting –
    I put the pot upon my head.
    They did not scream but stood and gaped.

    (The FOOL *arms himself with spit, cauldron lid and pot,*
    whistling 'The Great Herne's Feather'.)

CONGAL: Hush, that is an unlucky tune!
    And why must you kill Congal, Fool?
    What harm has he done you?

FOOL: None at all.

But there's a Fool called Johnny from Meath,
We are great rivals and we hate each other,
But I can get the pennies if I kill Congal,
And Johnny nothing.

CONGAL: I am King Congal,
And is not that a thing to laugh at, Fool?

FOOL: Very nice, O very nice indeed,
For I can kill you now, and I
Am tired of walking.

CONGAL: Both need rest.
Another drink apiece – that is done –
Lead to the place you have cleared of stones.

FOOL: But where is your sword? You have not got a sword.

CONGAL: I lost it, or I never had it,
Or threw it at the strange donkey below,
But that's no matter – I have hands.

(*They go out at one side.* ATTRACTA, CORNEY, *and donkey come in.* ATTRACTA *sings.*)

ATTRACTA: When beak and claw their work began
What horror stirred in the roots of my hair?
Sang the bride of the Herne, and the Great Herne's bride.
But who lay there in the cold dawn,
When all that terror had come and gone?
Was I the woman lying there?

(*They go out.* CONGAL *and* TOM THE FOOL *come.* CONGAL *is carrying the cauldron lid, pot and spit. He lays them down.*)

CONGAL: I was sent to die at the hands of a Fool.
There must be another Fool on the mountain.

FOOL: That must be Johnny from Meath.
But that's a thing I could not endure,
For Johnny would get all the pennies.

CONGAL: Here, take a drink and have no fear;
All's plain at last; though I shall die
I shall not die at a Fool's hand.
I have thought out a better plan.
I and the Herne have had three bouts,

He won the first, I won the second,
Six men and I possessed his wife.

FOOL: I ran after a woman once.

I had seen two donkeys in a field.

CONGAL: And did you get her, did you get her, Fool?

FOOL: I almost had my hand upon her.

She screamed, and somebody came and beat me.
Were you beaten?

CONGAL: No, no, Fool.

But she said that nobody had touched her,
And after that the thunder said the same,
Yet I had won that bout, and now
I know that I shall win the third.

FOOL: If Johnny from Meath comes, kill him!

CONGAL: Maybe I will, maybe I will not.

FOOL: You let me off, but don't let him off.

CONGAL: I could not do you any harm,

For you and I are friends.

FOOL: Kill Johnny!

CONGAL: Because you have asked me to, I will do it,

For you and I are friends.

FOOL: Kill Johnny!

Kill with the spear, but give it to me
That I may see if it is sharp enough.

(*The* FOOL *takes the spit.*)

CONGAL: And is it, Fool?

FOOL: I spent an hour

Sharpening it upon a stone.
Could I kill you now?

CONGAL: Maybe you could.

FOOL: I will get all the pennies for myself.

(*He wounds* CONGAL. *The wounding is symbolized by
a movement of the spit towards or over* CONGAL's *body.*)

CONGAL: It passed out of your mind for a moment

That we are friends, but that is natural.

FOOL: (*Dropping the spit*) I must see it, I never saw a wound.

CONGAL: The Herne has got the first blow in;

A scratch, a scratch, a mere nothing.
But had it been a little deeper and higher
It would have gone through the heart, and maybe
That would have left me better off,
For the Great Herne may beat me in the end.
Here I must sit through the full moon,
And he will send up Fools against me,
Meandering, roaring, yelling,
Whispering Fools, then chattering Fools,
And after that morose, melancholy,
Sluggish, fat, silent Fools;
And I, moon-crazed, moon-blind,
Fighting and wounded, wounded and fighting.
I never thought of such an end.
Never be a soldier, Tom;
Though it begins well, is this a life?
If this is a man's life, is there any life
But a dog's life?

FOOL: That's it, that's it;
Many a time they have put a dog at me.

CONGAL: If I should give myself a wound,
Let life run away, I'd win the bout.
He said I must die at the hands of a Fool
And sent you hither. Give me that spit!
I put it in this crevice of the rock,
That I may fall upon the point.
These stones will keep it sticking upright.
(*They arrange stones, he puts the spit in.*)
(*Almost screaming in his excitement*) Fool! Am I myself a
    Fool?
For if I am a Fool, he wins the bout.

FOOL: You are King of Connacht. If you were a Fool
They would have chased you with their dogs.

CONGAL: I am King Congal of Connacht and of Tara,
That wise, victorious, voluble, unlucky,
Blasphemous, famous, infamous man.
Fool, take this spit when red with blood,

Show it to the people and get all the pennies;
What does it matter what they think?
The Great Herne knows that I have won.
(He falls symbolically upon the spit. It does not touch him. The FOOL *takes the spit and wine-skin and goes out.)*
It seems that I am hard to kill,
But the wound is deep. Are you up there?
Your chosen kitchen spit has killed me,
But killed me at my own will, not yours.
(ATTRACTA *and* CORNEY *enter.*)

ATTRACTA: Will the knot hold?

CORNEY: There was a look
About the old highwayman's eye of him
That warned me, so I made him fast
To that old stump among the rocks
With a great knot that he can neither
Break, nor pull apart with his teeth.

CONGAL: Attracta!

ATTRACTA: I called you to this place,
You came, and now the story is finished.

CONGAL: You have great powers, even the thunder
Does whatever you bid it do.
Protect me, I have won my bout,
But I am afraid of what the Herne
May do with me when I am dead.
I am afraid that he may put me
Into the shape of a brute beast.

ATTRACTA: I will protect you if, as I think,
Your shape is not yet fixed upon.

CONGAL: I am slipping now, and you up there
With your long leg and your long beak.
But I have beaten you, Great Herne,
In spite of your kitchen spit – seven men –
(He dies.)

ATTRACTA: Come lie with me upon the ground,
Come quickly into my arms, come quickly, come
Before his body has had time to cool.

CORNEY: What? Lie with you?

ATTRACTA: Lie and beget.
    If you are afraid of the Great Herne,
    Put that away, for if I do his will,
    You are his instrument or himself.

CORNEY: The thunder has me terrified.

ATTRACTA: I lay with the Great Herne, and he,
    Being all a spirit, but begot
    His image in the mirror of my spirit,
    Being all sufficient to himself
    Begot himself; but there's a work
    That should be done, and that work needs
    No bird's beak nor claw, but a man,
    The imperfection of a man.

    (*The sound of a donkey braying.*)

CORNEY: The donkey is braying.
    He has some wickedness in his mind.

ATTRACTA: Too late, too late, he broke that knot,
    And there, down there among the rocks
    He couples with another donkey.
    That donkey has conceived. I thought that I
    Could give a human form to Congal,
    But now he must be born a donkey.

CORNEY: King Congal must be born a donkey!

ATTRACTA: Because we were not quick enough.

CORNEY: I have heard that a donkey carries its young
    Longer than any other beast,
    Thirteen months it must carry it.

    (*He laughs.*)

    All that trouble and nothing to show for it,
    Nothing but just another donkey.

PURGATORY

PERSONS IN THE PLAY

A BOY
AN OLD MAN

A ruined house and a bare tree in the background.

BOY: Half-door, hall door,
    Hither and thither day and night,
    Hill or hollow, shouldering this pack,
    Hearing you talk.
OLD MAN: Study that house.
    I think about its jokes and stories;
    I try to remember what the butler
    Said to a drunken gamekeeper
    In mid-October, but I cannot.
    If I cannot, none living can.
    Where are the jokes and stories of a house,
    Its threshold gone to patch a pig-sty?
BOY: So you have come this path before?
OLD MAN: The moonlight falls upon the path,
    The shadow of a cloud upon the house,
    And that's symbolical; study that tree,
    What is it like?
BOY: A silly old man.
OLD MAN: It's like – no matter what it's like.
    I saw it a year ago stripped bare as now,
    So I chose a better trade.
    I saw it fifty years ago
    Before the thunderbolt had riven it,
    Green leaves, ripe leaves, leaves thick as butter,
    Fat, greasy life. Stand there and look,
    Because there is somebody in that house.
    (*The* BOY *puts down pack and stands in the doorway.*)

211

BOY: There's nobody there.

OLD MAN: There's somebody there.

BOY: The floor is gone, the windows gone
And where there should be roof there's sky,
And here's a bit of an egg-shell thrown
Out of a jackdaw's nest.

OLD MAN: But there are some
That do not care what's gone, what's left:
The souls in Purgatory that come back
To habitations and familiar spots.

BOY: Your wits are out again.

OLD MAN: Relive
Their transgressions, and that not once
But many times; they know at last
The consequence of those transgressions
Whether upon others or upon themselves;
Upon others, others may bring help,
For when the consequence is at an end
The dream must end; if upon themselves,
There is no help but in themselves
And in the mercy of God.

BOY: I have had enough!
Talk to the jackdaws, if talk you must.

OLD MAN: Stop! Sit there upon that stone.
That is the house where I was born.

BOY: The big old house that was burnt down?

OLD MAN: My mother that was your grand-dam owned it,
This scenery and this countryside,
Kennel and stable, horse and hound —
She had a horse at the Curragh, and there met
My father, a groom in a training stable,
Looked at him and married him.
Her mother never spoke to her again,
And she did right.

BOY: What's right and wrong?
My grand-dad got the girl and the money.

OLD MAN: Looked at him and married him,

And he squandered everything she had.
She never knew the worst, because
She died in giving birth to me,
But now she knows it all, being dead.
Great people lived and died in this house;
Magistrates, colonels, members of Parliament,
Captains and Governors, and long ago
Men that had fought at Aughrim and the Boyne.
Some that had gone on Government work
To London or to India came home to die,
Or came from London every spring
To look at the may-blossom in the park.
They had loved the trees that he cut down
To pay what he had lost at cards
Or spent on horses, drink, and women;
Had loved the house, had loved all
The intricate passages of the house,
But he killed the house; to kill a house
Where great men grew up, married, died,
I here declare a capital offence.

BOY: My God, but you had luck! Grand clothes,
    And maybe a grand horse to ride.

OLD MAN: That he might keep me upon his level
    He never sent me to school, but some
    Half loved me for my half of her:
    A gamekeeper's wife taught me to read,
    A Catholic curate taught me Latin.
    There were old books and books made fine
    By eighteenth-century French binding, books
    Modern and ancient, books by the ton.

BOY: What education have you given me?

OLD MAN: I gave the education that befits
    A bastard that a pedlar got
    Upon a tinker's daughter in a ditch.
    When I had come to sixteen years old
    My father burned down the house when drunk.

BOY: But that is my age, sixteen years old,

At the Puck Fair.

OLD MAN: And everything was burnt;
    Books, library, all were burnt.

BOY: Is what I have heard upon the road the truth,
    That you killed him in the burning house?

OLD MAN: There's nobody here but our two selves?

BOY: Nobody, Father.

OLD MAN: I stuck him with a knife,
    That knife that cuts my dinner now,
    And after that I left him in the fire.
    They dragged him out, somebody saw
    The knife wound but could not be certain
    Because the body was all black and charred.
    Then some that were his drunken friends
    Swore they would put me upon trial,
    Spoke of quarrels, a threat I had made.
    The gamekeeper gave me some old clothes,
    I ran away, worked here and there
    Till I became a pedlar on the roads,
    No good trade, but good enough
    Because I am my father's son,
    Because of what I did or may do.
    Listen to the hoofbeats! Listen, listen!

BOY: I cannot hear a sound.

OLD MAN: Beat! Beat!
    This night is the anniversary
    Of my mother's wedding night,
    Or of the night wherein I was begotten.
    My father is riding from the public house,
    A whiskey bottle under his arm.

  (*A window is lit showing a young girl.*)

    Look at the window; she stands there
    Listening, the servants are all in bed,
    She is alone, he has stayed late
    Bragging and drinking in the public house.

BOY: There's nothing but an empty gap in the wall.
    You have made it up. No, you are mad!

You are getting madder every day.

OLD MAN: It's louder now because he rides
Upon a gravelled avenue
All grass today. The hoofbeat stops,
He has gone to the other side of the house,
Gone to the stable, put the horse up.
She has gone down to open the door.
This night she is no better than her man
And does not mind that he is half drunk,
She is mad about him. They mount the stairs.
She brings him into her own chamber.
And that is the marriage-chamber now.
The window is dimly lit again.

Do not let him touch you! It is not true
That drunken men cannot beget,
And if he touch he must beget
And you must bear his murderer.
Deaf! Both deaf! If I should throw
A stick or a stone they would not hear;
And that's a proof my wits are out.
But there's a problem: she must live
Through everything in exact detail,
Driven to it by remorse, and yet
Can she renew the sexual act
And find no pleasure in it, and if not,
If pleasure and remorse must both be there,
Which is the greater?
                               I lack schooling.
Go fetch Tertullian; he and I
Will ravel all that problem out
Whilst those two lie upon the mattress
Begetting me.
                    Come back! Come back!
And so you thought to slip away,
My bag of money between your fingers,
And that I could not talk and see!

You have been rummaging in the pack.

(*The light in the window has faded out.*)

BOY: You never gave me my right share.

OLD MAN: And had I given it, young as you are,
You would have spent it upon drink.

BOY: What if I did? I had a right
To get it and spend it as I chose.

OLD MAN: Give me that bag and no more words.

BOY: I will not.

OLD MAN: I will break your fingers.

(*They struggle for the bag. In the struggle it drops, scattering the money. The* OLD MAN *staggers but does not fall. They stand looking at each other. The window is lit up. A man is seen pouring whiskey into a glass.*)

BOY: What if I killed you? You killed my grand-dad,
Because you were young and he was old.
Now I am young and you are old.

OLD MAN: (*Staring at window*) Better-looking, those sixteen
years –

BOY: What are you muttering?

OLD MAN: Younger – and yet
She should have known he was not her kind.

BOY: What are you saying? Out with it!

(*The* OLD MAN *points to window.*)
My God! The window is lit up
And somebody stands there, although
The floorboards are all burnt away.

OLD MAN: The window is lit up because my father
Has come to find a glass for his whiskey.
He leans there like some tired beast.

BOY: A dead, living, murdered man!

OLD MAN: 'Then the bride-sleep fell upon Adam':
Where did I read those words?
     And yet
There's nothing leaning in the window
But the impression upon my mother's mind;
Being dead she is alone in her remorse.

BOY: A body that was a bundle of old bones
    Before I was born. Horrible! Horrible!
    (*He covers his eyes.*)
OLD MAN: That beast there would know nothing, being
        nothing,
    If I should kill a man under the window
    He would not even turn his head.
    (*He stabs the* BOY.)
    My father and my son on the same jack-knife!
    That finishes – there – there – there –
    (*He stabs again and again. The window grows dark.*)
    'Hush-a-bye baby, thy father's a knight,
    Thy mother a lady, lovely and bright.'
    No, that is something that I read in a book,
    And if I sing it must be to my mother,
    And I lack rhyme.
    (*The stage has grown dark except where the tree stands
    in white light.*)
                    Study that tree.
    It stands there like a purified soul,
    All cold, sweet, glistening light.
    Dear mother, the window is dark again,
    But you are in the light because
    I finished all that consequence.
    I killed that lad because had he grown up
    He would have struck a woman's fancy,
    Begot, and passed pollution on.
    I am a wretched foul old man
    And therefore harmless. When I have stuck
    This old jack-knife into a sod
    And pulled it out all bright again,
    And picked up all the money that he dropped,
    I'll to a distant place, and there
    Tell my old jokes among new men.
    (*He cleans the knife and begins to pick up money.*)
    Hoofbeats! Dear God,
    How quickly it returns – beat – beat – !

*

Her mind cannot hold up that dream.
Twice a murderer and all for nothing,
And she must animate that dead night
Not once but many times!
                            O God,
Release my mother's soul from its dream!
Mankind can do no more. Appease
The misery of the living and the remorse of the dead.

THE DEATH OF CUCHULAIN

PERSONS IN THE PLAY

CUCHULAIN
EITHNE INGUBA
AOIFE
EMER
THE MORRIGU, *Goddess of War*
AN OLD MAN
A BLIND MAN
A SERVANT
A SINGER, A PIPER, *and* A DRUMMER

A bare stage of any period. A very OLD MAN *looking like something out of mythology.*

OLD MAN: I have been asked to produce a play called *The Death of Cuchulain*. It is the last of a series of plays which has for theme his life and death. I have been selected because I am out of fashion and out of date like the antiquated romantic stuff the thing is made of. I am so old that I have forgotten the name of my father and mother, unless indeed I am, as I affirm, the son of Talma, and he was so old that his friends and acquaintances still read Virgil and Homer. When they told me that I could have my own way, I wrote certain guiding principles on a bit of newspaper. I wanted an audience of fifty or a hundred, and if there are more, I beg them not to shuffle their feet or talk when the actors are speaking. I am sure that as I am producing a play for people I like, it is not probable, in this vile age, that they will be more in number than those who listened to the first performance of Milton's *Comus*. On the present occasion they must know the old epics and Mr Yeats' plays about them; such people, however poor, have libraries of their own. If there are more than a hundred I won't be able to escape people who are educating themselves out of the Book Societies and the like, sciolists all, pickpockets and opinionated bitches. Why pickpockets? I will explain that, I will make it all quite clear.

(*Drum and pipe behind the scene, then silence.*)

That's from the musicians; I asked them to do that if I was getting excited. If you were as old you would find it easy to get excited. Before the night ends you will meet the music. There is a singer, a piper, and a drummer. I have

221

picked them up here and there about the streets, and I will teach them, if I live, the music of the beggar-man, Homer's music. I promise a dance. I wanted a dance because where there are no words there is less to spoil. Emer must dance, there must be severed heads – I am old, I belong to mythology – severed heads for her to dance before. I had thought to have had those heads carved, but no, if the dancer can dance properly no wood-carving can look as well as a parallelogram of painted wood. But I was at my wit's end to find a good dancer; I could have got such a dancer once, but she has gone; the tragi-comedian dancer, the tragic dancer, upon the same neck love and loathing, life and death. I spit three times. I spit upon the dancers painted by Degas. I spit upon their short bodices, their stiff stays, their toes whereon they spin like peg-tops, above all upon that chambermaid face. They might have looked timeless, Rameses the Great, but not the chambermaid, that old maid history. I spit! I spit! I spit!

(*The stage is darkened, the curtain falls. Pipe and drum begin and continue until the curtain rises on a bare stage. Half a minute later* EITHNE INGUBA *enters.*)

EITHNE: Cuchulain! Cuchulain!

(CUCHULAIN *enters from back.*)

                              I am Emer's messenger,
  I am your wife's messenger, she has bid me say
  You must not linger here in sloth, for Maeve
  With all those Connacht ruffians at her back
  Burns barns and houses up at Emain Macha:
  Your house at Muirthemne already burns.
  No matter what's the odds, no matter though
  Your death may come of it, ride out and fight.
  The scene is set and you must out and fight.

CUCHULAIN: You have told me nothing. I am already armed,
  I have sent a messenger to gather men,
  And wait for his return. What have you there?

EITHNE: I have nothing.

CUCHULAIN: There is something in your hand.

EITHNE: No.

CUCHULAIN: Have you a letter in your hand?

EITHNE: I do not know how it got into my hand.
I am straight from Emer. We were in some place.
She spoke. She saw.

CUCHULAIN: This letter is from Emer,
It tells a different story. I am not to move
Until tomorrow morning, for, if now,
I must face odds no man can face and live.
Tomorrow morning Conall Caernach comes
With a great host.

EITHNE: I do not understand.
Who can have put that letter in my hand?

CUCHULAIN: And there is something more to make it certain
I shall not stir till morning; you are sent
To be my bedfellow, but have no fear,
All that is written, but I much prefer
Your own unwritten words. I am for the fight,
I and my handful are set upon the fight;
We have faced great odds before, a straw decided.

(*The* MORRIGU *enters and stands between them.*)

EITHNE: I know that somebody or something is there,
Yet nobody that I can see.

CUCHULAIN: There is nobody.

EITHNE: Who among the gods of the air and upper air
Has a bird's head?

CUCHULAIN: Morrigu is headed like a crow.

EITHNE: (*Dazed*) Morrigu, war goddess, stands between.
Her black wing touched me upon the shoulder, and
All is intelligible.

(*The* MORRIGU *goes out.*)

Maeve put me in a trance.
Though when Cuchulain slept with her as a boy
She seemed as pretty as a bird, she has changed,
She has an eye in the middle of her forehead.

CUCHULAIN: A woman that has an eye in the middle of
    her forehead!
    A woman that is headed like a crow!
    But she that put those words into your mouth
    Had nothing monstrous; you put them there yourself;
    You need a younger man, a friendlier man,
    But, fearing what my violence might do,
    Thought out these words to send me to my death,
    And were in such excitement you forgot
    The letter in your hand.
EITHNE: Now that I wake
    I say that Maeve did nothing out of reason;
    What mouth could you believe if not my mouth?
CUCHULAIN: When I went mad at my son's death and drew
    My sword against the sea, it was my wife
    That brought me back.
EITHNE: Better women than I
    Have served you well, but 'twas to me you turned.
CUCHULAIN: You thought that if you changed I'd kill
    you for it,
    When everything sublunary must change,
    And if I have not changed that goes to prove
    That I am monstrous.
EITHNE: You're not the man I loved,
    That violent man forgave no treachery.
    If, thinking what you think, you can forgive,
    It is because you are about to die.
CUCHULAIN: Spoken too loudly and too near the door;
    Speak low if you would speak about my death,
    Or not in that strange voice exulting in it.
    Who knows what ears listen behind the door?
EITHNE: Some that would not forgive a traitor, some
    That have the passion necessary to life,
    Some not about to die. When you are gone
    I shall denounce myself to all your cooks,
    Scullions, armourers, bed-makers, and messengers,
    Until they hammer me with a ladle, cut me with a knife,

Impale me upon a spit, put me to death
By what foul way best please their fancy,
So that my shade can stand among the shades
And greet your shade and prove it is no traitor.

CUCHULAIN: Women have spoken so, plotting a man's death.
  (*Enter a* SERVANT.)

SERVANT: Your great horse is bitted. All wait the word.

CUCHULAIN: I come to give it, but must ask a question.
  This woman, wild with grief, declares that she
  Out of pure treachery has told me lies
  That should have brought my death. What can I do?
  How can I save her from her own wild words?

SERVANT: Is her confession true?

CUCHULAIN: I make the truth!
  I say she brings a message from my wife.

SERVANT: What if I make her swallow poppy-juice?

CUCHULAIN: What herbs seem suitable, but protect her life
  As if it were your own, and should I not return
  Give her to Conall Caernach because the women
  Have called him a good lover.

EITHNE: I might have peace that know
  The Morrigu, the woman like a crow,
  Stands to my defence and cannot lie,
  But that Cuchulain is about to die.

(*Pipe and drum. The stage grows dark for a moment.
When it lights up again, it is empty.* CUCHULAIN *enters
wounded. He tries to fasten himself to a pillar-stone with his
belt.* AOIFE, *an erect white-haired woman, enters.*)

AOIFE: Am I recognized, Cuchulain?

CUCHULAIN: You fought with a sword,
  It seemed that we should kill each other, then
  Your body wearied and I took your sword.

AOIFE: But look again, Cuchulain! Look again!

CUCHULAIN: Your hair is white.

AOIFE: That time was long ago,
  And now it is my time. I have come to kill you.

CUCHULAIN: Where am I? Why am I here?

AOIFE: You asked their leave,
When certain that you had six mortal wounds,
To drink out of the pool.

CUCHULAIN: I have put my belt
About this stone and want to fasten it
And die upon my feet, but am too weak.
Fasten this belt.

(*She helps him to do so.*)
And now I know your name,
Aoife, the mother of my son. We met
At the Hawk's Well under the withered trees.
I killed him upon Baile's Strand, that is why
Maeve parted ranks that she might let you through.
You have a right to kill me.

AOIFE: Though I have,
Her army did not part to let me through.
The grey of Macha, that great horse of yours
Killed in the battle, came out of the pool
As though it were alive, and went three times
In a great circle round you and that stone,
Then leaped into the pool; and not a man
Of all that terrified army dare approach,
But I approach.

CUCHULAIN: Because you have the right.

AOIFE: But I am an old woman now, and that
Your strength may not start up when the time comes
I wind my veil about this ancient stone
And fasten you to it.

CUCHULAIN: But do not spoil your veil.
Your veils are beautiful, some with threads of gold.

AOIFE: I am too old to care for such things now.

(*She has wound the veil about him.*)

CUCHULAIN: There was no reason so to spoil your veil:
I am weak from loss of blood.

AOIFE: I was afraid,
But now that I have wound you in the veil
I am not afraid. But – how did my son fight?

CUCHULAIN: Age makes more skilful but not better men.

AOIFE: I have been told you did not know his name
 And wanted, because he had a look of me,
 To be his friend, but Conchubar forbade it.

CUCHULAIN: Forbade it and commanded me to fight;
 That very day I had sworn to do his will,
 Yet refused him, and spoke about a look;
 But somebody spoke of witchcraft and I said
 Witchcraft had made the look, and fought and killed him.
 Then I went mad, I fought against the sea.

AOIFE: I seemed invulnerable; you took my sword,
 You threw me on the ground and left me there.
 I searched the mountain for your sleeping-place
 And laid my virgin body at your side,
 And yet, because you had left me, hated you,
 And thought that I would kill you in your sleep,
 And yet begot a son that night between
 Two black thorn-trees.

CUCHULAIN: I cannot understand.

AOIFE: Because about to die!
 Somebody comes,
 Some countryman, and when he finds you here,
 And none to protect him, will be terrified.
 I will keep out of his sight, for I have things
 That I must ask questions on before I kill you.

(She goes. The BLIND MAN of On Baile's Strand comes
in. He moves his stick about until he finds the standing stone;
he lays his stick down, stoops and touches CUCHULAIN's
feet. He feels the legs.)

BLIND MAN: Ah! Ah!

CUCHULAIN: I think you are a blind old man.

BLIND MAN: A blind old beggar-man. What is your name?

CUCHULAIN: Cuchulain.

BLIND MAN: They say that you are weak with wounds.
 I stood between a Fool and the sea at Baile's Strand
 When you went mad. What's bound about your hands
 So that they cannot move? Some womanish stuff.

I have been fumbling with my stick since dawn
And then heard many voices. I began to beg.
Somebody said that I was in Maeve's tent,
And somebody else, a big man by his voice,
That if I brought Cuchulain's head in a bag
I would be given twelve pennies; I had the bag
To carry what I get at kitchen doors,
Somebody told me how to find the place;
I thought it would have taken till the night,
But this has been my lucky day.

CUCHULAIN: Twelve pennies!

BLIND MAN: I would not promise anything until the woman,
The great Queen Maeve herself, repeated the words.

CUCHULAIN: Twelve pennies! What better reason for
killing a man?
You have a knife, but have you sharpened it?

BLIND MAN: I keep it sharp because it cuts my food.
(*He lays bag on ground and begins feeling* CUCHULAIN's
body, his hands mounting upward.)

CUCHULAIN: I think that you know everything, Blind Man
My mother or my nurse said that the blind
Know everything.

BLIND MAN: No, but they have good sense.
How could I have got twelve pennies for your head
If I had not good sense?

CUCHULAIN: There floats out there
The shape that I shall take when I am dead,
My soul's first shape, a soft feathery shape,
And is not that a strange shape for the soul
Of a great fighting-man?

BLIND MAN: Your shoulder is there,
This is your neck. Ah! Ah! Are you ready, Cuchulain!

CUCHULAIN: I say it is about to sing.
(*The stage darkens.*)

BLIND MAN: Ah! Ah!
(*Music of pipe and drum, the curtain falls. The music ceases
as the curtain rises upon a bare stage. There is nobody upon the*

stage except a woman with a crow's head. She is the MORRIGU. *She stands towards the back. She holds a black parallelogram, the size of a man's head. There are six other parallelograms near the backcloth.*)

THE MORRIGU: The dead can hear me, and to the dead I speak.
    This head is great Cuchulain's, those other six
    Gave him six mortal wounds. This man came first;
    Youth lingered though the years ran on, that season
    A woman loves the best. Maeve's latest lover,
    This man, had given him the second wound,
    He had possessed her once; these were her sons,
    Two valiant men that gave the third and fourth:
    These other men were men of no account,
    They saw that he was weakening and crept in;
    One gave him the sixth wound and one the fifth;
    Conall avenged him. I arranged the dance.

(EMER *enters. The* MORRIGU *places the head of* CUCHULAIN *upon the ground and goes out.* EMER *runs in and begins to dance. She so moves that she seems to rage against the heads of those that had wounded* CUCHULAIN, *perhaps makes movements as though to strike them, going three times round the circle of the heads. She then moves towards the head of* CUCHULAIN; *it may, if need be, be raised above the others on a pedestal. She moves as if in adoration or triumph. She is about to prostrate herself before it, perhaps does so, then rises, looking up as if listening; she seems to hesitate between the head and what she hears. Then she stands motionless. There is silence, and in the silence a few faint bird notes. The stage darkens slowly. Then comes loud music, but now it is quite different. It is the music of some Irish Fair of our day. The stage brightens.* EMER *and the head are gone . . . There is no one there but the three* MUSICIANS. *They are in ragged street-singers' clothes; two of them begin to pipe and drum. They cease. The* STREET-SINGER *begins to sing.*)

SINGER: The harlot sang to the beggar-man.
    I meet them face to face,
    Conall, Cuchulain, Usna's boys,

All that most ancient race;
Maeve had three in an hour, they say.
I adore those clever eyes,
Those muscular bodies, but can get
No grip upon their thighs.
I meet those long pale faces,
Hear their great horses, then
Recall what centuries have passed
Since they were living men.
That there are still some living
That do my limbs unclothe,
But that the flesh my flesh has gripped
I both adore and loathe.

(Pipe and drum music.)

Are those things that men adore and loathe
Their sole reality?
What stood in the Post Office
With Pearse and Connolly?
What comes out of the mountain
Where men first shed their blood?
Who thought Cuchulain till it seemed
He stood where they had stood?

No body like his body
Has modern woman borne,
But an old man looking back on life
Imagines it in scorn.
A statue's there to mark the place,
By Oliver Sheppard done.
So ends the tale that the harlot
Sang to the beggar-man.

(Music from pipe and drum.)

NOTES

CATHLEEN NI HOOLIHAN

Yeats, in a note dated 1903 and addressed to Lady Gregory, gives the source of this play (the title is later spelt as *Cathleen Ni Houlihan*) as a dream he had 'almost distinct as a vision, of a cottage where there was well-being and firelight and talk of a marriage and into the midst of that cottage there came an old woman in a long cloak. She was Ireland herself, that Cathleen Ni Hoolihan for whom so many songs have been sung and about whom so many stories have been told and for whose sake so many have gone to their death.' The play was first published in *Samhain*, October 1902, and first performed at St Teresa's Total Abstinence Association Hall, Dublin, on 2 April 1902, with Maud Gonne in the title role.

p. 1   *Cathleen* (or *Kathleen*) *Ni Houlihan* a symbol of Ireland.

p. 2   *Killala* in Co. Mayo, where a French force under General Humbert landed on 22 August 1798.

p. 5   *Ballina* town in Co. Mayo.

p. 6   *Enniscrone* G.B. Saul suggested not Inchicronan, Co. Clare, but Enniscrone, a small seaside resort, in the extreme west of Co. Sligo not far from Ballina is intended.

p. 8   *too many strangers* the English in Ireland.

        four beautiful green fields the four provinces of Ireland.

p. 8   *Kilglas* village near Killala, spelt Kilglass in later versions.

p. 9   *a red man* probably 'Red' Hugh Roe O'Donnell (*c.* 1571–1602), escaped from prison in Dublin, overran Connacht, shared in victory of Yellow Ford, failed

233

to reduce Kinsale, went to Spain for aid, and was
poisoned there.

a man of the O'Sullivans probably Donal O'Sullivan
Beare (1560–1618), received a Spanish garrison in
his castle of Dunboy, 1601; Carew demolished it.
O'Sullivan fought his way to Ulster, then went to
London, but failing to obtain restitution from James,
went to Spain, where he was killed by a refugee.

one Brian Brian Boru (926–1014), High King of
Ireland, killed in victorious battle with the Danes at
Clontarf, Dublin, 1014.

p. 11   *keening* Irish form of mourning over the dead.
white-scarfed riders white-robed priests at funerals.

ON BAILE'S STRAND

Yeats began to write this play in 1901, having thought it
out while walking in the Seven Woods of Coole Park, Lady
Gregory's seat in Galway. It is based on her translation of
'The Only Son of Aoife' in *Cuchulain of Muirthemne* (1902).
The original version was first published in 1903; its main
revision occurs in the version published in 1906. It was first
performed at the opening of the Abbey Theatre, Dublin, on
27 December 1904. It is dedicated to William Fay, an Irish
working man who with his brother Frank, an accountant's
clerk, had formed a company of actors. They were distinctive actors and were members of the Abbey company until
1907, when they resigned in protest against Miss Horniman's
reorganization of the company. See W.G. Fay and Catherine
Carswell, *The Fays and the Abbey Theatre* (1935).

p. 15   *William Fay* (1872–1947), Irish actor.

p. 16   *Cuchulain, King of Muirthemne* the warrior hero of the
Táin Bó Cuálnge, or 'The Cattle Raid of Cooley', a
Gaelic epic, contained in the Red Branch or Ulster
cycle of tales. These were probably transmitted orally
in the early Christian period, then written down by

monks, and incorporated in late manuscripts in the eleventh and fifteenth centuries.

Muirthemne area ruled by Cuchulain in modern Co. Louth. Early versions of the play show that Conchubar and other kings had come to consult Cuchulain about the rebuilding of Emain, burned down after the deaths of Deirdre and Naoise, told in tale of 'The Fate of the Sons of Usna', one of the remscéla of the *Táin Bó Cuálnge*.

Conchubar King of Uladh, or Ulster.

p. 17 *Dundealgan* modern Dundalk, Co. Louth.

p. 18 *Boann* (or *Boand*) Irish goddess, wife of Naada of the Silver Hand, who gave her name to the River Boyne which rose out of a secret well into which Boann looked, though this was not allowed. The water rose and drowned her. Cf. Eleanor Hull, *A Text-book of Irish Literature* (Dublin, 1906), I, pp. 8–9. For derivation of the name, perhaps 'Cow-white goddess', see T.F. O'Rahilly, *Early Irish History and Mythology* (Dublin, 1946), p. 3. See also Kuno Meyer, *The Voyage of Bran* (1895), p. 214.

Fand (or *Fann*) wife of Manannán Mac Lir, god of the sea. She fell in love with Cuchulain, when her husband forsook her; but he claimed her again and brought her back to his realm. Her name may mean a tear, or the moisture of the eye. Cf. Eleanor Hull, ibid., p. 22.

p. 19 *a young man* Conlaech, Cuchulain's son by Aoife.

Aoife's country Aoife was a warrior queen in Scotland, who was an enemy of Scathach (see note, p. 236). Cuchulain conquered her, and forced her to grant him three wishes. She was to become Scathach's vassal, to sleep one night with him, and to bear him a son.

p. 20 *Banachas and Bonachas* demons of the air, that screamed around warriors in combat.

Fomor head of the Fomorians, gods of darkness,

finally overthrown by the Tuatha de Danaan, gods
of life and light.

p. 23 *Maeve of Cruachan* Queen of Connacht, married to
Ailill; she was an amorous and warlike woman.
Cruachan (modern Rathcrogan, Co. Roscommon)
was the capital of Connacht.

the northern pirates Norse invaders, whose power was
finally crushed by Brian Boru in the Battle of
Clontarf, 1014.

Sorcha part of the Gaelic Otherworld.

p. 24 *your father* one tradition held that Cuchulain was the
son of Lugh, the god of light. In *At the Hawk's Well*
his father is Sualtam.

p.25 *Country-under-Wave* Tir-fa-tonn, Otherworld in Gaelic
mythology.

p. 34 *Laegaire* or Laeghaire Buadach, Leary the Triumphant,
a hero of the Red Branch.

p. 39 *Scathach* warrior woman of the Island of Skye who
taught Cuchulain the art of war.

Uathach daughter of Scathach, who was attracted by
Cuchulain's beauty and made him welcome when he
visited Scathach; he rewarded her by attacking her
and killing the champion who came to her aid.

p. 40 *Alba* Scotland.

Dubthach the Chafer character in *Táin Bó Cuálnge*.
He was sent by Conchubar as an emissary with
Fergus (see *Deirdre*, pp. 46–53) to bring Deirdre,
Naoise and his brothers back from Scotland. After
the murder of Naoise and death of Deirdre he joined
Queen Maeve.

DEIRDRE

Yeats probably began to write this play in prose; he was
working on it in 1905 and 1906, largely at Coole Park. He was
aware of the story of 'The Tragical Fate of the Sons of Usna' in

many forms (there were prose translations, by O'Flanagan in the *Transactions of the Iberno-Celtic Society* and by O'Curry in *Atlantis*; Sir Samuel Ferguson wrote his version in verse) but based his play on Lady Gregory's *Cuchulain of Muirthemne* (1902). It was first published in 1907 and first performed at the Abbey Theatre, Dublin, on 26 November 1906. The dedication is to Mrs Patrick Campbell who took the part of Deirdre in 1906, 1907, and 1908.

p. 43 *Mrs Patrick Campbell* (1867–1940), famous actress.

  Robert Gregory (1881–1918), son of Lady Gregory, painter and designer, shot down over Italy in 1918; for praise of his versatility see Yeats's poem 'In Memory of Major Robert Gregory'.

p. 44 *Fergus* MacRoy or Son of Rogh, former king of Ulster who was tricked out of his crown by Ness, the mother of Conchubar. He was the poet of the Red Branch cycle of tales.

  Naoise son of Usna; one of Conchubar's warriors.

  Deirdre formerly Conchubar's ward whom he kept in the hills in the care of an old nurse Lavarcham, intending to marry her. Naoise, one of his warriors, saw her, fell in love with her, and ran away with her to Scotland, accompanied by his brothers Ainle and Ardan. Deirdre prophesied she would bring suffering on Ulster.

p. 49 *Lugaidh Redstripe* a hero of the Red Branch.

  Queen Edain or Etáin, a beautiful woman, wooed, won, and taken to the Otherworld by King Midir. Here, she is changed into a fly by Fuamorach, Midir's wife, who blows her into this world, where she is reborn three times before Midir, in a game of chess, finally wins her back to the Otherworld. The account of this forms one of the major tales in the mythological cycle, *The Wooing of Etáin*.

p. 50 *a king of Surracha* possibly Sorcha, Gaelic Otherworld. O'Rahilly explains the name as originally *Syriaca*, Syria, influenced by the native word *Sorcha*, bright. In later romantic literature it denotes an exotic country with no precise geographical position.

p. 54   *The hot Istain stone, And the cold stone of Fanes* – the source for these images is Lady Gregory, *A Book of Saints and Wonders* (2nd ed., 1908, p. 154): 'The stone of Istien in the lands of Lybia is found in the brains of dragons after their death. The pools and the great lakes boil up by reason of it over their borders; it shines through water; it is like thunder in the winter time but in summer it has the sound of the winds. The stone of Fanes in the lands of Aulol out of the stream of Dara. Twelve stars there are seen in its side and the wheel of the moon and the fiery journey of the sun. In the hearts of the dragons it is always found that make their journey under the sea. No one having it in his hand can tell any lie till he has put it from him. No race or army could bring it into a house where there is one that has made away with his father. At the hour of matins it gives out sweet music that there is not the like of under heaven.' Lady Gregory's source was *Tenga Bithnua*, The Evernew Tongue; she used the version in the late fifteenth-century *Book of Lismore*, edited by Whitley Stokes, *Eriu* II, p. 117. This information is owed to Dr James Stewart of the University of Copenhagen.

p. 56   *a golden tongue* Fergus was occasionally called 'Honeymouth'.

p. 65   *The daughter of the King of Leodas* G.B. Saul, *Prolegomena to the Study of Yeats's Plays* (1958), p. 46, suggests Leodas may be 'an imaginary Pictish king? – the "Lord of Duntreon"?' Dun Treóin is in Argyll. Leodas is from Leòdhas, Gaelic name of the Isle of Lewis. Since rhyme in modern Irish is that of vowels only Treóin and Leòdhais (gen. of Leòdhas) would be interchangeable in the verse quoted, if it translated an original. In versions of the Deirdre story the woman who causes jealousy is the daughter of the Earl of Dún Treóin. I am indebted to the late Professor David Greene for this information.

THE PLAYER QUEEN

Yeats began to write this play in 1907 (cf. *Plays in Prose and Verse*, 1922, p. 429) with the intention of making a verse tragedy of it. He finished a prose draft in 1908, and was working on a further prose scenario in 1909. He continued to work on the play in 1914 and 1916. The first performance was at the King's Hall, Covent Garden, London, on 25 May 1919; the first published version is that of 1922.

p. 77 *Kubla Khan*, or *Kublai Khan* founder of Mongol dynasty in the thirteenth century.

p. 79 *the Bible says* Exodus 22: 18.

Candlemas celebrated on 2 February.

p. 84 *the donkey* see Matthew 21: 2–10.

p. 86 *The Tragical History of Noah's Deluge* probably *Noah and the Flood*, a Chester miracle play.

p. 88 *Saint Octema* an invented character.

p. 89 *Sleep of Adam* Genesis 2: 21.

p. 96 *Pasiphae* in mythology the daughter of Helios, married to Minos of Crete who, in order to secure the throne, prayed to Poseidon to send him a bull from the sea to sacrifice. The bull was so beautiful that Minos would not kill it, whereupon Pasiphae fell in love with it, disguised herself as a cow, and bore the Minotaur, half-man, half-bull, which lived in the labyrinth at Crete.

Leda in mythology the mother of the Dioscuri and Helen, Zeus having coupled with her in the shape of a swan. Leda was also the mother of Clytemnestra by her husband Tyndareus, King of Sparta.

p. 97 *Cato* Marcius Porcius Cato Uticensis (95–46 BC)
was a Roman stoic who supported Pompey and,
after his defeat, joined the Pompeians in Africa.
After Caesar's victory at Thapsus, he committed
suicide at Pharsalus.

Cicero Marcius Tullius Cicero (106–43 BC), Roman
orator, author, politician, led the opposition to
Antony and faced death bravely after Octavian
took Rome.

Athenian orator, *Demosthenes* (384–322 BC), who,
while in exile, tried to organize combined action
against Macedon after the death of Alexander. He
returned to Athens, which was subsequently occupied by a Macedonian garrison, and a decree for
his execution was passed. He took refuge in a temple;
being pursued there, sucked poison concealed in
his pen and died.

Petronius Arbiter Roman (*d.* AD 66), author of *Cena
Trimalchicius*, a former proconsul and Nero's *arbiter
elegantiae*, who, when Nero was turned against him
by Tigellinus, committed suicide, writing a docu-
ment denouncing Nero and his accomplices.

p. 98 *Xanadu* where Kubla Khan decreed a lordly pleasure
house, in Coleridge's 'Kubla Khan'; the source is
Purchas his Pilgrimes (1625).

Agamemnon husband of Clytemnestra, brother of
Menelaus, and leader of Greek armies against Troy.
He sacrificed his daughter Iphigenia at Aulis, was
murdered on his return to Argos by Clytemnestra
and Aegisthus, her paramour.

Helen wife of Menelaus, who went to Troy with
Paris, son of Priam, and was thus the cause of
the Trojan war.

p. 100 *Ionian music . . . Dorian scale* Yeats is making the
normal distinction here between these modes of
Greek music: the Ionic soft and effeminate, the
Dorian simple and solemn.

Delphi situated on slopes of Mount Parnassus, was the seat of a temple of Apollo and of a famous oracle, very influential between the eighth and fifth centuries BC.

p. 101 *The Christian Era . . . an end* an idea expressed by Yeats in 'A Vision' and in many poems, that history consists of opposing gyres, one age being the reversal of another.

THE DREAMING OF THE BONES

This play was first published in *The Little Review*, January 1919, and subsequently in *Two Plays for Dancers* (1919). It was first performed at the Abbey Theatre, Dublin, on 6 December 1931. Yeats mentioned Dermot (the Irish form is Diarmuid) and Dervorgilla in a story of 1897, 'Hanrahan's Vision', which has echoes of Dante's story of Paolo and Francesca. Lady Gregory's play *Dervorgilla* (1911) may have suggested the theme of the absolution of guilt. Yeats in his Introduction to *Four Plays for Dancers* (1921) said the prolonged penance of Dermot and Dervorgilla had warrant in the folklore of all countries. The need for penance was that Diarmuid Mac Murrough, King of Leinster, carried off Dervorgilla, daughter of the King of Meath, the wife of Tegernan O'Rourke in 1152. When subsequently driven out of Leinster by Dervorgilla's estranged husband in 1168, Diarmuid appealed to Henry II of England for permission to recruit among his subjects. He engaged the services of Richard Fitzgilbert de Clare, Earl of Pembroke (*c*. 1130–1176), known as Strongbow, who was to bring an army from Wales to Ireland. Diarmuid promised Strongbow his daughter Eva in marriage and the succession to his kingdom (though this was contrary to Irish law). The first Anglo-Norman force landed at Baginbun, Co. Wexford, in 1169, and Strongbow himself followed in 1170, becoming King of Leinster on Diarmuid's death in 1171. Dervorgilla outlived O'Rourke, Diarmuid, Henry and Strongbow, dying at Mellefont Abbey near Drogheda in 1193 at the age of eighty-five.

In his essay 'Swedenborg, Mediums, and the Desolate Places' Yeats acknowledged the influence of the Japanese Noh play, *Nishikigi*, in which a priest is wandering in an ancient village; he describes the journey and the scene. He meets two ghosts, dressed in old-fashioned clothes; they seem to the priest to be a married couple but he cannot understand why one carries a red stick, the other a piece of coarse cloth. They tell the priest that a young man had for three years offered a red stick, a token of love, at the young girl's window, but she had pretended not to see it and went on weaving. The young man died and was buried in a cave with his red sticks; the girl died too. They were never married in life and remain unmarried in death. The priest, who does not yet realize that the ghosts are telling their own story, asks to see the cave. The chorus describes the day's journey to the cave. The lovers slip into the shadows; the priest prays the lovers may be one. The cave is lighted up; the ghosts thank him for his prayer. Through his pity the love promises of long-past incarnations find fulfilment in a dream. He sees the love story in a vision, sees the lovers drinking from a bridal cup. All dissolves like a dream, the deserted grave left on the hillside.

The influence of the Noh on Yeats is thoroughly discussed in Masaru Sekine and Christopher Murray, *Yeats and Noh, A Comparative Study* (1990) – In *Irish Writers and the Theatre*, Ed. Masaru Sekine (1986) Sekine includes his own very useful essay on 'Yeats and the Noh' – who point out that *Nishikigi* is a typical dream play, that Yeats had earlier emphasized the supernatural in his story 'Hanrahan's Vision' but in *The Dreaming of the Bones* deals with the conflict between 'the individual and historical consciousness'.

p. 111 *Time–1916* Yeats put the essentials of the Japanese story of *Nishikigi* into an Irish setting by identifying its lovers with the historical Diarmuid and Dervorgilla; by turning the Japanese priest into a

young man who has been involved in the Easter
Rising of 1916 and is anxious to escape to the Aran
Islands he gave the play a contemporary political
reference which he feared might be 'too powerful'.
This is why the play was not performed in Ireland
until 1931.

old writers possibly writers in the occult tradition
such as Cornelius Agrippa (1486–1535), Henry More
(1614–1687) or Emmanuel Swedenborg (1688–1772).

Like wine . . . jade possibly suggested by the end of
Nishikigi where the ghosts of the two lovers finally
drink from a bridal cup when the priest has, through
his pity and his prayer that they may at last be one,
brought about the fulfilment of the love promises of
past incarnations in a dream.

p. 112 *Abbey of Corcomroe* situated in the northern part
of Co. Clare, it was associated with Donough
O'Brien, one of a group of Irish nobles who
invited the Scots to invade Thomond and take it
from the king. When they were defeated Donough
escaped from the battlefield at Athenry but fell in
1317, near the Abbey. The name is derived from
Corca Modhruadh, the children of Modhruadh, the
son of Maeve by Fergus MacRoigh. For Maeve see
note on p. 236; for Fergus note on p. 237.

bawneen traditional West of Ireland home-spun flannel
jacket without pockets or lapels.

the Post Office the General Post Office, Dublin, was a
centre of fighting in the Easter Rising of 1916. Yeats
refers to it in 'The Statues', *Yeats's Poems*, p. 460,
linking Patrick Pearse who was in command there
with the Irish hero Cuchulain (Oliver Sheppard's
statue of Cuchulain was placed in the rebuilt Post
Office).

p. 113 *Muckanish . . . Finvara* the first, the Promontory of
the Seals, is a promontory in Co. Clare near
Corcomroe Abbey, the second, the Wood by the

Sea, is a promontory on the coast of north Co. Clare.

when a man is born in Ireland . . . against us a general but one that relates to Diarmuid's bringing the Normans into Ireland.

Aughanish . . . Bailevelehan . . . Aughtmana these local names are introduced to give the scene an objective reality. Aughanish, the Promontory of the Horse, is in north Co. Clare; Bailevelehan, the Place of the Pathway, is also in north Co. Clare between New Quay and Corcomroe. Aughtmana, the Breast of the Mountain Pass, is in Co. Galway, a valley near Corcomroe Abbey.

p. 115 *a cloud* the element in which the lovers move.

cat-headed bird cat-headed birds appear in Yeats's *The Shadowy Waters*; they are the spirits of the dead.

p. 116 *Donough O'Brien* see note above on Abbey of Corcomroe.

the King of Thomond another of the regional kings, Diarmuid Mac Morrough being King of Leinster.

p. 118 *Helen* the Young Girl sees the crime of Dermot and Dervorgilla in terms of personal passion, but the Young Man sees their behaviour in terms of politics, resulting in the Rising of 1916 and his own situation after the fighting in Dublin ended in the surrender of the rebel forces. He refuses to pardon the lovers, to forgive their crime.

p. 119 *seven hundred years* a round number. Dermot carried off Dervorgilla in 1152; the first Norman landing was in 1169; Dermot died before Dervorgilla whose death occurred in 1193.

p. 120 *Music of a lost kingdom* possibly the supernatural music of the Irish faery world; perhaps also the music made by the spirits of the dead, described by Henry More in *The Immortality of the Soul* and quoted by Yeats in 'Swedenborg, Mediums, and the Desolate Places': 'thin melodious singing and

playing with an accent so sweet and soft as if we
should imagine air itself to compose lessons and
send forth musical sounds without the help of any
terrestrial instrument'.

THE ONLY JEALOUSY OF EMER

Yeats began this play in 1916 and finished it in January
1918. The story probably derives from the legendary tale
The Sickbed [or *Wasting-away*] of Cuchulain which is the basis
for Lady Gregory's 'The Only Jealousy of Emer' in *Cuchulain
of Muirthemne* (1902). The play was first published in *Poetry*
(Chicago), January 1919, then in *Two Plays for Dancers* (1919).
There were several revisions, the major ones contained in the
version included in *Collected Plays* (1934). The play was first
publicly performed in Holland with masks by Hildo van Krop.
Cf. W.B. Yeats, *Wheels and Butterflies* (1934), p. 69. A prose
version, *Fighting the Waves*, written in 1928, was performed
at the Abbey Theatre, Dublin on 13 August 1929.

p. 124 *Cuchulain* see note, p. 234.

    Emer Cuchulain's wife whom he won after a series
    of trials.

    Eithne Inguba Cuchulain's young mistress.

    Sidhe the gods of ancient Ireland.

p. 125 *Archimedes* (287–212 BC), of Syracuse, a mathema-
    tician and inventor.

p. 127 *Baile's tree* a reference to the story of Baile and
    Aillinn, lovers, to each of whom Aengus, the
    god of love, gave false news of the other's death.
    They died of broken hearts and were changed into
    white swans linked by a golden chain. A yew tree
    grew where Baile's body lay, a wild apple where
    Aillinn's.

p. 128 *Manannan, Son of the Sea* Manannán Mac Lir, the
    god of the sea.

p. 130 *Bricriu* the figure is here distinguishing itself from

Conchubar's poet Bricriu, known for his bitterness.

p. 133 *a hawk flew* this refers to Yeats's play *At the Hawk's Well*, where Cuchulain is deceived by the guardian of the well, half-hawk, half-woman.

p. 135 *Fand* wife of Manannán Mac Lir, see note p. 235.

THE RESURRECTION

Yeats drafted this play in 1925. It was first published in June 1927 in the *Adelphi*, then in *Stories of Michael Robartes and His Friends* (1921), and later in *Wheels and Butterflies* (1934). The first performance was at the Abbey Theatre, Dublin, on 30 July 1934.

p. 130 *Junzo Sato* a Japanese who met Yeats after a lecture in Portland, Oregon, and gave him a sword which is mentioned in 'Meditations in Time of Civil War, III', and in 'A Dialogue of Self and Soul'.

p. 141 *the Peacock Theatre* a small theatre (sometimes used for rehearsals) attached to the Abbey Theatre, Dublin.

Dionysus Greek god of an emotional religion which particularly affected women, who seized an animal or a child at the height of their ecstasy and, tearing it apart, ate the pieces, believing they were incorporating the god and his power within themselves in so doing. These lines draw a parallel between the myth of Dionysus and the death and resurrection of Christ. Ellmann (*Identity of Yeats*, 1954, p. 260) draws on Sir James Frazer's *The Golden Bough* (which Yeats read) for this explanation: Dionysus, child of a mortal, Persephone, and an immortal, Zeus, was torn to pieces by the Titans. Athene (the 'staring virgin' of the poem: 'staring' indicating that she acts as if in a trance because the events are preordained) snatched the heart from his body, brought it on her hand to Zeus, who killed the Titans, swallowed the heart, and begat Dionysus again, upon another mortal, Semele.

that beating heart in his introduction to this play Yeats gives Sir William Crookes's *Studies in Psychical Research* as a source for this image.

Magnus Annus this passage is explained by a passage in *A Vision* (1926), p. 149; (1990), p. 243, quoting Virgil's Fourth Eclogue: 'the cycles in their vast array begin anew; virgin Astrea comes, the reign of Saturn comes, and from the heights of Heaven a new generation of mankind descends . . . Apollo now is king, and in your consulship, in yours, Pollio, the age of glory shall commence.' The verses state Yeats's idea that Christianity brought a radical violence into the world and ushered in a new historical period. See also *A Vision* (1937), pages 243–54, where he discusses the idea of a Great Year. The Muses sing of Magnus Annus as a play because they regard the ritual death and rebirth of the god as a recurring event, part of the cycles of history. Ellmann points out that 'both Gods had died and been reborn in March when the sun was between the Ram and the Fish, and when the moon was beside the constellation Virgo, who carries the star Spica in her hand'. In these stanzas Yeats is thinking of Virgil, Eclogue IV, 6 'Iam redit et Virgo . . . ' where Virgo, daughter of Jupiter and Themis, is the last to leave Earth at the end of the golden age; but will return, bringing back the golden age. This Virgilian prophecy was later read as foretelling the coming of Mary (as Virgo) and Christ, the star of Bethlehem (as Spica).

Argo's Argo was the ship in which Jason sailed to fetch the Golden Fleece. The idea of a second Argo is in Virgil's Fourth Eclogue and also in Shelley's *Hellas*.

p. 142 *The Roman Empire stood appalled* because though there were but 6 million Christians in the Roman

Empire's 60 million, the world was to become Christian, and the Empire to be destroyed by Christianity (a view Yeats shared with Gibbon).

that fierce virgin Mary. Here R. Ellmann, ibid., p. 261, remarks that these lines daringly assert a parallelism and even identity between the three pairs, Astraea and Spica, Athene and Dionysus, and Mary and Christ. Cf. Lady Gregory, *Journal*, 263, for an early version reading 'Virgo [the constellation] and the mystic star'.

the fabulous darkness probably derived from a description of Christianity by Proclus, a fourth-century neo-Platonic philosopher (whom Yeats read in Thomas Taylor's translation of 1816, cf. F.A.C. Wilson, *Yeats and Tradition*, p. 59). Cf. *A Vision* (1937), pp. 277–8, *A Vision* (1926), pp. 185 *seq.* and *A Vision*, ed. A. Norman Jeffares (1990), p. 266 *seq.*

  ' . . . The irrational force that would create confusion and uproar as with the cry "The Babe, the Babe, is born" – the women speaking unknown tongues, the barbers and weavers expounding Divine revelation with all the vulgarity of their servitude, the tables that move or resound with raps – but creates a negligible sect. All about it is an *antithetical* aristocratic civilization in its completed form, every detail of life hierarchical, every great man's door crowded at dawn by petitioners, great wealth everywhere in few men's hands, all dependent upon a few, up to the Emperor himself who is a God dependent upon a greater God, and, everywhere in court, in the family, an inequality made law, and floating over all the Romanized Gods of Greece in their physical superiority . . . The world became Christian, "that fabulous formless darkness" as it seemed to a philosopher of the fourth century, blotted out "every beautiful thing", not through the conversion of crowds or general change of opinion, or through any pressure from below, for civilization was *antithetical* still, but by an act of power.'

the Eleven the disciples, minus Judas.

p. 143 *thirteen* Christ and the twelve disciples.

Jesus divided bread and wine see Matthew 26: 26–7.

Peter see Matthew 26: 37–75.

p. 144 *born of a woman* see Isaiah 7: 14.

p. 146 *Astrea's* Astrea, a daughter of Zeus, was said to have lived on earth and been a source of blessing to men during the Golden Age. She is mentioned in the passage from Virgil quoted above. G.B. Saul, *op. cit.*, p. 85, remarks, 'Astræa: goddess of justice, sometimes regarded as the daughter of the Titan Astraeus by Eos; in her heavenly transformation, Virgo.'

p. 147 *the goddess* Athene. Cf. W.B. Yeats 'The Phases of the Moon', *Yeats's Poems*, p. 267.

Achilles son of Peleus and Thetis, bravest of the Greeks in the Trojan war, was wounded in his heel (the only vulnerable part of his body, by which Thetis had held him when plunging him in the Styx) by Paris and died.

Lucretius Titus Lucretius Carus (*c.* 99–55 BC), Roman poet and author of *De Rerum Naturae*, a philosophical poem in which he tries to show that the course of the world can be explained without divine intervention.

p. 152 *the heart of a phantom* see note p. 247.

Heracleitus of Ephesus, wrote a work 'Concerning Nature' in which he asserted all things were in a state of flux.

Galilean turbulence foretold by astronomers in Babylon who reduce man's status by their science; Man is being taught that he is nothing in comparison to the universe; He is becoming featureless: cf. *A Vision* (1937), pp. 273 *seq.* and *A Vision* (1990), p. 264:

> 'The mind that brought the change, if considered as man only, is a climax of whatever Greek and Roman thought was most a contradiction to its age; but considered as more than man He controlled what Neo-Pythagorean and Stoic could not – irrational force. He could announce the new age, all that had not been thought of, or touched, or seen, because He could substitute for reason, miracle.'

Everything that man esteems a praise of man, who goes on creating heroically despite the fact that all things pass away. Cf. W.B. Yeats, *Autobiographies*, p. 315.

THE WORDS UPON THE WINDOW-PANE

The starting point for this play, according to Allan Wade, *The Letters of W.B. Yeats* (1954), p. 891 *n.*, was Yeats's finding in 1910 an inscription cut on a window in Oliver St John Gogarty's Dublin house 'Fairfield'. He wrote the play when he was reading deeply in Swift during 1930; it was finished in October and performed at the Abbey Theatre, Dublin, on 17 November 1930. It was first published in 1934.

p. 153 *Lady Gregory* Lady Augusta Gregory (1852–1932), Irish playwright, widow of Sir William Gregory; she co-operated with Yeats in establishing the Abbey Theatre.

p. 155 *the Corbets of Ballymoney* Yeats had Corbet relatives, but this name and that of Ballymoney (there are many villages or towns with this name in Ireland, for instance, in Co. Antrim, Co. Cork, Co. Wexford) are probably taken to indicate a young man of some social and intellectual standing.

p. 156 *Myers' Human Personality* written by F.W.H. Myers (1843–1901) and published in 1903 in two volumes.

a wild book either *A New Revelation* (1918) or *A History of Spiritualism* (2 vols., 1926) by Sir Arthur

Conan Doyle, perhaps more widely known for his
Sherlock Holmes detective stories.

Lord Dunraven, then Lord Adare introduced to 'place'
Dr Trench. The full title of this Irish peerage
created for the Quin family was Earl of Dunraven
and Viscount Adare. This reference is probably to
the third Earl, Edward Wyndham-Quin, a scholar
of literature and archaeology.

David Home presumably Daniel D. Home (1833–
1886), Scottish medium and spiritualist.

Emanuel Swedenborg (1688–1772), Swedish scientist
and mystic philosopher, devoted his life after 1745 to
interpreting the scriptures, his being a theosophical
system.

Harold's Cross Dublin suburb and situation of dog-
racing track.

p. 157 *Grattan* Henry Grattan (1746–1820), Irish barrister
and MP; carried an address demanding legislative
independence in 1782. The Irish parliament which
lasted until 1800 was known as Grattan's parliament.

Curran John Philpot Curran (1750–1817), Irish barrister and MP, who defended the prisoners in the
1798 trials and opposed the Union.

Jonathan Swift (1667–1745), Dean of St Patrick's
Cathedral, Dublin.

Journal to Stella Swift's letters (1710–1713) to Esther
Johnson and Rebecca Dingley, her companion.

Stella Swift's name for Esther Johnson (1681–1728).
They met in Sir William Temple's household when
he was secretary there; they were close friends till
her death. He was buried by her side in St Patrick's
Cathedral.

Vanessa Swift's name for Esther Vanhomrigh (1690–
1723), whom he met in London in 1708; she fell in
love with him, and Swift's poem 'Cadenus and
Vanessa' is an account of their unhappy relation-
ship.

p. 158 *Bolingbroke* Henry St John Bolingbroke, first Viscount (1678–1751), friend of Swift, author, orator, politician, in charge of the negotiations leading to the Peace of Utrecht in 1710. Dismissed on the accession of George I, he fled to France, but returned in 1723.

Harley first Earl of Oxford (1661–1724), friend of Swift, a moderate Tory who supported the act of Settlement. He remained in a Whig ministry until 1708. In 1710 he and St John led the Tory Ministry which brought about the Treaty of Utrecht (1713). He was dismissed in 1714 through the Jacobite intrigues of his colleague.

Ormonde James Butler, Duke of Ormonde (1610–1688), born of an ancient Anglo-Irish family, distinguished himself in the Strafford administration and in the rebellions of 1640 was appointed chief commander of the army. James Butler, second Duke of Ormonde (1665–1746), served in the army against Monmouth, at the Battle of the Boyne; Lord Lieutenant of Ireland three times 1703–13; impeached for high treason 1705, retired to Avignon. The Duke was greatly admired by Swift. Benjamin Yeats married into the family in 1773. Yeats's family valued this connection using 'Butler' frequently as a Christian name.

Brutus Marcius Junius Brutus (85–42 BC) joined Pompey, but was pardoned by Caesar after the battle of Pharsalia. Joined the conspiracy against Caesar; after the latter's murder Brutus and Cassius were defeated at Philippi and Brutus committed suicide.

Cato see note, p. 240.

p. 159 *Jean Jacques Rousseau* (1712–1778), born at Geneva, author and philosopher. His *Du Contrat Social* (1762) prepared the way for the French Revolution.

saeva indignatio from Swift's epitaph in St Patrick's Cathedral, Dublin (for Yeats's version, see *Yeats's Poems*, p. 361), which runs:

Hic depositum est Corpus
IONATHAN SWIFT S.T.D.
Hujus Ecclesiae Cathedralis
Decani,
Ubi saeva Indignatio
Ulterius
Cor lacerare nequit.
Abi Viator
Et imitare, si poteris,
Strenuum pro virili
Libertatis Vindicatorem
Obiit 19° Die Mensis Octobris
A.D. 1745 Anno Aetatis 78

p. 162 *the quotation*, Job 4: 13–15: 'In thoughts from the visions of the night, when deep sleep falleth on men, Fear came upon me, and trembling which made all my bones to shake. Then a spirit passed before my face; the hair of my flesh stood up.'

p. 164 *the Lord Treasurer* Robert Harley, first Earl of Oxford (1661–1724).

Plutarch (*c.* AD 46–120), Greek biographer, wrote parallel lives of twenty-three Greeks and twenty-three Romans.

p. 165 *Dr Arbuthnot* Dr John Arbuthnot (1667–1735) was Queen Anne's doctor, an author, and a friend of Swift and Pope.

a line of Dryden's 'great wits are sure to madness / Near allied', from Dryden's *Absalom and Achitophel*, I. 163.

p. 167 *Chrysostom* St John (*c.* AD 345–407), eloquent (Chrysostom = golden-mouthed) Greek Father of the Church, wrote commentaries on the Gospel of St Matthew and the Epistles to the Romans and Corinthians.

p. 170 *His brain had gone* probably not correct, but for an expert view of Swift's health see T.G. Wilson,

'Swift's Personality and Death Masks', *A Review of English Literature*, July 1962.

p. 170 *perish the day* from Job 3: 3: 'Let the day perish wherein I was born.'

A FULL MOON IN MARCH

Yeats developed this play, first published in 1935, from *The King of The Great Clock Tower* (1934), which was first written in prose, and on which he was working in 1933. He may have begun to work on the idea about 1929.

p. 173 *Pythagoras* a Greek philosopher of the sixth century BC who thought the universe had a mathematical basis. He believed in the Orphic doctrine of metempsychosis, the purificatory or punishing process in which souls transmigrated from man to man, or man to animal or animal to man.

p. 177 *An ancient Irish Queen* Queen Maeve of Connacht.

p. 178 *an innkeeper's daughter* the Empress Theophano, married by Romanus II, *c*. AD 956.

THE HERNE'S EGG

Yeats began to write this play in 1935. It was first published in 1938 and first performed by Lord Longford's company in 1939; it was later performed at the Abbey Theatre on 29 October and 5 November 1950. Mr Austin Clarke has suggested that the play is founded on a passage in Sir Samuel Ferguson's *Congal* (1872).

p. 182 *Congal* an Ulster king who rebelled against the High King Domnal in an attempt to reassert paganism; he was defeated at the Battle of Moyra.

Connacht one of the five ancient kingdoms of Ireland, its capital being Cruachan.

Aedh Irish for Hugh.

  Tara a hill in Co. Meath, seat of government of
  the High Kings of Ireland.

p. 183 *a great herne* a heron.

p. 186 *Danae's lap* Danae was the daughter of Acrisius, king
  of Argos, who shut her in a brazen tower as an oracle
  foretold he would be killed by his daughter's son.
  Zeus fell in love with her and visited her in a shower
  of gold; their son was Perseus, who eventually did
  kill his grandfather by accident.

p. 197 *Munster* southern province of Ireland.

p. 202 *Slieve Fuadh* (modern Sliabh Fuaid) the highest
  mountain in the Fews range in Armagh. Cuchulain
  when setting off from Dundalk to Emain Macha as
  a boy was told by his mother that he would have a
  hard journey as Slieve Fuadh lay in between.

PURGATORY

Yeats wrote this play between March and May 1938. It
was first published in *Last Poems and Two Plays* (1939) and
first performed at the Abbey Theatre, Dublin, on 10 August
1938.

p. 212 *the Curragh* district in Co. Kildare, famous for its
  race-course and as a breeding and training ground
  for race-horses.

p. 213 *Aughrim and the Boyne* two battles crucial in Irish
  and European history. At the Boyne on 1 July
  1690, William defeated James and thus brought
  about the triumph of Louis's European opponents.
  At Aughrim, twelve days later, Ginkle, William's
  Dutch commander, broke the Irish army, 11,000
  men of which left for France after the Siege of
  Limerick ended in October 1690.

p. 214 *the Puck Fair* an annual festival lasting three days
  and nights (Gathering Day, Market or Fair Day
  and Scattering Day), held at Kilorglin, Co. Kerry.

A goat is still crowned king as part of the ceremonies, which are attended by many of the tinkers of Ireland.

p. 215 *Tertullian* Quintus Septimus Florens Tertullianus (*c.* AD 160–225), lawyer and author, native of the Roman province of Africa, was converted to Christianity; his *Apology* rebuts charges against Christianity.

THE DEATH OF CUCHULAIN

Yeats began this play in the autumn of 1938, ending it before Christmas of that year. It was first published in *Last Poems and Two Plays* (1939) and first performed at the Abbey Theatre, Dublin, in 1949.

p. 220 *Cuchulain* see note, p. 234.
  Eithne Inguba see note, p. 245.
  Aoife see note, p. 235.
  Emer see note, p. 245.

p. 221 *Talma* François Joseph Talma (1763–1826), French tragedian.

p. 222 *Degas* Hilaire Germaine Edgar Degas (1834–1917), French painter.
  Rameses the Great (1311–1245 BC), Pharaoh of Egypt.
  Maeve see note, p. 236.
  Emain Macha capital of Ulster sited near modern Armagh, said to have been burnt in AD 332.

p. 223 *Conall Caernach* an Ulster hero, greatest in prowess after Culchulain.
  The Morrigu a crow-headed war goddess.
  At the Hawk's Well Yeats began *At the Hawk's Well* in 1915; it was first performed in Lady Cunard's drawing room in London in March 1916, first published in 1917. This play tells how Cuchulain is lured away by the woman of the well and begets a son on her.

Upon Baile's Strand Yeats's play *On Baile's Strand* (see pp. 15–42) tells the story of how Cuchulain kills his son.

The grey of Macha one of Cuchulain's two chariot horses, a kelpie or lake-horse.

p. 229 *Maeve's latest lover* the Queen was notoriously amorous.

her sons . . . these other men It is likely that Yeats is using poetic licence here. In the oldest version of the legend the hero is killed by Lugaid mac Con Roí and Erc mac Coirbri, by three magic spears prepared by the three sons of Calatín. Later versions add MacNiad mac Finn maic Rosa, to make one man for each spear. The fathers of all six had been killed by Cuchulain; this is the reason given for their combining to kill him.

Usna's boys Naoise and his brothers, Ardan and Ainle, who had accompanied him into Scotland when he ran away with Deirdre, King Conchubar's ward.

p. 230 *the Post Office* The General Post Office, Dublin, was held by the insurgents in the Easter Rising 1916, and was the scene of their surrender.

Pearse Patrick Henry Pearse (1879–1916), Irish poet and leader, shot for taking part in the 1916 Rising, when he was president of the provisional government.

Connolly James Connolly (1870–1916), Irish trade-union leader and organizer of the Irish Citizen Army, shot for his part in the 1916 Rising.

Oliver Sheppard (d. 1941), Irish sculptor.

SELECT BIBLIOGRAPHY

EDITIONS OF YEATS'S POEMS AND PLAYS

The Collected Works in Verse and Prose of William Butler Yeats (8 vols., 1908)
   Volumes II, III, and IV contain the texts of plays and notes.
Plays in Prose and Verse for an Irish Theatre (1922)
   Contains brief notes on the plays.
Plays and Controversies (1923)
   Contains essays on 'The Irish Dramatic Movement' and 'A People's Theatre'.
Wheels and Butterflies (1934)
   Contains very useful introduction.
Collected Plays (1934)
Last Poems and Plays (1940)
Collected Plays (1952)
   A good edition, though the dates supplied are misleading. Peter Ure, *Yeats the Playwright* (1963) gives useful information on the dates of composition, publication and performance; see also Allan Wade, *A Bibliography of the Writings of W.B. Yeats* (1951; 1958; 3rd rev. ed., 1968).
Russell K. Alspach (ed.), *The Variorum Edition of the Plays of W.B. Yeats* (1966)
Yeats's Poems, ed. A. Norman Jeffares (1989)

CRITICISM AND BIOGRAPHY

W.B. Yeats, *Essays and Introductions* (1961); *Explorations* (1962)
These two volumes contain essays by Yeats on the theatre and on particular plays and dramatists. Selections are contained in Pan Classics, *Selected Criticism & Prose* (1980).

W.B. Yeats, *A Vision* ed. A. Norman Jeffares (1990).
Several of the ideas in Yeats's later plays are related to this book.

Joseph Hone, *W.B. Yeats 1865–1939* (1943; rev. ed., 1963).

A. Norman Jeffares, *Yeats: Man and Poet* (1949; rev. ed., 1962).

A. Norman Jeffares, *W.B. Yeats: A New Biography* (1988; paperback rev. ed. 1990).

Birgit Bjersby, *The Interpretation of the Cuchulain Legend in the Works of W.B. Yeats* (1950).

Una Ellis Fermor, *The Irish Dramatic Movement* (2nd ed., 1954).

T.R. Henn, *The Lonely Tower* (1950; rev. ed., 1965).

G.B. Saul, *Prolegomena to the Plays of W.B. Yeats* (1958).

F.A.C. Wilson, *W.B. Yeats and Tradition* (1958).

F.A.C. Wilson, *Yeats's Iconography* (1960).

A.G. Stock, *W.B. Yeats. His Poetry and Thought* (1961; rev. ed., 1964).

A. Norman Jeffares (ed.), *A Review of English Literature* [Yeats number] (July 1963).

Peter Ure, *Yeats* [in *Writers and Critics* series] (1963).

Peter Ure, *Yeats the Playwright* (1963).

Helen Vendler, *Yeats's Vision and the Later Plays* (1963).

Denis Donoghue (ed.), *The Integrity of Yeats* (1964).

Edward Engelberg, *The Vast Design* (1964).

M.C. Bradbrook, *English Dramatic Form: A History of its Development* (1965).

Curtis Bradford, *Yeats at Work* (1965).

S.B. Bushrui, *Yeats's Verse-Plays: The Revisions 1900–1910* (1965).

Denis Donoghue and J.R. Mulryne (eds.), *An Honoured Guest: New Essays on W.B. Yeats* (1965).

A. Norman Jeffares and K.G.W. Cross (eds.), *In Excited Reverie* (1965).

D.E.S. Maxwell and S.B. Bushrui (eds.), *W.B. Yeats 1865–1965: Centenary Essays* (1965).

Shotaro Oshima, *W.B. Yeats and Japan* (1965).

B. Rajan, *W.B. Yeats: A Critical Introduction* (1965).

Corinna Salvadori, *Yeats and Castiglione: Poet and Courtier* (1965).

Robin Skelton and Ann Saddlemyer (eds.), *The World of W.B. Yeats* (1965).

Alex Zwerdling, *Yeats and the Heroic Ideal* (1965).

Donald T. Torchiana, *W.B. Yeats and Georgian Ireland* (1966).

Austin Clarke, *The Celtic Twilight and the Nineties* (1969).

A. Norman Jeffares, *The Circus Animals: Essays on W.B. Yeats* (1970).

A. Norman Jeffares and A.S. Knowland, *A Commentary on the Collected Plays of W.B. Yeats* (1975).

Katharine Worth, *The Irish Drama of Europe* (1978).

Richard Taylor, *A Reader's Guide to the Plays of W.B. Yeats* (1984).

A. Norman Jeffares, *A New Commentary on the Poems of W.B. Yeats* (1984).

Masaru Sekine (ed.), *Irish Writers and the Theatre* (1986).

Masaru Sekine and Christopher Murray, *Yeats and Noh: A Comparative Study* (1990).